PENGUIN BOOKS

FEARLESS

Sylvia Yu Friedman is an award-winning author, philanthropy adviser, TV host, film-maker, and inspirational speaker. She has pioneered philanthropic initiatives for some of the world's wealthiest families, transforming countless lives while exposing some of the most egregious human rights abuses of our time.

For two decades, she has fearlessly investigated the human trafficking underworld, risking her own life in the process—shattering barriers, and charting a course for a new generation of philanthropists and activists.

Her tireless efforts have been instrumental in raising awareness about human trafficking in Asia and have been recognized with prestigious international awards. Sylvia's life story and bestselling memoir, *A Long Road to Justice: Stories from the Frontlines in Asia*, have inspired a TV series that is currently in development.

She is the author of four books and the editor of the highly acclaimed book *Rethink the Couch: Into the Bedrooms and Boardrooms of Asia with an Expat Therapist* by Allison Heiliczer.

Her LinkedIn interview show, *Inspiring YOU with Sylvia Yu*, reflects her passion for highlighting remarkable individuals. Sylvia's inspiring work reminds us that through the transformative power of love, courage, and dedication, we can make a difference in the world and motivate others to do the same.

ADVANCE PRAISE FOR *FEARLESS*

'Sylvia Yu Friedman's book is the best antidote for all those who initially doubt themselves or doubt to be up to someone else's expectation. A must-read for all young people in search for their own truth. Through her personal experience, which will resonate in many minds, she also makes us realize that self-love is not narcissistic, but a condition to reach one's potential and help others. This book should also guide parents who wish the best for their children but sometimes have difficulty drawing the line between teaching principles and not accepting enough of their children as they are, to help them to become the best version of their true selves.

And finally, Sylvia's book is also a universal story of acceptance, forgiveness, and courage. As she says, "In your greatest pains lies your superpower."'

—Cyrille Vigneron, CEO of Cartier

'Sylvia's *Fearless* is a remarkable guidebook for all ages, filled with wisdom, humanity, and valuable life lessons. It is an incredible journey that inspires and encourages growth for those who are brave enough to continue on their own path in life. Bravo, Sylvia!'

—S. Alice Mong, president of the
Asia Society Hong Kong Center

'Sylvia's book spoke to me at a time when I was going on a journey of self-discovery and finding my identity again. Her stories, courage, and fearlessness challenged me to reflect [on] stories of my own, acknowledge my past, and redefine a new calling to drive impact. More than the book, *Fearless* is a movement that Sylvia sets to impact many others to embrace the essence of fearlessness and find meaning in our lives.'

—Derek Tan, co-founder of Viddsee

'This book shows how compassion can be a strength and proves how pain can be turned into purpose and power. An essential guide for my teenage daughter—and her dad.'

—Daryl Kho, author of *Mist-Bound: How to Glue Back Grandpa*

'I have read many books in my life but *Fearless* is one of those books that will remain with me forever. It explores resilience, purpose, and courage in facing adversity, while also uncovering the significance of each struggle through the lens of love.'

—Detina Zalli, doctor, leader, author of *Good Morning, Hope: A True Story of Refugee Twin Sisters and Their Triumph over War, Poverty, and Heartbreak*

'Sylvia Yu Friedman's *Fearless* is full of inspiration for those who find themselves at the crossroads of uncertainty and aspiration. From her wealth of experience as a philanthropist, journalist, filmmaker, and believer, Friedman offers a treasure trove of wisdom that transcends the pages of mere autobiography. Her global odyssey addressing critical challenges such as HIV/AIDS, human trafficking, and the legacy of comfort women, coupled with her own personal trials, makes for a riveting read that is as educational as it is motivational. It is a compelling guide that empowers readers to confront their fears and embrace their full potential across all facets of life—from nurturing love and friendships to achieving career milestones, fighting racism, and healing from past wounds.'

—Hyepin Im, president, CEO, and founder of Faith and Community Empowerment (FACE)

'*Fearless* is captivating and a must-read for anyone interested in philanthropy, leadership, embracing identity, women's rights, and making a positive impact in the world. It's a powerful guide for aspiring changemakers.'

—Jin Kang, divisional vice president, East Global of Fellowship of Christian Athletes (FCA)

'Sylvia's book *Fearless* is a powerful call to action, urging us to recognize the struggles we face as women. Her message inspires us to fight for a fair and just world as we strive to overcome the biases that hold us back. Let us heed her words and work together to build a better future for all.'

—Irene Tse, past president of
Rotary Club of Hong Kong

'With *Fearless*, Sylvia has written a trailblazer! Maintaining a rare balance of courage and vulnerability, the author deals candidly with both personal and professional challenges that have led her to champion marginalized women across East Asia. Just one example: Friedman's commitment to North Korean sex-trafficking victims in China was on full display when, as a journalist, she documented the hair-raising flight of refugee women that our NGO was guiding to safe havens beyond the rim of China.

An entire generation of up-and-coming women in Asia—and beyond—will benefit from Sylvia Yu Friedman's transparency, humility, words of faith and encouragement . . . all tethered to her example of sheer tenacity.'

—Tim Peters, founder and director of operations of
Helping Hands Korea, https://helpinghandskorea.org/

ALSO BY SYLVIA YU FRIEDMAN

A Long Road to Justice: Stories from the Frontlines in Asia (2021)
Rethink the Couch: Into the Bedrooms and Boardrooms of Asia with an Expat Therapist (2023, editor)

Fearless

A Guide to Freedom and Fulfilling Your Fullest Potential

Sylvia Yu Friedman

PENGUIN BOOKS
An imprint of Penguin Random House

PENGUIN BOOKS

Penguin Books is an imprint of the Penguin Random House group of companies whose addresses can be found at global.penguinrandomhouse.com

Published by Penguin Random House SEA Pte Ltd
40 Penjuru Lane, #03-12, Block 2
Singapore 609216

Penguin Random House SEA

First published in Penguin Books by Penguin Random House SEA 2024

10 9 8 7 6 5 4 3 2 1

The views and opinions expressed in this book are the author's own and the facts are as reported by her which have been verified to the extent possible, and the publishers are not in any way liable for the same.

ISBN 9789815233100

Typeset in Garamond by MAP Systems, Bengaluru, India
Printed at TK

Fearless includes elements that might not be suitable for some readers. Sexual violence and exploitation, trafficking, and modern slavery are present in the story. Readers who may be sensitive to these elements please take note.

www.penguin.sg

MIX
Paper from responsible sources
FSC® C043100

Non nobis solum nati sumus.
Not for ourselves alone are we born.

—Marcus Tullius Cicero

I dedicate this book to my beautiful mother, Anne.

You have touched countless lives with your extraordinary love, godliness, and wisdom.

My sister Jayne and I often say that if there's anything good in us, it's from our mom.

It's because of you, Umma, that I have done anything useful in this life. I owe it all to your unconditional love, unwavering support and prayers, and special wisdom. No words can express how grateful I am for you.

Contents

Foreword

On your journey to self-improvement, you've probably read plenty of self-help books and scrolled through countless inspirational quotes. Perhaps you've taken some courses or consulted a therapist or guru. Or even gone on a retreat. Maybe you've tried it all and are still searching for more.

What you will read in this book is nothing like what you've tried before. It will outrage, humour, humble, and inspire you. And it will challenge you to consider: what if you could transcend the expectations and limitations placed on you by yourself and others? What if you could change your relationship with fear so it was no longer in the driver's seat? What would reaching your full potential look like?

The stories in this remarkable book have answers to these questions but be warned: it's no magic carpet ride. Pain is necessary for growth. This journey requires not only curiosity, creativity, and humility but also blood, sweat, and tears—not to mention perseverance and a whole lot of faith.

Along the way, you'll learn the importance of creating meaning in all that you experience. Self-improvement is often a mysterious, arduous process but at its heart is a simple truth: reaching one's potential is possible through experience not intellect.

Sylvia Yu Friedman will be your guide as she takes you on her own journey, from the place of her birth in Busan, South Korea, to her childhood haunts in Canada and her work across Asia as an adviser to philanthropists, a television journalist, and an advocate for social change. You'll hear about the many scrapes and close calls this dangerous line of work involved, from sitting with trafficked North Korean women in the homes of their impoverished and elderly Chinese husbands, being surrounded by soldiers with machine guns in Myanmar, and visiting Sichuan, China, days after a magnitude eight earthquake that killed tens of thousands of people.

You'll also hear about her personal struggles, from experiencing racism as a child and questioning her identity and heritage to her run-ins with toxic work colleagues, her search for Mr Right and her recovery from the pain of divorce.

In Sylvia's stories, you'll hear the echoes of endless women who have lived lives shackled by the narratives others forced on them.

For most of us, as the years pass, our limiting beliefs are fed not only by the narratives of others but by the stories we come to tell ourselves. We end up imprisoned in a life that doesn't belong to us.

What sets Sylvia apart in her bid to break out of this cage is her willingness to reckon with her own soul—territory few of us dare to tread. Plenty of us will ponder the external influences on our lives but few of us are prepared to confront the enemy within. Mainly, it is fear that stops us; if we stare into the abyss, we fear what might stare back, so we do our best to look away.

Fear is something we all experience and can sometimes be a force for good. Yet, all too often, it is fear that prevents us from escaping that jail that's been built around us. We fear being humiliated. We fear being unlovable. And, as outlandish as it may seem, even after all our limiting beliefs have been deconstructed, we can fear our own potential.

How many of us fear the unknown, the possibility of what's out *there*, and decide instead to stay safe, small, and shackled?

For Sylvia, breaking these chains began when she learned the power of forgiveness. Finding an anchor in life—in her case, service to others—is what ultimately set her free.

Read her story, and it will dare you to change your relationship with fear. It will challenge you to make the choice we all must face: to frame experiences as meaningless or meaningful, to sleepwalk through life hypnotized by limiting scripts, or to live it wide-eyed and alive.

It takes a brave person to make that choice, yet doing so is the first step to weaving together the messiness of being human into a purpose that far exceeds what most of us believe is possible.

With deep admiration for the *Fearless*,

—Allison Heiliczer
Psychotherapist and author of *Rethink the Couch: Into the Bedrooms and Boardrooms of Asia with an Expat Therapist*

Introduction

This book is a result of my nostalgic journey through the corridors of time, mining the memories that shaped me into who I am today.

Many of the stories I am about to share explore what I would have told my younger self about my career and life during times of intense pain, confusion, and sadness, when I felt the most lost.

Reliving these memories was a beautiful yet humbling time of self-discovery, where breakthroughs emerged amid the chaos.

These pages are a letter to my younger self, offering her wisdom gained through the highs and lows of my adventurous career. I share insights on overcoming self-doubt and hardships, navigating toxic environments, and embracing one's true identity.

From the perils of rushing into marriage to confronting imposter syndrome, learning to ignore critics, and escaping toxic environments, each tale is a stepping stone towards self-realization and empowerment.

If I could go back in time, I would tell my younger self to:

- not be paralysed by what others think
- laugh uncontrollably at least once a week, if not once a day
- not rush into a marriage—it ended in divorce after a year
- believe in yourself and tell that creeping imposter syndrome to go to hell
- ignore the critics
- remember that just about everyone feels insecure at large networking events
- run as far as you can from a toxic office
- stop diving into work mode all the time.

Always, always forgive. Otherwise, you're the one imprisoned by bitterness. And when necessary, let go and have a good ugly cry, even in front of people. (There's nothing wrong with showing vulnerability, and remember, there's no need to care what people think anyway.)

During the early years of my career, I had a naive belief that the world was a happy and supportive place. I thought I would quickly succeed with everyone's support and ride into the clouds of glory on a white unicorn with a powder blue horn.

Looking back, I cringe at how innocent I was. Trusting too easily, I learned the hard way that not everyone had my best interests at heart. It's a revelation that could have been softened by the guidance of a mentor.

Recently, a profound realization has reshaped the trajectory of my work. From advocating for the voiceless to producing films and writing books, a newfound focus has emerged for me—educating and inspiring the younger generation. I feel compelled to share my lessons to encourage those searching for meaning and purpose.

Fearless is my personal guidebook, a last lecture to my younger self and it's for those seeking direction and meaning in their own journeys. It's an anthology of unconventional and adventurous experiences in Asia, pearls of wisdom drawn from philanthropy, journalism, and cross-cultural workplaces. This is also my gift to those in their teens and twenties—a reminder that they are unique and destined for something greater.

In crafting this book, my beautiful mother's influence loomed large. Her unwavering love and encouragement continue to provide the foundation for every achievement. Indeed, this book is a tribute to the unspoken heroes who shape our narratives.

This memoir goes beyond a simple reflection on the past—it's a road map for those navigating the twists and turns of life. It's a call to laugh unabashedly, to believe in oneself, to stand tall amid insecurities, and to acknowledge that tears are not a sign of weakness but a pathway to healing.

Prepare to embark on a fearless odyssey—a journey through the mountaintops and valleys, the triumphs and tribulations.

Let these pages be your companion to self-discovery and the pursuit of your highest potential.

Chapter 1

Rejected at Birth

In your greatest pain lies your superpower.

For as long as I can remember, I strove for my father's approval.

Perhaps it's because long before I came along, he had made up his mind that a son was better than a daughter.

I was born in Busan, South Korea. When I came into this world, instead of pride and joy, my father felt disappointment. My Korean name made his feelings clear: its first part 'Sae' is a masculine name, meaning 'world'.

My earliest memories are of him treating me like the son he never had. Though my father never talked to me about it, his preference for a son overshadowed my entire life.

I felt a profound sense of rejection.

We spent time together only when we were playing sports. When I was too young to play with a proper ball, we used a balloon instead.

He was good at running, swimming, soccer, and most other sports too.

I don't recall him ever treating me gingerly, like a little girl.

I soon learned to embrace the sporting life to bask in his fleeting attention. I would play volleyball with him, my tiny hands bouncing the pink balloons back and forth. Later, it was soccer and badminton, kicking the ball around or swatting the birdie in the air. I wonder if this is where I get my finely tuned hand–eye coordination from. My high school volleyball coach once told me I had the most accurate bump he had ever seen—I could set up a spike from anywhere on the court.

I also played floor hockey, basketball, and softball on an all men's team and often as the only woman.

From an early age, I sensed that my father had little interest in me beyond my sporting potential. But it was only much later, when I was in counselling, that I learned how this had fuelled the self-hatred, insecurities, and desperation of my school years. To prove my self-worth, I felt compelled to excel at everything I put my mind to. For years, I built my self-esteem and identity on how well I performed any given task.

I remember panicking one semester in the eleventh grade when I didn't top the honour roll. I feared the families of the Korean students who went to my church would find out and my parents would lose face. In previous semesters, I had always been at the top or at least in the top three, so I felt like a dismal failure.

My mom, an exceptionally supportive mother with a dash of the tiger in her, murmured about why my name was missing. 'What went wrong?' she asked. 'Are you hanging out with your friends too much?'

I was depressed for the next month. It was as if my identity was a house built on shifting sands—always on the brink of collapse due to criticism or a less-than-perfect grade. I lacked a strong foundation and didn't know how to believe in myself, since I did not know who I was. As a result, I became more self-absorbed and self-conscious, as I constantly worried about what others thought of me. My insecurities were magnified in my own eyes.

It wasn't until decades later that I learned about the psychological phenomenon known as the 'spotlight effect', where people mistakenly believe there is a glaring light on them, showcasing their flaws and blunders for everyone to see. It's a cognitive bias, a tendency for people to overestimate how much others are observing and evaluating them. In reality, everyone is too self-absorbed and caught up in their own lives to notice much about anyone else.

Better than Ten

When I was younger, I always tried to show my father, 'Look, I'm better than ten sons!'

It was exhausting. I was constantly pushing myself, yet I was never satisfied with my achievements for long. I felt inadequate, as if I kept falling short of some undefined gold standard just out of my reach. So, I pushed myself ever harder.

I dreaded getting less than 86 per cent, an 'A' grade, on tests because of my mom's inevitable reaction, 'What happened to the other 14 per cent? Why didn't you get 100?' Only if I scored a near-perfect grade would I get a passing nod of approval.

It was her way of motivating me. The parents of most of my Asian friends had a similar approach. Fortunately, studying, writing essays, and taking exams came easy to me. In my mom's circle of friends and at church, I became known as the 'really smart one'. I began to link my identity to how well I did at school. My younger sister, Jayne, who was called the most perfect-looking Korean girl by countless boys, was the 'pretty one'. She had a large fan club in high school and her nickname was 'Queen of Korea'.

I am embarrassed to admit that, for most of my life, I believed I was ugly and unattractive. I never felt feminine and, perhaps due to my father's gender preference, I was not encouraged to embrace my identity as a young woman.

There is an ingrained discrimination against women in the Korean and Asian cultures at large. It leads to many girls and women being treated as burdens and being rejected as worthless because of their gender. The objectification of women, where they are valued only based on their beauty, virginity, and ability to bear children, is part of this prejudice. Male children are prized because they can carry forward the family lineage. Women bear all the blame if a couple cannot conceive.

Over the centuries, it was common to withhold from women the rights to own property, to have a voice in their own lives and marriages, and to access education. In some parts, genital mutilation has been enforced as a way of controlling and subjugating them.

I was always finding fault in my almond-shaped eyes, skinny legs, or the natural bulge of my stomach. During my senior years in high school and in my twenties, I often piled on make-up and overcompensated by dressing up—this became an impenetrable armour to cover up my insecurities. Or I swung the other way and wore tomboyish sports shirts like New York Yankees baseball tops and jogging pants.

'Watch and learn,' I would taunt the boys at the gym or in class, where I would always be competing with them. I saw other girls as too weak to bother competing with. But all the while, I felt a nagging pain that I couldn't put my finger on. In hindsight, I understand it was connected to my very being as a girl. I had been born into this identity crisis and it was only as I grew older that I began to fathom how pervasive this condition is for girls across the world.

Since the age of eighteen, I started exercising obsessively and went overboard to achieve a muscular physique. I even hired a personal trainer and eventually was certified as one. I would often examine the flab on my upper thighs as one would appraise a diamond. All my energy was focused on the few flaws that I perceived.

Later, I realized this was a form of body dysmorphia—a type of mental health condition where a person spends an inordinate amount of time obsessing over and worrying about perceived flaws in their appearance, causing anxiety and shame. The condition goes beyond not liking something about your appearance, such as freckles or crooked teeth. It's more than fleeting dissatisfaction with a perceived imperfection in one's appearance. Depending on the severity of the disorder, it could be an all-consuming obsession. Usually, these flaws are unnoticeable to others, but the sufferer loses the ability to see themselves objectively.

If you are concerned about not fitting in or being rejected—like I was—then you may be susceptible to developing thought patterns that lead to body dysmorphia. Body Dysmorphic Disorder (BDD) affects up to 2.9 per cent of people in the United States or roughly up to 10 million people, according to pioneering researcher Katharine Phillips, MD.

It's most common among teenagers and young adults and can affect both men and women. Interestingly, it is more prevalent among men who work in dermatology and cosmetic surgery.

Breaking Sad

My own breakthrough came in my early thirties.

I attended a one-day seminar on the generational power of our words conducted by the well-regarded author and pastor, Terry Bone.

He gave me the gift of quality time that day and mentored me. After a long and honest conversation, Pastor Bone urged me to forgive my father and embrace who I was as a strong, fun-loving woman. I was surprised to hear someone in authority describe me that way. I felt seen. I saw Pastor Bone then as a father figure, affirming me and speaking life and truth to me.

I told him of my divorce and how I had impulsively rushed into my first marriage years ago because I didn't fully appreciate my self-worth. A decision that shattered my heart and took years to fully get over. He prayed for me and said he hoped I would marry well and not just fall for any man who would hitch his wagon to mine.

He said that so many Asian women get plastic surgery and obsess about their looks because their fathers and grandfathers reject them at birth. It was a light bulb moment for me and crystallized all my struggles over the years. I recalled many Asian women friends who were rejected by their fathers as children and as adults, and still felt ugly, even though they were attractive.

'You need to be with a guy who will appreciate you for who you really are,' Pastor Bone said, adding prophetically, 'You're going to help other women in Asia who are struggling with the same issue.'

I bawled like a baby. For the first time, I felt self-acceptance. My hardened exterior melted away. That simple conversation changed my life. I wished I had this revelation a lot earlier, as it would have saved me a lot of grief and unnecessary anxiety over my appearance. I had no idea that I harboured anger and resentment towards my father for so long.

While I had a successful career in journalism at that time and lots of friends, there was a nagging sense of emptiness that something was still missing in my life.

It was sobering to discern that my inability to forgive my father had affected all areas of my life. It had turned me into a workaholic as I drove myself into the ground in search of achievements that would bolster my self-esteem. It had also played a part in my impulsive decision to marry my ex-husband, whom I didn't love and who—it slowly dawned on me—mistreated me badly. He treated me the way I felt about myself.

Several friends who knew my ex-husband from years ago warned me not to marry him because they felt he was untrustworthy. In my gut, I knew they were right, but I ignored the red flags because he had some great qualities. He, at least, had them as a friend. When we started dating, he was drastically different.

There were numerous warning signs that I ignored while we were dating. I made compromises to my values and needs that I wouldn't make today. For instance, he insisted that we split the bill every time we went out, which shocked me, initially. But I downplayed my feelings and convinced myself that things would change after marriage. Unfortunately, our 50–50 financial arrangement continued even after we got married, and I despised the cold, transactional, and sickening way of dealing with our money. I believed that a married couple should share everything, but instead, I had my separate bank account, and I always paid for my flights and half of our holiday expenses, dining out, and almost everything else was split down the middle.

It was like living with a frugal roommate, and I rarely felt cherished or cared for.

I postponed our wedding for almost a year because I wasn't sure I was making the right decision. A second time, I called things off a month before the ceremony after he screamed at me in a crazy rage over the phone about something insignificant. He was often critical and hurtful with his words and nothing was ever his fault.

I proceeded with the wedding anyway because I felt stuck. The ceremony venue and all the vendors were booked, hefty deposits were paid, and I felt too embarrassed to cancel. I walked down the aisle crying with a heavy heart.

Right after our wedding ceremony, my husband literally grabbed all the monetary gifts, including the ones from my relatives, and claimed them as his own, arguing that he had paid for more than half the wedding.

I tried to reason with him, explaining that my family and I had contributed our fair share, but he refused to listen. That was the earliest pivotal moment when I perceived that our marriage was in deep trouble and I would deeply regret my decision. I knew in my heart that it was doomed.

After about a year of marriage, he told me that he wanted a divorce. Soon after, I learned of his adultery through a friend who had met the other woman and heard her admit to the affair during a church home group meeting. He denied everything. It was a one-in-a-billion chance, a kind of miracle, to have his affair exposed like that.

This miserable first marriage left me traumatized and distrustful of men for a while.

During a counselling session to process my actions that had led to divorce, my therapist told me that my ex-husband was abusive because he essentially blamed me for everything that was wrong and because he screamed at me.

In retrospect, I see that I took advice from the wrong friend at the wrong time. Before the wedding, a friend had convinced me that the sort of conflicts I was experiencing were common and that I should proceed with the marriage because it would all work out. I naively listened to this friend because I was too scared to end the relationship after all the time and energy I had put into planning a wedding.

I am anguished as I look back at that fork in the road when I could have ended the relationship. We should have remained friends, since we had little chemistry, passion, or affection back then.

I made this reckless decision due to anxiety. I was convinced I needed to get married by the time I turned thirty because I mistakenly believed my choices for a partner were dwindling each year. In hindsight, I can see that was nonsense, but I've heard from countless Asian women who have felt the same pressure to marry. They feel a sense of shame and failure at being single as if it means they are somehow defective.

One discerning British woman in China told me that this extreme longing to get married comes from my Asian culture and the fact that historically women were virtually considered property and not given names until they had a husband.

This woman established a non-profit to rescue women from sex trafficking and saw countless women facing the same pressure. It left many young women susceptible to being ensnared by traffickers posing as Romeos or fake boyfriends who love bombed them then deceived them into selling their bodies to pay off an alleged debt.

As a strong professional woman, I might not have seemed the sort of person who would tolerate a verbally abusive partner. But, deep inside, I didn't feel deserving of love. Despite my outward tenaciousness, I struggled internally with feelings of unworthiness and inadequacy. It's taken years for me to admit this inner turmoil.

Looking back, it struck me that my unresolved anger towards my father and the oppressive patriarchal systems he was bound up in played a role in shaping my choices and experiences. Unfortunately, I found myself trapped in a cycle of mistreatment that many women face.

My father, as a traditional Korean man, was usually oblivious to my internal struggles, and I was never able to communicate my pain to him. But, eventually, I came to conclude that I needed to make peace with both me and my father.

After I forgave him, I felt lighter and liberated, and I had a better idea of what I wanted in life.

I strongly believe now that generational reconciliation is the key to a fulfilling existence.

Over the years, I have seen people who are estranged from one or both parents. They usually hit a glass ceiling of some kind that stops them from reaching their full potential and leading a prosperous, happy life.

That's why I urge everyone to make peace with their parents.

My Superpower

Over time, I have learned to embrace how I look. I try to accept my flaws now, rather than obsess over what I want to change or camouflage with make-up. I am most content when I am free to be me with all my imperfections. I went to see a counsellor who helped relieve some of the anxiety related to my body dysmorphic disorder.

Years later, I married my husband Matt. His unwavering love and complete acceptance of me have been a tremendous source of support. And thankfully, Pastor Bone helped me to see that I could help other women with similar experiences.

It's become my passion to support the women's movement in Asia and around the world, to celebrate and uplift women, and to see an end to their exploitation. The rejection I once felt for being a girl has inspired my life's mission as an advocate for gender equality.

Over the years, countless women, of all ages and cultural backgrounds, have told me how the same ghosts have haunted their lives and relationships.

Here is the advice I give them:

- Forgive your father. His mindset has caused you pain but that mindset is a product of generational and cultural influences.
- Look inward to recognize your positive character traits and inner beauty.
- Never allow others to influence your identity and self-esteem in negative ways.
- Celebrate being yourself—your strong, beautiful self.
- Finally, remember the words of the American memoirist Maya Angelou: 'Each time a woman stands up for herself, without knowing it possibly, without claiming it, she stands up for all women.'

Truly, my greatest pain has become my superpower.

Yangban Women

Putting ghosts to rest is not only about forgiving ancient mindsets. Researching the female ancestors in my family tree has helped me to grow and better understand myself.

It's taught me how generations of indomitable women on both the paternal and maternal sides of my family have shaped me. Over the years, I have thought a lot about my great-grandma and my paternal grandma and am grateful to have them as role models. If anything, their influence has been all the greater due to the distance between us—I grew up in Canada while they remained in South Korea.

As an infant, my great-grandma raised me for nearly a year while my mother went back to school. Later, we spent time together during trips to Korea or whenever she travelled to Vancouver. I saw my paternal grandma last when I was two before our family emigrated to Canada.

Both were strong, impressive women who carved a niche for themselves to give back to others despite living in an oppressive, patriarchal society where they had few rights and no access to higher education.

My great-grandma and paternal grandma came from a long line of Yangban families, the aristocracy or ruling class in Korea. Their parents grew up in the twilight years of the Joseon period, during which women were considered inferior and were mostly prohibited from being educated, hidden away from the outside world, while men could have both a wife and several concubines.

The women of that era were dominated by men and their firstborn sons and forced to conform to Confucian ideals of purity, obedience, and chastity. Most of these cultural restrictions on women were still in place in my great-grandma and grandma's time, yet they navigated life the best they could and became leaders in their own right despite the limitations.

I admire everything about great-grandma. She truly knew herself and with humility, she embraced the prominent role she played in her community. She exuded love. She was a compassionate woman who helped run a social service for the impoverished and homeless. She and my great-grandfather offered free meals to the needy every week in their home and would give them the clothes off their backs in an instant. What's more, she did so while honouring the dignity of those she helped. She was the epitome of using one's influence to make a difference.

Great-grandma was also known for her sophisticated and elegant style. She would wear fashionable custom-made clothes and hanbok, a Korean traditional dress with a full skirt and short jacket. These were made of beautiful, brightly coloured silks. Complementing these outfits would be gorgeous jewellery in the form of a glittering, flower-shaped diamond brooch on her jacket, sparkling rings on her fingers, and a dainty handbag on her arm. I remember once seeing her brush her waist-length hair, which she usually wore swept up into a bun. It was jet-black even when she was in her eighties.

She had natural leadership qualities, was incredibly charismatic, and had a smile that lit up the room. Once, when we visited her church in Gyeongju, she was swarmed by a group of children who called out, 'Grandma's here, she's here!' She looked at each of them and gave them her dazzling smile and the kids squealed and hugged her. I have never seen anything like it since; it was as if she were a K-pop star. Children can sense a person's loving nature.

My paternal grandma was known as the smartest person in her village. She was the go-to person for reading and writing letters in Korean and Japanese. She had chutzpah and knew how to write a diplomatic letter to get something done. During the long and ugly history of the Japanese colonial period between 1910 and 1945, when Korea was considered a part of Japan, the Japanese empire waged an all-out war on Korean culture. Everyone was forced to adopt the Japanese language and forbidden to speak in their native tongue. Freedom of speech, assembly, and the press were abolished.

Grandma was forced to become fluent in Japanese during this time and became a talented linguist. Later in her eighties, she would travel around Japan as a solo tourist. I'm convinced that her adventurous spirit and love of travel has been passed down to me.

There is a story that my cousin has relayed to me with a sense of awe: When grandma's two eldest children were less than three years old, she took a train to the northern part of the peninsula to yank her husband out of the *giaseng* house, a place where women entertained Yangban or ruling class men. She literally forced him to go back home with her. I cannot imagine what she said to him to convince him to leave that place.

Grandma was known for her bold and direct, take-no-prisoners communication style. She was expected to be subservient in that era yet she had an independent spirit, with an unusual boldness and a sassy personality.

I have so much admiration for how she went against the grain of her culture and challenged the expectations of how women of her generation were supposed to act. While her second son, my uncle, served in the

Vietnam War in a government office, she sent a message directly to the official in charge, persuading him to give special permission to her son to return home immediately to Korea. With great admiration and respect, my uncle described her unprecedented message as fearless and forceful. Against all odds, he was sent back.

How did she develop this derring-do attitude? Clearly, it would not have been encouraged by those around her. It must have been innate.

'Missing' Women

Gender discrimination and inequality are all-pervasive.

Throughout Asia, there has been a long-standing preference for sons. The economist Amartya Sen wrote, in an article for the *New York Review of Books*, about the profound cultural impact of misogyny, particularly in Asia, which has led to an estimated 100 million 'missing women'. These women have been 'missing' due to a combination of neglect and discrimination, which has resulted in the infanticide of countless girls. Tragically, many girls have died from a lack of access to healthcare and proper nutrition. The high price that women must pay simply for being born is truly devastating. Even more disturbing, many girls have been denied the chance to live because of sex-selective abortions.

Daughters are usually the first to be taken out of school so that sons can continue their education. In China, the ancient practices of polygamy and the binding of women's feet by breaking them and binding them to change their size and shape are manifestations of the devaluing of women. Foot binding was a status symbol that allowed families to marry their daughters off to wealthy suitors for a better life. It limited girls' mobility—consequently their power—and was meant to symbolize obedience. It was banned in 1912.

Lauren Bossen, author of *Bound Feet, Young Hands*, says that foot binding served a critical economic purpose because it ensured young girls, as young as seven, sat still doing boring tasks for hours each day to help make handicraft objects—such as cloths, mats, shoes, and fishing nets—to contribute to their families' livelihoods. This tradition declined as factory-made goods became more prevalent.

In the world's two most populous countries, India and China, parents have long turned to sex-selective abortions to ensure they have sons. They do so because they see sons as more likely to support them in their twilight years. Daughters are expected to live with their husband's family; sons can pass on the family name.

China's one-child policy, which was in practice from 1979 to 2015, amplified the problem because it meant parents-to-be had just one chance to ensure they had a boy. So, it should be no surprise that men now outnumber women at a staggering scale in the two nations. According to the United Nations Population Fund (UNFPA), India accounted for 45.8 million missing females as of 2020 and China accounted for 72.3 million.

This is an unprecedented situation in human history and already has alarming and far-reaching consequences. We have yet to see the long-term effects of too few women in these societies. But there are already bride shortages and China's population is beginning to fall, raising a question mark about its continued prosperity.

China, for its part, appears to have recognized the error of its ways. In recent years, it has banned sex-selective abortions, and since 2021, a significant policy shift has been allowing parents to have up to three children.

But there are other factors behind the 'missing' women, too. Violence, social and economic instability, and an increase in bride trafficking all play a part, according to Human Rights Watch.

We must work to end this discrimination and ensure that all girls have the opportunity to live, thrive, and contribute to society.

Chapter 2

Trafficked Women and Sex Slaves

In Asia, women are trafficked from across the world, many coming from places like Myanmar, North Korea, Cambodia, Vietnam, Indonesia, and even from as far away as Pakistan.

Years ago, I had a flash of insight into this dark trade when I visited a shelter for survivors of sex trafficking in China. I was managing an HIV/AIDS fund for a philanthropist at the time and wanted to interview some of the women for a book I was writing.

Each woman I met was formidable in her own right, but 'Mei' was nothing less than a walking miracle. Short and stout, she wore dark eye-shadow and pink lipstick on her heart-shaped face and had caramel highlights in her chin-length hair. Trafficked as a young bride at fourteen, Mei had been bought by an elderly farmer who kept her chained up like a dog for years on end. Workers at the shelter told me this type of enslavement—chains and all—was common.

Mei, who was around nineteen years old when I met her, recounted to me how she had been trapped in this nightmarish existence. Shortly before her abduction, her father had pulled her out of school so that her much younger brother could continue his education. The family had been struggling with their farm, and Mei's father wanted to prioritize their only son, since he was their 'insurance policy' and would be expected to care for his parents in their old age.

Mei, naturally, had been angry. So, she had run away from home and visited a friend, Ting, and vented about this cruel and unfair treatment. Ting's 'auntie', a family friend, overheard the conversation and offered to take the two shopping in a nearby town. Once they left the city, Ting was sent back home while Mei was taken to an apartment where the aunt's husband was waiting.

Mei had been shoved into a room with only a wastebasket to relieve herself and was starved for two weeks until her will to resist was completely broken.

During that time, several men had come to inspect her like a piece of meat. Among them was a farmer with a wizened face who was in his seventies. He scrutinized her body as if looking at an animal for slaughter. Instinctively, she resisted, and he began to hit her. She sobbed and promised to do whatever he wanted if only he would stop. Instead, he handed over a wad of bills to the aunt, grabbed Mei, and grunted that he had paid for her and was now taking her home.

He had taken Mei back to his village home and kept her chained in a room except when he wanted to use her. So traumatic was her time in captivity that even today, Mei struggles for words to describe it. About a year in, she became confused, as her stomach began to swell. She did not know it, but she was pregnant with a baby girl.

Mei had gone on to have that child, but she was to face a decision no mother should have to make. She adored her daughter yet knew that to escape her 'husband', she would have to abandon her.

After scrimping and saving money that she had found around the house, she ran away. She made it to the bus depot and got on the first bus she could find. It took her from the frying pan straight into the fire. When she got off, a female trafficker sensed her vulnerability and pounced, luring her with a false promise of a good job. The pimp took Mei to a brothel and forced her to work there. Then, Mei contracted HIV. To cope, she turned to hard drugs and alcohol.

I was shocked to hear her story. *How could this happen in this day and age?* I thought. Yet, there was also an evil familiarity to it, a sense that I had heard this story before. The aged faces of the women forced into prostitution by the Japanese Imperial military before and during World War II—sex slaves known by the awful euphemism, 'comfort women'—flashed before my eyes.

Up to 400,000 women and girls as young as eleven years old were forced into systemic sexual servitude on the frontlines of World War II alone. In Japanese-occupied China, there were more than 1,000 'comfort stations' or military brothels. Many girls were Mei's age, fourteen or fifteen when they were deceived into thinking they were going to work as a nurse or a factory worker before being taken to a comfort station on the frontlines of war and raped repeatedly by Japanese soldiers.

I had spent nearly fourteen years writing a book on the wartime sexual exploitation of young women across the Asia Pacific, and this felt like a profound moment for me. It confirmed my calling as a documenter of these atrocities against women and as a witness to mobilize others into action.

The cycle of sex trafficking keeps repeating with no end in sight. Worldwide, there are an estimated 29 million women and girls in modern slavery—more than the population of Australia—according to the International Labour Organization, Walk Free, and the International Organization for Migration. Of those, 6.3 million are sex slaves.

Mei eventually glimpsed a route to freedom. Shelter workers monitoring the brothel helped her leave and offered her treatment for HIV, drug addiction, and therapy for her trauma. They offered her an opportunity to learn new skills and start a new life. Most importantly, they gave her hope. Despite struggling with suicidal thoughts and self-hatred, Mei seized her escape route with both hands.

When we sat together, she smiled brightly after sharing her story and said she wanted to prevent others from suffering as she had. She didn't want any more girls or women to be sold as brides. Her raw, simple courage inspired me.

I have often thought of Mei in the years since I visited that shelter. I thought of her when a video showing a woman in rural China chained by the neck in a dilapidated hut with a faded silver metal padlock racked up 2 billion views on Chinese social media in 2022. The woman in the video was Xiao Huamei, whose name means 'little plum blossom'. She was wearing only a long-sleeve shirt in the frigid weather. Her hair was dishevelled and her face looked like she hadn't washed it in a long time. Her vacant eyes suggested that she wasn't fully aware of what had happened to her.

According to news reports, the authorities stepped in. Xiao was taken to hospital for an extended stay while the eight children she had borne her captor went into state care. A court sentenced six people to prison terms ranging from eight to thirteen years for human trafficking and abuse of a woman.

If there could possibly be such a thing as a silver lining in a case as horrific as this, it is that it led to a public outcry and a debate about the treatment of women in China. A sense of outrage at Xiao's exploitation has been rising in the nation, especially among professional women. Even now, this collective outrage has not died down, and it gives us hope that we can help exploited women.

We have seen how a collective outcry can lead to change. In 2012, a young Indian medical student named Jyoti Singh died after being brutally gang-raped on a bus in New Delhi. During the trial, she came to be known as Nirbhaya, which means 'fearless'. The public uproar over Jyoti's shocking case resulted in the overhaul of India's laws on violence against women.

We must continue to speak out collectively and demand change, as it is within our power to make a difference.

Trafficked from North Korea

Since the 1990s, due to famine and the economic downturn, North Koreans have been crossing the border illegally into China in search of medical help or work to be able to send money back home to their struggling families.

Traffickers in China and North Korea prey on the vulnerability of these North Koreans in search of a better life. According to Korean NGOs, these traffickers drug, rape, and coerce up to 80 per cent of these women into forced prostitution and sexual exploitation or sell them as brides to elderly or disabled Chinese men who cannot marry the traditional way.

While there are no statistics on the exact number of women in modern slavery, the US State Department's *2022 Trafficking in Persons Report: North Korea* stated that as many as '30,000 children born in the PRC (Peoples' Republic of China) to DPRK (Democratic People's Republic of Korea) women and PRC national men have not been registered upon birth, rendering them stateless and vulnerable to possible exploitation. If found by PRC authorities, trafficking victims are often forcibly returned to the DPRK, where they are subject to harsh punishment, including forced labour in labour camps, torture, forced abortions or death.'

Thousands of these stateless children, who have no access to education or medical care, are abandoned by their mothers if they escape to a safe third country or if they're sold again to another 'husband'. They remain virtual prisoners inside their homes out of fear of being caught.

I have witnessed an underground railroad in China where frontline workers rescue North Korean victims of bride trafficking and forced pornography. This secretive network of clandestine safe homes spans more than 3,000 miles across a few nations and offers medical and spiritual care to people who escape North Korea. It is managed by courageous people, mostly missionaries with family ties in the country, who must operate in the stealthiest ways due to the danger of being arrested by undercover police or reported on by citizen spies. Their sole motivation is to bring North Koreans to the safety of a third country, such as South Korea.

Through a friend, I met a South Korean man—'Mark'—in his fifties, in a café. He explained that they usually do not speak with journalists and that I was a special exception because of my friend's recommendation. I told Mark that I wanted to help raise awareness of the plight of these women.

For the next hour, I was interrogated about my past experiences, my faith, and my integrity. Then, he cryptically said to me, 'Don't call us, we'll call you.' Mark's poker face gave nothing away and I felt I had failed to persuade him. But, a few months later, I received word I was to meet 'Johnny' in another city.

Johnny was a heavy-set Chinese man in his fifties and seemed to view me and another journalist as a burden. I didn't feel totally comfortable trusting Johnny with my life but it was too late to bail. We got in a car and he told us many stories of North Korean women who had crossed the border into China only to be snatched by traffickers and sold as brides or into brothels and online pornography businesses.

I initially felt intense fear, as we were close to the border area, and I was paranoid about being found out. I was blindfolded for parts of the journey but when I did have the opportunity to look out of the window, my eyes drank in the scenery of the rural farmlands marked by green and yellow vegetable stalks and grassy mountains. Our car was moving at a fast speed, but I could make out tiny figures of farmers with their leathery brown faces, broad straw hats, and outfits covering their faces and arms. *Time stands still in this part of the world*, I thought. Was that why women are bought and sold here as if they were still living in medieval times?

In hindsight, I would never do a trip like this again. We had to switch cars at least a dozen times, and I was troubled by the blindfold. Still, I calmed myself by thinking of the women's suffering and the need to tell the world what was happening.

Looking back, I'll never forget sitting with trafficked North Korean brides in the homes of their impoverished Chinese farmer husbands. Most of these women looked beyond depressed, in quiet despair and shame, barely whispering responses to my probing questions.

That was back in 2007. The shock and sadness I felt that day has remained with me ever since. Never have I ever felt more helpless for them or more saddened for our divided Korean peninsula. There was very little I could do for these women trapped in poverty-driven sexual slavery and that frustrated me intensely. But I found comfort in the fact that there are humanitarian workers like Johnny and his team mates—unsung heroes who are risking their lives going into some of the darkest places on earth to help suffering girls and women.

These Korean and Chinese men are transforming one life at a time. Their selfless, noble work touched me to my core.

Against the Grain of Culture

At one of the safe homes, Johnny introduced me to 'Su-jin'. She was a survivor of forced marriage and when we met, her skin was such a dull yellow tone that I did a double take. I soon learned that her jaundice had been the least of her hardships over the past few years. As we sat down, she told me that she had been lured by traffickers from North Korea and promised a good job to be able to support and wire money back to her parents.

In reality, as soon as she had arrived in China, she was sold for 1,000 RMB (US$140) to a Chinese man in northeast China. They lived in a dank cave because he was too poor to afford a decent home in town. She had a few children with this man and sobbed when she first talked about it. I felt deeply sad for her while I sat there listening to her. She couldn't talk about her kids. She told me she was sold for a second time, to a Chinese farmer, and then miraculously escaped.

But her freedom was short-lived. She was then forced to work in prostitution in a bar by an ethnic Korean who claimed to be rescuing her. Like so many women in her situation, to cope with her trauma, she turned to alcohol and began drinking heavily every night. The situation worsened when she was diagnosed with liver cancer. While that bar was very nearly the death of her, it was also where she found her salvation.

She began talking to a group of Christians there who began sharing with her about their faith. Over time, she decided to convert and a profound peace settled over her. She found she was able to sit quietly to pray and read the Bible, which was something she had never been able to do before due to her deep anxiety and trauma. One day after saying her prayers, her cancer symptoms suddenly disappeared and her doctor confirmed that she was cancer-free. She believes it was a miracle; that God healed her.

I wanted to spend the entire day with Su-jin, but Johnny interrupted us after a few hours and said we had to leave immediately in case the neighbours got suspicious. This saddened me, but I promised Su-jin I would tell the world her story and those of other North Korean women.

She looked lighter than when we had first met. After I thanked her and we said our goodbyes, she turned around to walk to her hiding place, her room. My eyes lingered as she shut the door.

The Real Cause of Trafficking

Gender discrimination is the underlying cause for both brides being trafficked and the enslavement of women. Addressing this issue is crucial for ensuring the safety and freedom of all women.

There are various forms of trafficking: forced labour, domestic servitude, debt bondage, forced criminality, scam rings, and begging rings. But the vast majority of victims in any of these forms and anywhere in the world are women and girls.

Combating gender inequality, including misogyny and sexism, is essential to fight the sex trade because men have normalized the buying of sex. Female victims are economically and socially vulnerable and have limited access to education and employment. They are often from single-parent homes and are not seen as a priority, as poor families in Asia often prefer schooling their boys. A lack of education and job skills further disadvantages young women later in life.

It's easy to get discouraged when you see only the big picture of 6.3 million girls and women suffering as sex slaves. But when you hear some of the individual stories, of bravery and survival against all odds, there is room for hope too.

A New Hope

Having grappled with the rejection of my gender since early childhood, my personal search for my identity began in earnest in my teens. For most of my youth, I was truly lost. I lacked purpose and a sense of cultural identity. I was broken and insecure, and it manifested in shyness and fear of what others thought of me. I was also discouraged that I had so many barriers to navigate, such as racial discrimination in an all-white neighbourhood.

After years of processing my personal experiences, I learned that embracing myself was key to my breakthrough—it helped me understand myself and be honest about my strengths and weaknesses. It also freed me from depending on the approval of others. I became happier and clearer about who I was, and this improved my confidence.

I have learned to embrace and celebrate my forthrightness—I speak my mind. When utilized constructively, it empowers me to advocate for others. However, if not used with care or used destructively, it can be downright scary and may intimidate others.

This newfound self-acceptance has helped me love and value myself, warts and all, and ultimately allowed me to reach my full potential in my calling as a writer, speaker, and campaigner.

I believe that by embracing our identity, we can set a powerful example for other Asian women and show them that it is possible to be successful while being true to yourself. I feel humbled thinking I could help challenge the stereotypes and biases often attributed to Asian women.

Something good and redemptive has come from my personal pain. My personal awakening and the two decades I have spent investigating the underworld of trafficking have come from the most challenging moments in my life—my rejection as a girl and my first terrible marriage and subsequent divorce. These trials changed me profoundly and transformed my life purpose to focus on helping others and mobilizing resources for those in dire need, especially women and girls.

I have experienced challenges while reporting on human rights issues like wartime sexual slavery and sex trafficking. I have been exposed to untold human suffering, which has expanded my heart and mind in profound ways that have made me more empathetic to others. I feel grateful. Throughout my life, I have come to understand that the most incredible growth comes from stepping outside my comfort zone. I never imagined the incredible adventures and unconventional experiences that would shape my personal growth and understanding of the world. It is only by pushing myself to my limits that I have truly discovered who I am and what I am capable of achieving.

I used to believe that gender inequality was not an issue that affected me in my work bubble, whether I was in Canada, Beijing or Hong Kong. That was primarily because I hadn't been exposed to the statistics and what was really going on.

Having learned about the countless ways that women and girls are held back in society—from their education and health to their participation in public life and the workforce—I have become convinced that empowering more women and fighting against the biases they encounter is an incredibly important cause, one that I am committed to dedicating my life to.

In most countries, the average woman still gets paid less than the average man and faces a 'glass ceiling'. According to *Harvard Business Review*, women earned an average of 17 per cent less than men in 2022. This means that for every dollar earned by men, women earned only 82 cents.

Forbes magazine has stated that globally, on average, women earn 77 cents for every dollar earned by men, which indicates a significant global gender pay gap. According to estimates by UN Women, Asia and the Pacific, it will take around 257 years to close this gap if the current rate continues and more than 340 million women and girls could be left in poverty by 2030. To make matters worse, an alarming 4 per cent could face severe food insecurity by the same year. In 2020, the highest gender pay gap in the European Union was in Latvia at 22.3 per cent while the lowest was in Luxembourg at 0.7 per cent. In comparison, Korea has the largest gender pay gap in the world at 31.5 per cent, whereas Belgium has one of the smallest gaps at 3.4 per cent.

According to UN Women, Asia and the Pacific, the gender pay gap in East Asia and the Pacific stands at 20 per cent, while in South Asia, it's a staggering 33 per cent. Globally, the average is 24 per cent.

There are fewer women in decision-making roles due to discrimination, direct or otherwise, in the world of work. Even when comparing women and men who have the same job title, seniority level, and work the same hours, a gender pay gap of 11 per cent still exists.

We've come a long way since foot binding times, yet so much more needs to be done across Asia to target the root issue of gender discrimination. A UN Women report, *Progress on the Sustainable Development Goals: The Gender Snapshot 2021*, says that the world will not achieve gender equality by 2030, the lofty goal the United Nations set itself in September 2015 at the UN Sustainable Development Summit in New York. Indeed, for many women, things are getting worse.

'Violence against women remains high; global health, climate, and humanitarian crises have further increased risks of violence, especially for the most vulnerable women and girls; and women feel more unsafe than they did before the pandemic,' states the report's summary.

Raising awareness is the first step towards making a change. As professionals, particularly as women, it's our responsibility to take the initiative and help our sisters and daughters who are struggling with the pressing issues of our era.

I foresee a global women's movement that will be bigger than anything we've ever seen. We have more influential women and Asian women than at any other time in history. They're breaking barriers in various fields with their achievements.

It's incredible to witness the moment that I thought would never happen in my lifetime. Hollywood, known for being ageist and sexist, has very few high-profile Asians in the industry. But in 2023, Michelle Yeoh, a sixty-year-old actress, won an Oscar. Her win was a historic moment that inspired women worldwide to break through barriers and push past hindrances.

During one of her rousing speeches, Yeoh emphasized how women were put in a box, and she called on everyone to demolish the door of discrimination. According to a *Malay Mail* report, she declared to all female artists, no matter their age, 'I am holding the door open for you. We will never let it be closed again [. . .] For too long, we as women have been left out of rooms and conversations. We have been told the door is closed to us [. . .] There is still work to do, we have a long way to go before we can say we are on equal footing [. . .] So, what I would like to say is keep fighting, keep pushing, keep telling your stories. Your voices are important and your vision is vital.'

For the past twenty years, I've shared the personal stories of victim–survivors across Asia, as well as those of human traffickers and frontline workers, in the hopes of inspiring more people to help. It's crucial that the international community understands the urgent need to take coordinated action against sexual slavery.

I have devoted my life to fighting for the rights of women and girls, and other gender-related issues. Through my speaking engagements, and TV and film projects, I will continue to raise awareness about these issues and motivate the next generation to become changemakers, empowering them to help those in need.

Remember, you are unique and have a significant role to play in this world. You have an incredible opportunity to make a difference—to do something that only you can accomplish. This is your calling, your sweet spot, where everything aligns to create a convergence, and you can create a positive impact.

I leave you with the words of William Wilberforce, who helped abolish the transatlantic slave trade more than 100 years ago: 'If to be feelingly alive to the sufferings of my fellow creatures is to be a fanatic, I am one of the most incurable fanatics ever permitted to be at large.'

Here are some examples of gender inequality alongside relevant goals from the UN Women report, *Progress on the Sustainable Development Goals: The Gender Snapshot 2023*. Will you take action?

- **No poverty:** Over 340 million women and girls live in extreme poverty, living on less than US$1.90 a day. If current trends continue, in sub-Saharan Africa, even more women and girls will live in extreme poverty by 2030.
- **Zero hunger:** Globally, nearly one in three women experienced moderate or severe food insecurity in 2021. Rising food prices are to blame for this hunger around the world.
- **Quality education:** 54 per cent of girls who do not have access to formal education worldwide live in crisis-affected countries. Protracted conflicts, wars, and renewed efforts to keep girls out of school perpetuate gender gaps in access to school and learning.
- **Good health and well-being:** Unsafe abortion is a leading but preventable cause of maternal mortality and morbidity. Today, over 1.2 billion women and girls of reproductive age live in countries with some restrictions on access to safe abortion.
- **Gender equality:** At the current rate of progress, it may take another 286 years to remove discriminatory laws and close prevailing gaps in legal protections for women and girls. Globally, more than one in ten women and girls aged fifteen to forty-nine were subjected to sexual and/or physical violence by an intimate partner in the previous year.

  It was only in 2021 that 4,475 communities finally made public declarations committing to eliminate female genital mutilation (FGM). According to the UNICEF, worldwide, over 230 million girls and women have undergone FGM. Africa accounts for the largest number of girls who have been cut—over 144 million of them. It is mostly carried out on young girls between infancy and age fifteen.

Women hold only one-third of seats in local decision-making bodies.

The glass ceiling remains intact. Close to one in three managers or supervisors is a woman. At the current pace of change, parity will not be achieved for another 140 years.

- **Clean water and sanitation:** The lack of clean water claims the lives of more than 800,000 women and girls every year.
- **Affordable and clean energy:** Affordable and clean energy, key to life-saving care and productivity, remains out of reach for millions of women and girls in Asia and sub-Saharan Africa. Rising energy prices are making matters worse.
- **Decent work and economic growth:** Women's labour force participation in 2022 is projected to remain below pre-pandemic levels in 169 countries and areas.
- **Industry, innovation, and infrastructure:** Women hold only two in ten jobs in science, engineering, and information and communication technology globally.
- **Reduced inequalities:** By the end of 2021, some 44 million women and girls had been forced to flee their homes due to climate change, war, conflict, and human rights violations.

Chapter 3

The 'C' Word

I was often called a 'chink' growing up. People would pull their eyes back into exaggerated slits as they passed me by. And that was often just the adults. Children could be even crueller, particularly teenage boys. They would not only taunt me with abusive words but do so in a 'sing-song' way to mimic the sound of an Asian language. So stinging was the humiliation to a little girl that I tried to distance myself from my Korean heritage in elementary school.

The problem, as I saw it then, was that I stuck out. In class photos, not only was I the sole Asian girl but I was also always in the front row, as I was the shortest and they seated us by height. It was a mostly Caucasian elementary school in a Vancouver suburb, and the students who towered over me had not been exposed to Asian culture before meeting me. They did not even know that Korea was a country.

Some of the kids laughed at the food I ate for dinner—the usual staples of rice, kimchi, and meat-plus-vegetable side dishes marinated the Korean way. So, I learned to hide and lie about my meals. I couldn't have fathomed then that years later, Korean food would become so popular.

Every time I heard a racially charged 'joke'—like someone saying 'chink you' instead of 'thank you'—I would feel crushed and embarrassed. I desperately wished I was a blue-eyed blonde or brunette in those moments.

Ashamed of my cultural heritage, I vowed never to speak Korean at home and asked my parents never to address me by my Korean name, Saejung, ever again. I swore I would never again wear a Hanbok, the traditional Korean dress my parents liked for me to wear to church on Christmas and New Year's Eve.

I totally rejected the Korean part of my identity and began focusing on speaking English without an accent. I had decided English was the best language. It was perfect, I told myself, much better than Korean. But, in time, this led me into a linguistic limbo. By third grade, I had lost fluency in Korean yet my English remained heavily accented because I mirrored how my parents spoke it.

I would be teased about this yet remain defiant, as I was convinced my parents were the smartest and, therefore, an authority on everything, English pronunciation included.

'No, it's Je-jus! Not Je-ZUS!' I would insist as I tried to correct others in my usual sassy way of pronouncing words from the Bible.

It's no wonder that I was mocked.

Racist Mrs Reed

One particularly traumatic event sticks out from my childhood. It was when I mispronounced the word 'adjective' in an advanced reading group in the fifth grade. The teacher, 'Mrs Reed'—a wispy older woman in her late fifties with dark hair and dark energy—laughed out loud at me. That gave the other kids permission to laugh, too.

I wanted to shrink into a corner and disappear. It was scarring and confirmed the instinctive distrust I had felt for 'Mrs Reed' from the beginning. I had always sensed something cold and disdainful in her eyes when she looked at me. I was highly sensitive and had a radar for discrimination even then. In hindsight, I was right.

Mrs Reed treated me differently because I looked different from the other children in her class—in so doing, she broke my trust in authority figures. When older people are bigoted, it has a magnified effect on a child because children work on the assumption that adults should know better and do what's right. I have many Asian friends in the West whose memories of racist teachers, like mine, linger decades later.

In my case, I wouldn't make sense of the full extent of the damage Mrs Reed had done until three decades later when this memory came up in counselling and I learned that to heal and get closure, I would need to forgive her. But forgiving is easier said than done. It was hard for me to forget how, around the time of the Mrs Reed incident, I had begun to play an incredibly foolish game with my friends, in which we would sprint across the highway for fun. Often, we would do so just seconds away from a speeding car; had one of us tripped, we likely would have died.

I shudder to think of that game now. Was it a way to process the pain of feeling rejected? The impact of racism on the self-esteem and self-worth of children begins as early as age four. It affects their identity formation for life, according to a 2021 article in the *Journal of Canadian Academy of Child and Adolescent Psych* headlined, 'What's Race Got to Do with It?' The article notes that experiences of systemic discrimination in childhood can lead to rage and hopelessness, substance abuse, depression, anxiety, and even suicide.

Stress during childhood can develop hypervigilance among children who sense they are living in a threatening world, points out Dr Maria Trent, a professor of paediatrics at Johns Hopkins School of Medicine. This can lead to chronic stress that can cause hormonal changes, inflammation, and potentially chronic disease.

The emotional scars I bear from racism, both veiled and overt, are long-lasting. Even though I have a dual identity as a Korean and a Canadian, for most of my life, I felt I didn't fit in on either side. Self-rejection and identity issues took root in my childhood and devastated my self-esteem. These experiences continued to haunt me decades later, even after I emigrated back to Asia, in the opposite direction as my parents, to live and work in Beijing.

I couldn't speak Mandarin and when I did, people laughed at my bad pronunciation, and that triggered memories of my childhood in Burnaby, B.C. Often, I was asked if I was Japanese. When I replied that I was Korean and Canadian, the local Chinese people couldn't understand what I meant until I explained my parents had emigrated when I was two.

'So, basically, I'm a white person on the inside,' I would cheekily tell them.

Still, living in Beijing as a foreigner forced me to re-examine my Korean identity in a way I might never have done had I stayed in Vancouver. This is the silver lining to these traumatic memories—they instilled a greater sensitivity to the marginalized and the underprivileged and catalysed my early interest in human rights. These early wounds led to my calling as an agent for social justice and as a writer, campaigner, and filmmaker.

Today, I can say in earnest that I am grateful I didn't remain bitter.

What Could Have Been

My mother and father emigrated to Vancouver in the early 1970s. It was barely two decades after the Korean War had ended and the South was still rising from the ashes of its tattered economy. It was unimaginable back then that South Korea would become the economic miracle it is today, home to global brands like Samsung, K-pop bands like BTS and Blackpink, and all-conquering Netflix hits like *Queen of Tears, Crash Landing on You* and *Squid Game*.

My parents settled in Vancouver because a close relative had already moved there and they hoped it would offer better opportunities for their children. My father's work at a company that made rubber products meant it was there or Tokyo.

I shudder to think how life might have turned out had he chosen Tokyo in the 1970s or if we had remained in South Korea. In Japan or South Korea, I would have likely grown up to become a housewife and happily raise children in my twenties, like my cousins in Korea who are around my age. I don't have anything against being a housewife but, in hindsight, I feel I dodged a bullet, as I love my work and I'm grateful to have grown up valuing independence and freedom. There was another reason that growing up in Japan would have radically altered my life's course, one that wouldn't become clear for decades yet. But I'll get to that later.

Even growing up Canadian left me conflicted. On one hand, I was taught Western values of direct communication and independence. On the other hand, my Asian mindset was to avoid conflict or any action that might dishonour the family name.

Perhaps the one place I did feel a sense of belonging was at church with the other Korean immigrant children. Being with them was a great boost to my confidence. We would hang out every Wednesday and Friday night during church services and all day on Sunday, waving goodbyes late at night when our parents decided it was time to go home.

I found camaraderie, mischief and even young love among this group of good friends. We played games and sometimes scared ourselves by playing Bloody Mary, a silly game calling on the ghost of Queen Mary in the mirror. A few of the younger kids cried and I once swore I saw a ghost. A few times, we played an icky kissing game with the boys we had a crush on.

I was still in elementary school when my parents divorced and I struggled with abandonment, as I no longer saw my father on a daily basis. My mother found it even harder to be a single parent. I grew up fast and didn't have much of a childhood. I did my best to help clean the house and translate documents when necessary. She found solace and support from her friends at our church.

As we drove home on Sunday evenings, I knew it was time to switch gears mentally and emotionally and get ready to hang out with my Caucasian friends at school, even if they didn't entirely 'get' me and my Korean culture.

A Writing Dream

The Chinese American broadcaster Connie Chung was the only Asian news anchor in my era. I felt excited to see her on TV and inspired by her breaking barriers. There was hardly anyone who looked like me on the TV screen or in the movie theatres back then. It made me feel invisible.

My friends raised in Asia, who were surrounded by Asian faces in the media and advertisements, often do not understand what it's like to grow up as an ethnic minority in the West with no Asian role models or other authority figures such as teachers.

One way I coped with my identity issues and all the related baggage was by burying myself in a mountain of books. When I came home from school every day, I read fiction and non-fiction for hours. To my mother's consternation, I read novels at the dinner table. I was so drawn into the magical world of words that I couldn't put books down. It was an escape from reality. And I read everywhere.

One summer, my mother—a single parent at the time before she remarried—travelled to Korea, leaving us kids at home and asking her friend's nineteen-year-old daughter to babysit us. My babysitter told everyone how surprised she was that instead of going out to party and have fun, I sat around all day reading books and magazines like *Time* while eating oranges and apples.

My mom also instilled in me a love of the *Anne of Green Gables* book series by L.M. Montgomery. When she took a Western name in her teens, years before arriving in Canada, she chose Anne with an 'e' because she identified with the feisty yet sensitive main character's love of poetry and her strong bond with best friend Diana.

Mom had all the qualities Anne displayed in the book and a similar bond with her own high school best friend in Korea, whom she called Diana. We used to recount beautiful parts of the novel together and cry as we talked about Anne's kind adopted father figure, Matthew, and the loyal dog that waited in vain for its deceased master. I'll treasure these core memories forever.

Mom told me it had been her childhood dream to write a book. She wrote essays and poetry and was published in the newspaper. She planted a seed, and I too began to dream of becoming an author.

One teacher, in particular, nurtured my writing and love of words. 'Mrs Hall', my twelfth-grade English Literature and English AP teacher, was one of the most influential educators in my life. She was the antithesis of Mrs Reed and was one of the few teachers who showed sincere interest and respect for my Korean heritage.

I once shared with her that I wanted to write a book. To my surprise, she encouraged me. She was articulate and charismatic and when she taught English Literature, she captured our imaginations—probably because she truly loved the material and cared deeply about her students. She reminded me of the larger-than-life inspirational English teacher, Mr Keating, the main character in the movie *Dead Poets Society*, portrayed so memorably by the late Robin Williams.

Recently, I felt compelled to track down Mrs Hall. I had thought of her often over the years and finally decided to act. I was surprised to find her email online and I reached out immediately. Of course, I felt teary as I wrote my message:

> Hi Mrs Hall!
>
> It's Sylvia! I was in your English Lit and English AP course many years ago when I was a teenager and your teaching changed my life.
>
> I'm an author now. I also host a digital TV show and do other work in the philanthropy realm.
>
> I wanted to say hello and let you know that you had the most significant impact on my life as a student. Thank you for being an incredible teacher.
>
> Love and blessings,
> Sylvia

I was delighted when Mrs Hall wrote back immediately to say she remembered me.

> Hi Sylvia!
>
> I am so glad to hear from you; I vividly remember you being in my classes. Thank you for your very kind words. It is wonderful to teach young people—like yourself—the amazing wealth seen in fine literature.
>
> So you are an author of several books? Could I wire you the $ and you send me a signed copy of one of your books—I am thrilled to know an actual published author. I knew you would be highly successful in whatever you undertook!
>
> Take care and hope to chat again. Cheers!

Tears rolled down my face as I read her message. It was not until this moment that I fully appreciated how great a role her encouragement and infectious love for literature had played in my life. Mrs Hall demonstrated the power of one—it takes only one person to profoundly impact another.

I mailed Mrs Hall my latest book and, of course, I did not allow her to pay for it. I was thrilled to be able to honour what she had done for me.

Thank you, Mrs Hall for believing in me. You made a world of difference to this nerdy and awkward immigrant kid. As the American historian Henry Adams once put it: 'Teachers affect eternity; no one can tell where their influence stops.'

The Healing Power of Telling Your Story

During my teens, a lack of Asian role models in the media made me feel worse about my appearance. I struggled with feeling invisible and my body dysmorphia flared up. There were times I simply believed I was ugly and inferior and that only Caucasian girls embodied the ultimate standard of beauty.

For a teen girl, that's a devastating belief, and it wreaked havoc on my emotions and confidence. And yet, there were times when I received a lot of attention and special treatment for being a 'pretty girl'. I knew how to wield this power over the boys when I needed a ride, computer support or immediate help at a store.

Still, for the most part, I thought my eyes were too small, my nose too flat, and I would have happily traded my features for those of my Caucasian friends. I wished I had blonde hair and blue eyes and in senior high school, I even used colour contacts to change my irises to a light bluish grey.

I was full of contradictions.

Had I grown up seeing more Asians on TV and in the media in general, my life might well have turned out very different. When I was hooked on hip-hop dancing at sixteen, I longed to be African American and wore little braids in my hair. I watched the fluid poetry of my African Canadian friend Michelle's dance moves with envy and wondered why I couldn't move as naturally as her. Sadly, I wanted to be like everyone else—anyone, that is, other than me.

It was a hollow feeling and stemmed from a lack of confidence in who I was. I was like a jellyfish, with no backbone and no sense of self. There's a scientific basis for why teenagers are desperate to fit in and feel anxious when they are not part of the 'in crowd'. According to the Stanford Medicine Children's Health Organization, the rational part of the human brain isn't fully developed until around twenty-five.

As we grow into adults, our brains undergo significant changes in the way we process information. Adults tend to use the prefrontal cortex, the rational part of the brain, to think and make decisions. However, in teenagers, the amygdala, which is responsible for emotional behaviour and motivation, is more active. This difference in brain function explains why teenagers often experience emotional turmoil, impulsivity, social anxiety, and poor judgement. Understanding these neural underpinnings is crucial for parents, educators, and mental health professionals to support and guide teenagers through this challenging phase of their development.

In my twenties and thirties, I often joked that I was a white person trapped in a Korean body—a 'banana' or 'twinkie'—white on the inside, yellow on the outside.

I was twenty-five when my dear friend 'Felicity's' Korean Canadian husband 'Morris' mentioned feeling trapped in a 'Korean person's body'. He had suffered mortifying incidents of racial discrimination while growing up in all-White schools. I thought it was the most apt description of how I had felt growing up, so I adopted Morris's phrase and used it liberally. I wanted to take the sting out of the racial abuse I had endured. It truly conveyed how I didn't want to be Korean. I didn't want to be different from the herd in my childhood.

Where Are You Really From?

From an early age, I was asked by both friends and strangers, 'Where are you from?'

When I would respond that I was Canadian, there would be the inevitable follow-up question, 'No, where are you *really* from?'

It was extremely painful to hear that word 'really', as if I were not a bona fide Canadian. It gave me that 'in-between' feeling that I wasn't entirely accepted as a Korean by South Koreans nor as a Canadian by Caucasian Canadians. This sentiment of never entirely fitting in, of being stranded in the middle, has helped sensitize me to those struggling for acceptance and the oppressed—asylum seekers and refugees, minorities, and victims of racial and sexual discrimination.

But it wasn't until my late twenties that I understood the importance of knowing one's identity more deeply. I'll never forget the words of Professor Edward Chang, founding director of the Young Oak Kim Centre at UC Riverside, at a conference I once attended: 'If you don't know your identity, then you cannot know your destiny and purpose in life.'

I thought about his words for a long time, wondering how one found one's identity. Culture, society, family, the people around us, our experiences and memories, the events we witness, the environment that shapes us—all these things help form our view of ourselves and where we fit in the world. Recognizing this and getting to know ourselves is critical because it shapes our choices and influences our relationships and every aspect of our lives. And as with many journeys of understanding, this one must begin in our past.

Processing Pain

It was not until years later, in my twenties, that I came to appreciate the value of looking back. To my surprise, I was hired at a local newspaper and then recruited to work at the Canadian public broadcaster, CBC. I heard whispers of resentment from a handful of Caucasian colleagues and bosses about more diversity hires and I wondered if I had been given the job simply for being Asian.

It was the first time being different was a perceived advantage, yet it also put me on edge. I overcompensated and worked twice as hard as the rest to prove that I belonged there because of my talent and hard work. I was afraid people would accuse me of getting a free ride. Other minority journalists told me that they too drove themselves harder to shut down the resentful critics.

A turning point in my identity crisis came when I was working as an executive editor at *Ricepaper*, an Asian Canadian arts and culture magazine envisioned as a platform for Asian authors, artists, and emerging voices who were underrepresented in the mainstream. A well-known community organizer and author Jim Wong-Chu asked me to consider taking on the role and I accepted. I was working full-time at the CBC, yet something special about this magazine—more like a newsletter at the time, stapled together and assembled in a basement—compelled me to take on the role.

Though I had no idea how to edit a magazine or assemble a team, I quickly brought on board talented editors, Angela Mackenzie and Yen To, and later designers and more writers. We talked about our experiences with racism as the only Asian kids in class—something we had not discussed with anyone.

I was surprised they had gone through the same things I had. They were also asked the dreaded question, 'Where are you really from?' and we included this in one of the magazine's issues to foster more discussion. It felt gratifying and highly empowering to be heard and to write about our collective pain while promoting other Asian Canadian artists, activists and writers. It helped immensely to process our experiences together.

Again, there is a scientific basis for this. According to *Psychology Today*,

> Every time you tell your story and someone else who cares bears witness to it, you turn off the body's stress responses, flipping off toxic stress hormones like cortisol and epinephrine and flipping on relaxation responses that release healing hormones like oxytocin, dopamine, nitric oxide, and endorphins. Not only does this turn on the body's innate self-repair mechanisms and function as preventative medicine – or treatment if you're sick. It also relaxes your nervous system and helps heal your mind of depression, anxiety, fear, anger, and feelings of disconnection.

Who knew? From this I have learned that it's vital to have a group of friends to remind you of your worth and purpose. Don't ever let the critics get you down. I was not alone and that was a profound lesson.

As part of my identity search, I volunteered for Asian Heritage Month in Vancouver, a series of events celebrating Asian artists, writers, and culture in the month of May in 2000. A few years later, I launched the first Asian Heritage Month in Victoria, B.C., a predominantly Caucasian city, after moving there to work as a news reporter and host of a lifestyle programme at a TV station. It was an incredible experience to spotlight Asians and their achievements.

Several Asian Canadian friends and those of mixed heritage told me how they felt a real sense of belonging for the first time. New connections were forged and some of them became life-long friends. My good friend Dorothy Wong met her husband Yin Lam through one of these events. She brought the community together by hosting unforgettable dinners at her home.

This month of celebrating Asian culture is now a big deal in the West. Companies are embracing it and bringing in speakers to raise awareness about the importance of appreciating and respecting cultural diversity.

Today, the Greater Vancouver region is vastly different from when I was coming of age. Back then, new immigrants were a relatively rare phenomenon. Now, more than half of Vancouver is made up of ethnic minorities. In the past decade or so, a growing resentment has been simmering towards wealthy mainland Chinese who snap up properties as investments rather than as somewhere to live. This has caused property prices to soar and squeezed young families who must move further out into smaller cities with cheaper homes. Sometimes, this frustration boils over in the form of racial slurs directed at anyone who looks Asian—whether they are from China, Hong Kong, Korea, or elsewhere.

During the pandemic, there was a spike in violence and hate crimes directed at Asians in North America, particularly towards young Asian women who were physically attacked by mostly larger Caucasian men. In a 2021 Pew Research Centre survey, 32 per cent of Asian Americans, more than any other ethnic group, feared someone might threaten or attack them, and 27 per cent of Asians in the US, more than other groups, said they had been told to go back to their home country.

The glimmer of hope that has come out of this tragedy is that it has helped mobilize Asians to speak out in the West and brought them together as a community in unprecedented ways. Asian immigrants in the West are usually stereotyped as being 'model minorities', and the myth is they're successful with little to no need for social or economic support and they're nice, obedient, and hard-working.

Often, our pain leads to our greatest contributions. That's true for Gina Wong, the founder of the Asian Gold Ribbon campaign, a social change platform taking a stand against anti-Asian hate and racism. We had a Zoom conversation before the campaign in May 2022, and I felt an immediate connection with her over our shared childhood experiences. Gina and I commiserated over our scars from growing up as the only Asian girls in our schools and neighbourhoods.

She visibly recoiled as she recounted being called 'China girl' in her teens. It was the title of a well-known David Bowie song. I was called the same and empathized with how she initially responded by rejecting her Chinese heritage. I surprised myself by breaking down and sobbing during a video interview for the campaign with Gina and Samantha Louie-Poon. They asked brilliant questions and were incredibly empathic. In the interview, I reflected on feeling alone during my identity crisis and how I'd had no one to process the pain with. It was my first time speaking publicly about this childhood trauma. At first, when I watched the interview, I was incredibly embarrassed. But later, I was buoyed by the thought that my on-screen vulnerability might have been exactly what someone out there needed so they would know they were not alone.

If I'd had an Asian Gold Ribbon campaign to join when I was younger, I might have embraced my cultural identity a lot sooner. I admire Gina for turning her challenges into something powerful by uniting a group in the fight against racial discrimination. That campaign sent a message that we Asians deserve respect and equal treatment. When we celebrate our culture and tell our stories, we show through our actions how inclusion, acceptance, and understanding can build a stronger society.

Here are some words of advice to help you tell your story effectively and impactfully:

- Mine and explore your personal experiences by reflecting on any remarkable moments in your life, such as a watershed experience or a big mistake. Consider how these experiences made you feel and what lessons you learned. The cringier, the better. Remember, the more embarrassing the experience, the more powerful your story can be.
- When crafting a story, think about the message you want to convey. Be honest—warts and all—including both positive and negative aspects.
- Use quotes, data, and visuals that are relevant to your message to make it stronger.
- Before sharing your story with the world, seeking feedback from a trusted friend is helpful.

Remember that your story and experiences can help and inspire others like nothing else. As the American author of *Return to Love* Marianne Williamson said, 'As we let our light shine, we unconsciously give other people permission to do the same. As we are liberated from our own fear, our presence actually liberates others.'

Mining the Past

Understanding our family history can illuminate who we are.

This realization came to me when my philanthropy work took me to numerous parts of China between 2004 and 2011. Traces of ancient village systems still exist in the country, and as I met the various community elders, it dawned on me that I was walking in the shoes of my ancestors.

I had a flash of insight that my paternal great-grandfather and grandfather, who had leadership roles in local government in Korea, must have been involved in similar meetings long ago. I remembered, too, how my maternal great-grandparents loved and served the poor free meals in their home and gave away clothes—even their long johns—in the winter to those in need. Everyone said our great-grandpa loved justice. That was his greatest passion and he walked his talk. He pointedly chose to have one wife only and to forego concubines.

I cannot express enough how grateful I feel to be part of a lineage of Koreans who have devoted their lives to serving their community. This awakening was a turning point and helped me embrace my heritage. It's ironic that I had to move from Canada to China to appreciate it fully. It opened my eyes to the significance of giving back to society, and I now take pride in carrying forward the legacy of my ancestors.

One summer, my sister Jayne and I travelled to several cities in South Korea to explore our roots. I interviewed my uncles and relatives about their memories of my late maternal grandfather and great-grandparents. It was incredibly meaningful to hear them talk about our close family members and to gain insight into their personalities.

No one in my family had mentioned one word of the Korean War until this trip. But the shadows of it had been cast over our family for many years. Generational pain from war is real. I was seven during the last sombre gathering with relatives to observe my maternal grandfather's death. A black and white photo of his beautiful oval face with piercing eyes, frozen in time, was the centrepiece on the table, along with an abundance of fruits and other Korean foods. We looked down at his photo and stood around in silence. I heard sniffling and crying. I felt a palpable sadness. This is a traditional Korean way to honour the dead, a tradition that my Christian relatives abandoned once they found out it didn't align with our faith to 'worship' the dead.

That trip to Korea was a life-changing one for me, and I was able to pick up some missing puzzle pieces of my identity by getting to know my family history. It altered how I see myself culturally. A few weeks into the trip, I realized no one had spoken of my late grandfather.

I started to poke around the topic and found my grandfather's youngest brother tearing up. I decided to change tactics and ask more direct questions. I was merciless and kept asking questions even when he cried because I truly believed I was helping him release his grief. I asked him daily about my grandfather, and the tears flowed often as he spoke.

At the end of my visit, he said, 'Wow, I feel so refreshed, I feel like I've been cleansed at a spa.'

I was shocked that he hadn't spoken of his brother to anyone for decades. I learned my grandfather had held my mom as a baby before he left to fight in the Korean War and never returned. He went missing in action during the early days of the war. He was only twenty-four. Had he lived, my mother's life would have been entirely different.

My family was unable to mourn him fully because his body was never found. This was a great trauma for my mother and my great-grandparents. My grandfather's mother, my great-grandmother, was so grieved that she travelled all over Korea to find the most accurate shamans and fortune tellers to find out if he was still alive. She spent a small fortune to find closure. She later converted to the Christian faith and stopped believing in shamans.

Family and friends dearly loved my grandfather. Even decades later, mentioning him brought tears to my grandfather's younger brothers. He was a natural leader, a gifted guitar player, and athlete who loved to compete in shotput and baseball. One relative said you could tell he was a teacher by the way he spoke. He inspired young people and was charismatic and strong.

A passionate man, he even wrote a letter in his own blood to his wife during their courtship. They were from opposite sides of the track and unlikely to be matched in marriage at that time. Somehow, they met and fell in love. He was an eligible bachelor from a wealthy family while his wife was ivory-skinned with a pretty porcelain doll-like face. She was quiet, demure, and from an impoverished village in Daegu. He treated her like a queen.

After losing her husband in the war, my grandmother remarried a man from her home village and left the opulence of her in-laws' home with its servants. Her new family struggled financially.

Her eldest daughter, my half-aunt, told me my grandmother never recovered from my grandfather's death. Her love for him did not diminish one bit over time. He was the love of her life. She lost her will to be a mother and often left my eldest aunt when she was five at home alone to care for her infant siblings. Most of the child-rearing work, such as washing the children's hair, was clumsily done by their father.

Meanwhile, my mother was raised by her loving grandmother and had the opposite experience of being cherished and treated as a little princess. She was given tailored clothes and the best of everything, and lavished with attention and extravagant love.

My great uncle told me my outgoing personality reminded him of his older brother, my grandfather. His life was brimming with immense passion and great promise but was tragically cut short by the North Korean forces or their allies, the Communist Chinese army. It only occurred to me recently that he could have died at the hands of the Communist Chinese. If I had known that the Chinese killed him, would that have changed my view of China? Would that have caused barriers in loving the Chinese people while I lived in Beijing?

Thinking of my grandfather and even writing of him now causes the tears to fall for someone I have never met. I mourn because I'm connected with him intricately through the generations—his death affected my life through the impact on my mother, as if there were no distance in time. Tears mingle afresh with the joys of celebrating his brief yet meaningfully splendid life. Both tears and happiness in equal measure. The beauty of life is its brevity—a reminder to cherish every moment.

By the end of my time in Korea, I had a greater appreciation for my parents' homeland, a far-off place an ocean away, of which I had previously known so little.

Our past holds the key to who we are today. Knowing where we come from shapes the way we view ourselves and the world. Having a fuller picture of my family line, passed down by my relatives, illuminated some things for me. I now know that my great-grandpa and grandpa were very passionate, and I inherited this trait from them. I also learned I come from a lineage of warm-hearted and fiercely strong Yangban women with strong social consciences and landowners with a royal lineage that can be traced back to King Gyeongsun, the last ruler of the Silla kingdom (897–978 CE).

Our roots run deep, and our history is a vital part of who we are. By delving into our past, we can gain valuable insights that help us navigate the present. The character, values, and legacy of our ancestors are woven into our very being, and it's up to us to carry that forward and make our own mark on the world.

I feel incredibly fortunate to be able to carry on the incredible legacy of some of my ancestors and will do my best to make a positive impact.

Fifty Years of Silence Shattered

In the midst of my teenage angst, the opportunity to explore my Korean heritage suddenly presented itself one day.

It began when my mother shared a newspaper article on an elderly South Korean woman, Kim Hak-soon. Kim, sixty-eight, a slight, pepper-haired woman, was wearing a traditional white dress at a press conference in Seoul on 14 August 1991, where she bravely chose to do something utterly alien to women of her culture: speak out.

She testified tearfully that as a seventeen-year-old, she had been forced into sexual servitude during the Japanese war against China and recounted being raped by up to thirty Japanese soldiers a day in a tiny cubicle in a military brothel in Manchuria.

The teenage Kim was one of the estimated 200,000 to 400,000 girls and women forced to work in Japanese military brothels during World War II and the years leading up to it—sex slaves euphemistically called 'comfort women'. There were more than 1,000 'comfort stations' in China alone. The sole reason these girls and women were forced to serve was to 'comfort' lonely Japanese soldiers traumatized by war to prevent military secrets from being leaked.

Because the Japanese military wanted to protect its men from sexually transmitted diseases, there was a greater demand for younger girls and women who were virgins. The victims came from across the Asia Pacific: Chinese, Koreans, Japanese, Dutch (Indonesia was a Dutch colony then), Indonesians, Taiwanese including the Indigenous people, Eurasians, Filipinos, Burmese, Malays, Vietnamese, Thai, Pacific Islanders, and more.

Between 1931 to 1945, countless girls and women were forced into prostitution and systemically raped, some by up to sixty soldiers a day. But in the years since the end of the war, elements of Japanese society—led by ultranationalists and right-wing conservatives and at times with the Japanese government's backing—have tried to obscure their place in history, belittling the accounts of survivors and claiming instead that the 'comfort women' were, in fact, voluntary and willing prostitutes who joined the brothels to make money.

Kim was moved to recount her experiences after the Japanese government outright denied ever having forced women and teens like her into brothels. She campaigned for an unequivocal, sincere apology from the Japanese government for the rest of her life. She knew that with the passage of time, it became ever more important to challenge the lies and distortions of Tokyo because, with every passing year, fewer women like her could bear witness to the truth.

So, with a brooding intensity on her wrinkled face, she took the stand. 'How did I become a public witness? When I read newspapers and watched the news, Japan kept denying the truth,' Kim told the press conference. 'They took us forcibly, put us directly in the military compound, and turned us into comfort women.'

Her testimony catalysed a global movement, motivating many other survivors to bear witness in public and researchers to begin looking into this tragic and untold chapter of history. Kim had suffered profoundly from her secret for fifty years before breaking her silence. With those words, she set the truth free.

Since 2018, the date that Kim broke her silence on 14 August is a national memorial day for all survivors of Japanese military sexual slavery. Hearing what Kim went through made me want to learn more about the history of Korea.

In the public and high school libraries, I searched through more than twenty history books for mentions of 'comfort women' and wartime sexual slavery but could find none. I was disturbed by how the suffering of Asian women in war, many of them the same age as me, had been erased from history. And I was surprised at how a wave of profound generational anger, seemingly embedded in my DNA and passed down from my ancestors, welled up inside me.

I learned more about the plight of the wartime sex slaves from reports by the United Nations. And the more I learned, the more I felt pain and anger towards the people group responsible for these and other wartime atrocities in the Asia Pacific. I saw that a lack of closure by the Japanese government after World War II and this unresolved issue of Japanese war crimes and wartime sexual violence and forced prostitution still affects Asian race relations.

I suddenly began to feel uneasy around my good friend 'Betty', a Japanese Canadian, and another Japanese family who rented the basement of our house. Although this feeling was fleeting, it led me to accept the impact of our biases and how they can affect our relationships with others.

I also took more notice of the anti-Japanese attitudes of those around me. I recalled how my great-uncle spoke fluent Japanese but owned no Japanese electronics and vowed never to buy a Japanese car. Growing up in South Korea under the Japanese occupation, he had experienced unjust treatment from the teachers at his Japanese government-run school. He drives an American vehicle to this day. Young and old in the Chinese and Korean communities whispered that no one liked or trusted the Japanese. 'No one wanted to date Japanese men,' said some young Chinese and Korean women as they laughed.

For a *Ricepaper* magazine article in 1999, I interviewed renowned civil-rights lawyer Gay McDougall who, a year earlier as a UN special rapporteur, had authored a report on Imperial Japanese military sexual slavery. It was a watershed conversation. McDougall told me that the Japanese government had spent a lot of time and money trying to bury her report. I knew I was dealing with something bigger and more menacing than I had the skills and experience to handle. I was scared. Nevertheless, I decided to keep moving forward, but I didn't know where to find survivors to interview.

My opportunity came a few years later, in 2001, when I worked as a TV reporter in Victoria. A well-connected Chinese Canadian activist dedicated to raising awareness of Japanese war crimes told me that Kim Soon-duk, an eighty-year-old survivor of Japanese military sexual slavery, would speak at a news conference at the US State Department in Washington, DC.

Three hours later, I called my mentor Nancy Patterson, a pastor's wife at my church, to ask for her advice on whether I should go on this spontaneous trip to meet Kim. Her support was instrumental and led me to buy a plane ticket online. I immediately took a ferry and then drove like crazy to Seattle to catch a flight.

When I met Kim in DC, I was in awe of her. She was a walking history book. During our time together, Kim told me that as a sixteen-year-old, she had been promised a job as a nurse but was instead taken forcibly to a military brothel in Shanghai with fifty other Korean teenage girls.

For three years, she was forced to serve as a sex slave for Japanese soldiers and subjected to the most abhorrent living conditions. After the war ended, she was too ashamed to return to her family home and migrated to Seoul, where she became a domestic worker.

In 1992, after her partner (they were not married) passed away, Kim finally testified to the horrors of sexual violence she had endured at the hands of the Japanese military. In an interview with me in DC, Kim said she did not harbour prejudice towards the Japanese today. 'We have to recognize in Japan, there are many good citizens. I do not hate the younger generation,' she said. 'We can only get healing if we solve this problem. Solving the problem means the Japanese government issues an official apology.'

I learned for the first time from Kim that even after all these years, the Japanese government was still unwilling to accept unequivocal responsibility for its direct involvement in forcibly and deceptively recruiting girls and women into this military forced prostitution system.

Tokyo was unwilling to apologize without ambiguity for destroying the lives of so many girls and women. Kim asked me to tell the world about her experience and that's when I decided in my heart to write a book.

Several years later, I moved to Beijing in 2004 to do more research. I asked people daily what they thought of the Japanese. Young and old, atheists and Christians—even pastors—all said they hated the Japanese for what they had done to the Chinese during the war, for enslaving women and for the Rape of Nanking (Nanjing) or what's also known as the Nanking Massacre, where 150,000 Chinese male prisoners of war were slaughtered, elderly and infants executed, and tens of thousands of women raped.

It began on 13 December 1937, during the Second Sino-Japanese War and ended six weeks later. Even the Nazis were purportedly horrified by the brutality of Japanese soldiers who did live burials, roasted people, disembowelled and castrated, and allowed them to get torn apart by dogs.

The Chinese learn about Japanese war crimes as early as kindergarten. 'The Japanese government hasn't properly apologized to us,' I heard repeatedly. 'They need to apologize!'

Through the years, Japanese prime ministers and politicians have repeatedly and publicly denied historical facts and direct responsibility for forcing women into military sexual slavery. Late prime minister Shinzo Abe once said there was no evidence that Japan's wartime government coerced women into prostitution for the Japanese Imperial Army.

As a result, the Japanese government has refused to give symbolic government compensation to victims. Abe had even said he wanted to revise the Kono Statement, the first apology given by the Japanese government in 1993, which was rejected by survivors and activists for its ambiguity and insincere tone.

Several survivors including those from Korea, the Netherlands, China, and Taiwan have demanded an official apology and reparations for being forced into Japanese military sexual servitude and subjected to constant abuse and rape. Tragically, they still await an official apology from Japan's prime minister that honours and fully acknowledges the unspeakable suffering of all victims and survivors of imperial Japanese military sexual slavery.

Since 2007, the governments of Canada, the Netherlands, South Korea, Taiwan, and the European Parliament have all passed resolutions demanding that the Japanese government take moral and legal responsibility for directly planning and implementing the system of military sexual slavery. They have called on the Japanese government to offer the survivors an unequivocal apology and compensation.

In recent years, during a two-day review of Japan's record, the UN Committee on the Elimination of Racial Discrimination urged the government of Japan to do more for victims of wartime sexual slavery and offer full redress and reparations. Gay McDougall, the vice chair of the UN committee, said what the survivors have been saying all along: 'It is a wound that has been festering for far too long.'

A New Reconciliation Journey

While visiting friends in Hong Kong in 2008, I attended a meeting with a reconciliation team, a group of Japanese Christians who had travelled to China in an attempt to heal the divide.

During our meeting, which was held at a local church, they did something radical and out of the ordinary—they apologized sincerely, tears streaming down their cheeks, to the Chinese in the pews for the past conduct of the Japanese forces—killing and torturing civilians and forcing women into wartime sexual slavery.

The Chinese looked surprised at first, then couldn't control their weeping. The loving gesture of the Japanese had hit a chord too deep to articulate in words. I sat rigid and stony-faced as they faced me to apologize to the Koreans. I doubted their apology would affect me, a 'banana' who felt little connection with the place of my birth. Besides, however sincere, no civilian apology could ever replace an official apology from the prime minister.

To my surprise, I wept until I had no more tears. I had blown my nose so often that I was struggling to breathe. Their simple apology, compelled by love, triggered an intense release of pain and generational hatred towards the Japanese in the room. Just imagine what effect an official government apology from Tokyo would have.

I later filmed a different reconciliation team led by Tomoko Hasegawa called Healing River-Rainbow Bridge from Japan for a documentary, *Healing River*, and wrote about them in my books, *A Long Road to Justice* and *Silenced No More: Voices of Comfort Women.*

They knelt on the ground and held a sign that expressed how deeply sorry they were for Japanese war crimes against humanity. Their humility and love transformed lives. Wherever they went in China, people wept after reading their sign. Their sincerity touched ancient pain. As the Book of Psalms describes: 'Deep calls unto deep.'

My documentary *Healing River* and book *Silenced No More* were showcased at the Comfort Women Museum in Nanjing for a time.

Sadly, the Japanese involved in grassroots reconciliation face persecution and rejection from their compatriots and family members. One woman in Tokyo was ordered by her husband never to participate in the reconciliation work again and asked us to blur her face in the documentary.

Online attacks and harassment from the right wing or ultranationalists occur regularly against Japanese involved in raising awareness of comfort women and World War II war crimes.

Most Japanese still have not learned about the forced prostitution system of 'comfort women' or other Japanese war crimes in their history books, so they do not understand the issue and how it impacts other Asian people.

When I showed my documentary about the Japanese reconciliation team *Healing River* in schools and universities in Hong Kong, China and the US, many people, including teenagers, wept. One student said she was touched that there were Japanese willing to apologize and that she didn't know there were good people in Japan. Others said their grandparents or parents were affected by the Japanese invasion of China and they hated the Japanese still.

I hid my identity for a year and wrote under a pen name to protect myself from harassment. I'm grateful that I wasn't a target of the right-wing in Japan; however, there were a handful of strange encounters and online incidents. An American who had lived in Japan for many years angrily confronted me at a conference and asked why Korean soldiers weren't being held accountable for raping Vietnamese women during the Vietnam War.

After my initial shock, I expressed my disappointment and directly informed him that his beliefs echoed those of Japanese right-wing groups who deny the existence of women who were systematically forced into Japanese military sexual slavery. These groups aim to divert attention from the Japanese military's war crimes. I noticed he seemed to be unaware of this fact.

I once had a book lined up with a Japanese publisher; the book was almost ready to be published, but the Japanese male executives at the publishing house cancelled it. I have wondered whether after my book *Silenced No More* is published in Japanese, I should go to Japan to speak on the issue and call for racial justice. It would be like an African American going into the heart of segregation in the Deep South during the Jim Crow era to talk about lynching.

A Japanese citizen involved in community issues in Chicago once connected with me on LinkedIn. As soon as I mentioned that I had written a book on Japanese wartime sexual slavery, she blocked me. Shockingly, she made a snap judgement and didn't want to connect professionally or understand more.

At a stop in Macon, Georgia, during our 2016 speaking tour on modern slavery, I told the audience about the racial hatred of the Chinese and Koreans for the Japanese and how protesters in China had smashed glass at Japanese businesses and overturned Japanese cars. I recounted how I had witnessed crowds in Beijing chanting, 'Down with Japan!', and that in Korea, one man had chopped his fingers off and another self-immolated to protest the whitewashed history books that failed to mention the full extent of Japanese war crimes and atrocities.

The audience of Caucasians and African Americans was shocked that seemingly well-behaving Asians would display such anger. I told them such scenes demonstrated the rawness of the generational pain and racial hatred in East Asia and showed the pressing need to heal it.

During my talks, I usually show my film of the Japanese Christian reconciliation team and conclude by noting the need to release lingering feelings of hatred. In Georgia, several members of the audience—both Caucasians and African Americans—came up to thank me and tell me that my talk had struck them like a parable of race relations in America and that it had broadened their thoughts on race. Until then, I hadn't even been conscious of the fact that anti-racism and conciliation were at the heart of my awareness campaign.

Reporting on these survivors changed my life. Meeting these women helped me see that the cycle of slavery continues and inspired me to write and make films about human trafficking and human rights violations. I've interviewed girls and women forced into prostitution and their traffickers, 'mamasans', and pimps.

Today, there remain only a handful of survivors of Japanese military sexual slavery around the world. These elderly women in their twilight years have long fought for a powerful, sincere apology that brings healing. Yet, most of the survivors I have interviewed have since passed away, denied the closure, healing and reconciliation that are so urgently needed.

Back when my mom shared about the newspaper article of Kim Hak-soon's story, little did I know it would take me fourteen years to research and write a book on her and women like her. In hindsight, I have been surprised at how writing that book helped me explore my Korean history and the concept of generational pain and ultimately, accept my Korean heritage.

To this day, I'm amazed at how Kim's story led me out of an identity crisis and shaped the direction of my life. It is Kim and all those who shared her indescribable suffering who inspired me to fight for the rights of girls and women globally, for gender equality.

I used to feel pain at not fitting in as a Canadian or Korean, at being stuck and 'in between' cultures. Now, I love it because it means I can be a bridge. This is my gift. A redemptive gift that has shown me how our greatest pain can become our greatest power. I wrote the books I wanted to read as a teenager in Vancouver, Canada, when I couldn't find anything written by strong Asian women role models, or the ones that reflected my Korean heritage. Doing so helped me understand that documenting the untold stories of the oppressed and those suffering from exploitation is an act of justice and an act of love and compassion.

But my real light bulb moment came when I discovered that documenting and bearing witness to the sufferings of past generations of women could help those still facing exploitation today.

As the philosopher George Santayana said in 1905, in a quote famously paraphrased by British leader Winston Churchill in the aftermath of World War II, 'Those who do not learn from history are doomed to repeat it.'

Letting Go

When I eventually became comfortable in my own skin in my thirties, it was incredibly liberating. Finally, I felt freedom.

Learning to let go can be a powerful tool in overcoming past hurts. Forgiving those who have hurt me, particularly through experiencing racism as a child or other forms of discrimination, brought freedom from the weight of anger and resentment. Also, recognizing that there are some things I cannot change—in myself or others—helped me move forward and focus on positive growth.

I have found that releasing this hurt has been more meaningful than I ever could have imagined. Harbouring a grudge is like drinking poison and expecting your enemy to fall ill. Hanging on to anger, bitterness, and a desire for revenge hurts only the one experiencing those emotions. Letting go led to finding myself, accepting myself, celebrating my capabilities, and learning to be content in all circumstances. This is how I found peace.

I cannot trace it back to a single moment. As I reflected on my past, I experienced a gradual epiphany that releasing the pain of my childhood was the key to unlocking my fullest potential. It became clear to me that only by letting go of the hurt and wounds of my past could I embrace a bright and hopeful future. Releasing all the blockages and hindrances within, resisting less, and having a growth mindset has been pivotal to living out my life's purpose.

I saw a counsellor for several months. By the end of those sessions, I felt as though a great weight had been lifted off me. Sharing my story in my books also helped me to learn about myself and heal.

Adversity has been my greatest teacher. It has tested me to my limits and has been a crucible for building resilience and finding creative solutions. I believe that if we handle it well, adversity can give us the motivation to succeed. It is when we are challenged that we find out who we really are and what we're made of. It is only when we're faced with challenges that we discover our true identities and learn to use our abilities to rise above our weaknesses. I'm thankful for my worst experiences because they forced me to learn from my mistakes, and this has given me the wisdom to navigate through life's ups and downs.

The gender and racial discrimination I experienced were about rejection at their core, and dealing with rejection can be difficult. How do you deal with rejection or the fear of rejection? Ultimately you need to know who you are—understanding and embracing who you are is the cornerstone upon which one can build the perseverance necessary to achieve enduring success.

This is the first piece of advice I would give anyone. Know your identity.

When my memoir, *A Long Road to Justice,* was published in 2021, my friend Grace Chae, a brilliant professor, gave me a gorgeous yellow and pink silk hanbok. Grace's timing was uncanny, as I had been so moved by the woman in the hanbok on the cover of my book, and suddenly, I longed to wear one as a symbolic act.

As a child, I had vowed never to wear a traditional Korean outfit. Now, I wanted to reclaim a sense of pride in my heritage, to show that I no longer saw it as a curse but an honour and a gift.

Since then, my book has been in development to be a TV series that is inspired by my life and my investigation into the trafficking underworld with a Korean Canadian woman lead. And I have been connecting with many Koreans in Seoul in the entertainment industry and have been asked to coach a new K-pop girls group.

It's like my homecoming journey has come full circle. I have found freedom by embracing my cultural identity and gained a sense of pride in who I am. When we embrace our ethnic identity, we send a message that our worth does not depend on the validation of others. By accepting ourselves, we give permission to others to do the same, and we show that it is okay to be different.

Chapter 4

Finding Your Calling

My roles in philanthropy, film-making, and journalism over the past few decades have taken me on many thrilling, and often dangerous, adventures in China and Southeast Asia.

I've interviewed human traffickers—criminals who buy and sell people.

I've been followed by undercover police.

I've walked across a river on a log to sneak into another country because that was the only way aid workers could get in.

I've been groped by a strange man in Bangkok while filming a documentary on sex trafficking.

I've been lifted by a humongous elephant in Southwest China.

I've sat in brothels interviewing scary pimps and teenage victims of sex trafficking.

I've travelled through rubble in Sichuan, China, days after a magnitude 8 earthquake killed tens of thousands of people.

I've spoken with strung-out addicts with AIDS who had heroin needles sticking from their arms as they eyed my diamond earrings.

I've documented an underground railroad of people dedicated to rescuing trafficked North Koreans and been led, blindfolded, to their safehouses.

I've been surrounded by soldiers with machine guns in Myanmar.

And I've lived to tell the tale.

I often find myself getting bored when people complain about minor issues like bad hair days or insignificant problems. It never ceases to surprise me when I reflect on my journey and reflect on how many crazy and out-of-the-ordinary experiences I've had on my journey, all in the name of my work.

I am grateful for all these encounters, for they have enlarged my heart and transformed my life. I am grateful even for all the brutal and sad things I've witnessed: orphans, exploited children in Southeast Asia, trafficked brides, heroin addicts, modern slavery victims, and more. These encounters have shaped who I am today and helped me put my personal setbacks, in perspective.

Around the time of my divorce, I was venturing into uncharted waters on the work front by launching two funds, one for HIV/AIDS and one for non-profit programmes that helped migrants and their children in Beijing. As part of this, I had to edit a white paper for a billionaire philanthropist on HIV/AIDS in China and write one from scratch on migrants. As neither of these had been done before, I had nobody to turn to for guidance. It was daunting.

I was a beginner Mandarin language student and found it nerve-wracking that I was pioneering something so consequential in a cross-cultural context that would impact so many people, yet, simultaneously, I was excited to challenge and push myself to the limits to grow. I was pleasantly surprised that ultimately, despite the language barriers and self-doubt, I was able to establish the funds and finish the paper smoothly.

In dark moments, I found solace in the words of John Maxwell who reminded me that fear is a natural part of progress, especially when you're venturing into uncharted territory. He believes that it is our inner drive or burning desire to reach our goals that enables us to defeat our fears. That burning inner drive, a 'deep-calls-unto-deep', is a divine signal that shows us what we were created to do.

Not All Jobs Are a Calling

So how do we find our calling? Or does our calling find us?

I believe it is confirmed organically as we go on a journey of discovery and pursue our passions. While our jobs take up a lot of our time and become a part of our identity, a sense of calling is something quite different. It captures what we were born to do, what we were made for. You could even describe it as the work you would do for free because it is so enjoyable. It's part of your destiny and can inspire a broader, more outward perspective of how we can benefit others.

The author Os Guinness once said, 'A sense of calling should precede a choice of job and career, and the main way to discover calling is along the lines of what we are each created and gifted to be. Instead of, "You are what you do," calling says: "Do what you are."'

Sometimes, following our calling is not easy. There can be obstacles and hindrances, but we must press on, sometimes alone and sometimes at the risk of being misunderstood, especially if we're forging our own path.

It's not easy to break away from the norm, veer off the beaten track, and go where no person has gone before. It takes a certain level of courage and idealism to do so. I've kissed goodbye to the traditional career path and, instead, embraced life as an author, media entrepreneur, speaker, and campaigner. This has challenged me to my limits—physically, mentally, and spiritually—and taken me out of my comfort zone. It has also caused me to grow exponentially in ways I never thought possible. I had to crush the fear and anxiety of failure to achieve my goals.

In choosing the path less travelled, I have become a different person from the naive young woman I was when I emigrated to Asia in 2004. Living in a different culture challenged me in ways that I hadn't been in my hometown of Vancouver, Canada.

Before living overseas, I was rigid and my world was confined to my local community. The options of where to work and live were limited and it was expected that young people would get married, buy a house, and gather with the same group of friends for years to come. Our future was laid out for us in simple black and white and no one really coloured outside of the lines.

My friends had the same background as me; we grew up in similar suburbs, graduated from similar universities and worked similar jobs as young professionals. We had no communication challenges or cultural barriers to navigate.

Years later, when I re-connected with childhood friends, I saw they had followed the conventional path of getting married, going to work every day, having kids and paying off mortgages. They hadn't changed much at all since I first met them. They had stayed the same, met the same friends, and repeated their familiar routines like a scene out of the movie *Groundhog Day*. We talked about it and marvelled at how our paths diverged and that there's a transformation that takes place when one lives in a foreign country or travels the world.

While I was living in Beijing, in addition to working in philanthropy for ultra-high-net-worth families and in journalism, I served as a foreign expert for a few years at the All China Women's Federation, a powerful, government-backed national organization for women and children.

The office was frozen in time as if it were the 1950s. All the staff had to take part in afternoon group exercises that involved swinging our arms and marching on the spot, to the direction of a voice coming from a speaker at the top of the wall. Even the voice sounded old-fashioned and Communist. It was an incredible experience to immerse myself in a work environment in another culture.

Still, I could feel lonely at times. There were only two Chinese colleagues in the office with whom I could converse. They were the only ones fluent enough in English and not intimidated by the prospect of speaking with me.

The trade-off was that I had an extraordinary window into the Chinese mindset and workplace. This opened my mind and expanded my understanding of human nature. I was forced to examine myself more deeply in a cross-cultural context at work and in relationships with people from several cultural backgrounds. It was more taxing to find common ground. I learned a lot and grew exponentially from dealing with frustrations and misunderstandings I would not have encountered in Vancouver.

I learned the hard way that my direct, Western style of communication was difficult for the local Chinese, who preferred to be more subtle and avoid conflict. My Chinese colleagues valued the concept of saving face, whereas my enthusiasm for direct conflict resolution was perceived as aggressive, causing them to feel less respected and even a little fearful of me. I learned to adjust my communication style and speak more gently.

If I hadn't moved to Beijing, I would have ended up like my old friends. I would have been working for a Vancouver-based company, living in a house in the suburbs, attending the same church and socializing with the same group of people. No doubt, I would have loved my life had I stayed and wouldn't have been aware of the adventures I was missing out on overseas.

Eventually, my mind and heart opened up to another culture and world through learning a new language, Mandarin. To my surprise, the more I immersed myself in the Chinese culture, the more I began to embrace my Korean identity. It may have been easier to do in Asia because here I was an international citizen, surrounded by a handful of expats and a majority of people who looked like me.

Hailing a taxi or asking for directions before an important meeting could turn into a huge ordeal if the driver didn't understand my Mandarin. I had to learn how to be flexible and open-minded, and problem-solve on the go.

The flipside of missing my old friends and family in Canada was that life had become a continuous adventure, full of tumult and excitement, and I got to meet talented and fabulous new friends from all over the world.

Once in a while, even now, I feel shocked that I ended up living in Asia. There had been no hint of my life overseas or my calling to help the trafficked and the poor back when I was a geeky kid struggling in a Vancouver suburb.

When Dreams Are Born

Looking back at my career trajectory, I see that I was not as intentional about finding my calling as I could have been but rather stumbled into finding work that I was passionate about and that matched my talents, personality, and dreams. I believe there were early signs in my childhood.

Dreams are often birthed when you're young. I believe these dreams give a sense of purpose and meaning and they are indicators of one's calling and purpose. When I was ten years old, I had dreams that were as big as they were unusual. I dreamed of winning an Oscar, giving millions of dollars to poor countries, including North Korea, and writing many books.

All of these dreams have come to pass, with the exception of one: I have *yet* to be nominated for an Oscar! I have written books and produced films, and indeed, I have travelled all over Asia for philanthropists to direct funding to humanitarian projects, North Korean aid, some of the first anti-trafficking programmes in China and Southeast Asia, schools for migrant kids, programmes to empower girls and women and the blind, and more. And I'm working with a film company in Singapore to create a TV series based on my recent memoir, *A Long Road to Justice*, and developing other feature film projects.

To this day, I often wonder how a nerdy encyclopaedia-loving Korean Canadian immigrant kid with braces like me ended up fulfilling most of my wildest dreams. There was absolutely no indication that I would be able to achieve these goals when I was a child and had so many identity and rejection issues. I have no idea where these early fantasies—or my audacity—came from.

My friend Allison Heiliczer, a therapist based in Singapore and author of *Rethink the Couch: Into the Bedrooms and Boardrooms of Asia*, recommends that we stop actively searching for our purpose in life and let it come naturally. She says:

> This idea of searching for purpose can feel very heavy and burdensome so I suggest pausing the search and focusing instead on it being a creative process – one that is often edited and co-created throughout a lifetime. Purpose is something that some do feel is a calling and can name early on as something singular such as their work, family, volunteering, or spiritual practice.

She also suggests turning that question of 'What is my purpose?' into a prayer or meditation and focusing instead on 'How can I be of service to others?' Heiliczer adds:

> Marinating in that question helps redirect focus from self to others and will often bring some insight. Yet, the key to purpose is less about insight and more about taking action. Shift your focus on

doing something for others and remove the pressure that this action has to be directly tied to your purpose. This approach can help you discover a sense of fulfilment and purpose in unexpected ways.

Many will only take action when they're convinced that it will lead to "finding" purpose, and because they believe it won't become immobilized. That immobilisation, though, is often the barrier to interacting with a sense of purpose.

Here are six life lessons I've learned that might help you to find your own 'dreams with a purpose':

Your dreams and desires are a clue to your purpose. What makes you happy? Where do you see yourself near the end of your life? What are your life goals? Explore these desires first, then look for a job that aligns with these dreams.

Get out of your comfort zone. Trying new things and experiences stretches us to our limits and helps us to learn more about ourselves and what we're genuinely passionate about. Find friends with a growth mindset who will encourage you to keep pushing against any self-imposed barriers and hold you accountable.

Dream big—take bigger risks. Don't settle for anything less. Like most Asian parents, mine wanted me to be a lawyer, doctor, or accountant and live a white-picket-fence life in Vancouver. Instead, I followed my heart and moved to Beijing without a job. I chose an unconventional and uncertain path of working abroad that allowed me ultimately to achieve my dreams.

Ignore the doubters and stick to your dream. Never give up on your vision for what you want in life. When I was writing one of my books, a handful of jealous and competitive people working on a similar project tried to sabotage my research. I'm so glad I persevered and reached my goal, not only for myself but for the victims who had asked me to tell their stories to the world.

Transform adversity into something good. I had a near-death experience while gathering video footage in a notorious red-light district. It was frightening and traumatic, and it duly changed me. But something good came from it, too. It made me more able to identify with victims of abuse and channel that empathy into my writing and philanthropy.

Don't waste your time. In a keynote speech I delivered at a gala for more than 700 students from thirteen universities in Hong Kong, I talked about how we have more women in positions of influence now in Asia than at any other time in history. I urged the audience, especially the young women, to do all they could to reach their fullest potential. 'Don't get distracted by boys and small issues. Don't waste your opportunities,' I urged them.

And I say the same to you: Don't waste your time, talents, and potential. Just go for it!

Milestone in Mexico

I have a distinct memory of my former Sunday School teacher, Peter, visiting me and my mom at our home when I was in the tenth grade. This memory persists to this day out of the billions in the storehouse of my mind. Peter was a short Korean Canadian man in his mid-twenties with a dark, tanned complexion and metal-rimmed glasses that framed his eyes, and he had a penchant for knit cardigans. His broad smile showed remarkably even white teeth. He was gentle and kind, and spoke in a melodic tone.

He had just returned from a church-sponsored mission trip to an African nation and was fired up about helping impoverished communities. We sat on our couch, eating apples and snacks my mom brought us. We were chatting about school work when suddenly he urged me not to be materialistic but to remember and care about the poor. He even cried as he implored me. It suddenly occurred to me that this was the reason he had come to see me.

I was shocked and puzzled by his tears and the fact that he thought that I was materialistic. I had no self-awareness of that, but upon reflecting a while after that conversation with Peter, I came to a sober understanding that I cared too much about how I looked. Peter knew I enjoyed dressing up in fashionable clothes because he would see me at church.

On any given Sunday, my friends and I dressed up: one day, I would wear striped flare pants with a silk top, a sharply tailored black blazer, and a navy wide-brimmed hat. Another day, I would wear a lavender linen short jumpsuit with vintage black block heels.

Since then, I've come to see his emphasis on helping the poor as prophetic, the first sign my life would one day revolve around human rights. My mom helped low-income families at the church for more than 35 years. I grew up watching her minister to and weep with people suffering financial difficulties or illnesses like cancer. She and dad would serve them hot meals and help with repairs at their small businesses when there were break-ins or emergencies.

When an opportunity to join a two-week missions trip to Tijuana, Mexico, presented itself at church several months later, I jumped at the chance. As a church group of people of all ages, we delivered programmes for the children who came from homes with dirt floors in nearby villages. Their faces were dirty and their hair was dishevelled and filled with dust; water was precious and not to be wasted on washing hair. We held precious orphan babies.

When I returned to Vancouver after a drive that took longer than twenty hours, I saw my mom waiting for me and wept as I hugged her. The exposure to impoverished families living in deplorable conditions that I'd just had was unforgettable.

It was depressing and made me aware of my privilege. I became sensitized to those less fortunate and the plight of those in poverty overseas, in disaster areas and war zones. Suddenly, my appetite for dressing up was gone and a commitment to justice work was beginning to take root.

Race Riots

There was a pivotal moment in my teenage years that fuelled my passion for justice and human rights. I can still vividly recall the scenes that played out before my eyes. I was in the eleventh grade and had just returned home from school, eager to complete my homework. As I snacked and switched on the TV, chaos and destruction loomed on the screen.

Smoke billowed, looters pillaged stores, armed men stood guard on rooftops. At first, I thought I was watching a news report from a war-torn region overseas.

Yet, to my utter shock, it was happening in Los Angeles, home to golden beaches and Hollywood. The beating of African American

Rodney King and the acquittal of the four White policemen involved had led to utter pandemonium over five days marked by senseless violence and the killing of more than sixty people, looting, and arson—the 1992 Los Angeles riots.

While the beating that caused King's death did not involve an ethnic Korean, its effect was to enflame racial tensions between the African American and Korean communities of LA. These tensions had festered for decades, dating back to the Watts riots of 1965 during the Civil Rights era, when rioters had killed thirty-four people and damaged countless businesses. The Watts riots prompted Jewish business owners to leave South Central LA in droves, and Korean immigrants took their place; many in the African American community resented this, feeling the Koreans were taking from them.

After King's death, all this resentment welled up. The rage towards the LA police quickly turned into rage against the Korean Americans, especially business owners.

The ensuing carnage caused damages estimated at US$1 billion, of which 40 per cent was suffered by the Korean immigrant community.

Watching this painful cycle repeat itself left me feeling bereft and sad for weeks. It was especially gut-wrenching for me because I had African Canadian friends from middle-class families who identified and sympathized with the African Americans during the riots. For the first time in our friendship, we confronted our racial identities—something that had been largely invisible to us before as friends.

We had Korean Canadians, Chinese Canadians and African Canadians in our group—and suddenly, we were having uncomfortable conversations about the strife. There were allegations of racial discrimination on both sides. My friends started to look at me differently, as if I were guilty of discrimination too. I became anxious and embarrassed and distanced myself even further from my Korean heritage.

The LA riots scarred the Korean American community in LA and overseas and left an enduring mark on me. It was a watershed event because it opened my eyes to the frailty of race relations and showed how things could so quickly descend into hate and violence. It highlighted, to me, the importance of fighting against racial discrimination. I dug deeper to ponder my ethnicity and to delve into why I felt such strong empathy for all of the victims and why I identified with the traumatized immigrant Korean American community.

I wasn't the only one. Other Koreans in the West expressed similar shock and sorrow over the destruction on all sides. But, perhaps, the most surprising thing to me personally was that this tragic event had ultimately helped me identify with being Korean for the first time in years.

I didn't understand it fully then, but this period lit a flame within me, what would become a burning desire to fight against injustice and racial hatred. Around this time, I had what I would describe as a 'justice awakening' as I became drawn to inspirational leaders involved in social justice.

I was mesmerized by writings on the work of Martin Luther King Jr, Gandhi, Nelson Mandela, and Mother Teresa. They raised the bar for what is possible through a life that's lived sacrificially for one's convictions. In hindsight, their remarkable experiences shaped me at a pivotal time.

King's non-violent struggle for racial justice through peaceful protests and eloquent, impassioned speeches advocating for an equitable and just world free of racial discrimination were awe-inspiring. He and his wife Coretta Scott King grew up in an era where the segregation or separation of people based on their race was not only acceptable but enforced by law.

His courageous stand to abolish systemic racism led to historic social change—in 1964, the landmark Civil Rights Act was passed, making racial segregation illegal in publicly owned facilities. In 1964, he won the Nobel Peace Prize. Sadly, he was assassinated on 4 April 1968. But his legacy endures beyond the grave.

King and his wife made a pilgrimage to Gandhi's home in 1959, eleven years after the death of the Indian independence leader. He asked specifically to spend the night in his room in the hopes of catching his 'vibrations'. Gandhi's ideals and his movement for truth and non-violent resistance called 'Satyagraha' inspired King and many other activists. Gandhi's fight against British colonial rule was a 'David and Goliath' scenario—a diminutive Indian man dressed in a white loin cloth standing up to the might of the British empire.

Against all odds, his campaign was victorious in 1947 when India became independent. Gandhi is revered as a saint by many, and I was an admirer myself when I was a high school student.

During a trip to South Africa in 2001, I travelled to Pietermaritzburg to spend time at a Christian organization and during that time, I visited the landmark bronze statue of Gandhi.

The statue shows Gandhi as a young man, a working lawyer, and marks where he was notoriously thrown off the train because, as a man of colour, he was not allowed to sit in first class and refused to move to third.

It was a seminal moment in his life. It influenced his decision to stay in South Africa and get involved in peaceful resistance against the oppression of Indians in the nation. But his early attitudes on race and sex have come under scrutiny in recent years.

Another global human rights activist who moved me was Nelson Mandela and his long dedication to the fight against racial injustice and the oppressive system of apartheid in South Africa. He dreamed of seeing a democratic society in which people of all races were treated equally and was willing to lay down his life for it: 'It is an ideal for which I hope to live for and to see realized. But my Lord, if it needs be, it is an ideal for which I am prepared to die.'

Mandela was the global face of the anti-apartheid movement, and forgiveness and reconciliation were his legacy. He said, 'No one is born hating another person because of the colour of their skin or his background, or his religion. People must learn to hate and if they can learn to hate, they can be taught to love.'

He led the African National Congress' non-violent campaign against apartheid; then, he was a part of an armed resistance and was ultimately imprisoned for twenty-seven years for charges that included treason and acts of sabotage. He was released in 1990. The first eighteen of his twenty-seven years were spent in a jail on Robben Island, where he spent his days and nights in a tiny cell with no plumbing and no bed. He had to do hard labour in a white quarry for several hours daily, damaging his eyesight.

In 2001, I visited the prison on Robben Island and I stood in front of his cell, a tiny space with bars and imagined what it'd be like to live there for nearly two decades. I lingered there in awe of Mandela's moral conviction, trying to imagine what it must have been like to be imprisoned for something you believe in and are willing to die for.

I also walked around that bleached white quarry. Staring at the jagged ivory walls for only a few minutes hurt my eyes so much that I could barely keep them open and used my hands to shield them from the rays.

I learned from Mandela that there can be a great personal cost to acting on your values and dreams of a better world. Eventually, he became the first democratically elected president of South Africa and called for a national reconciliation and a new country where everyone could prosper. Famously, he said, 'Forgiveness liberates the soul. It removes fear. That is why it is such a powerful weapon.'

I was also drawn to Mother Teresa, a diminutive woman, usually pictured in a white sari with royal blue edges, who served India's poorest of the poor for nearly half a century after 1950. She cared for the forgotten poor—the orphans, the sick, and the dying—and gave them a dignified death. Like Gandhi, Mother Teresa also had her fair share of critics of her celebrity, legacy, and character.

Learning about the sacrifices of Mandela, King, Gandhi, and Mother Teresa awakened in me the desire to fight for something greater—to live for something bigger than myself and to stand for what is right, whatever the opposition.

Mandela and King, like me, had experienced racial discrimination (though, of course, my own experiences were on a far lower level than what they went through). Yet, they overcame it with forgiveness and non-violence and led a movement to bring social change.

They turned their pain into power and showed me the possibility that I could, too. Had I not gone through my early experiences with racial discrimination, I would be a different person today. I would most likely be less empathetic to those who are discriminated against and abused.

In this season of my life, of my justice awakening, seeds were sown for my future work. Several years later, I delved into investigating the Japanese military's systemic enslavement of Korean women and other women from occupied countries in brothels during World War II. Through my work, I have been able to articulate my observations of the Asian communities in Canada and East Asia, and the deep-seated animosity towards the Japanese. It's shocking how these gaping generational wounds have been left open for so long due to the lack of genuine remorse from the Japanese government. The need for closure was palpable, yet it seemed like an impossible dream.

In my writings and speeches in universities, high schools, and corporations, I try to channel my inner-Mandela as I call for peace, forgiveness, and racial reconciliation.

My Aha Moment

My inner turmoil and search for identity carried on from my childhood to my twenties as I struggled to find my calling and place in this world.

I was confused about my career path, though I found I had one advantage—my knack for speaking calmly under pressure and presenting confidently in job interviews. This helped me score numerous jobs in the media—in newspapers, radio, and television. Yet, I was insecure and constantly questioning whether I was in the right field.

It didn't help that I had no career-oriented mentors to advise me or share how they found their purpose and calling. I also did not know who I was and was woefully unaware of what I was good at, oblivious to my talents and what work I truly loved doing.

The moment I felt in my bones that I was made for a greater purpose came one dark rainy evening in Burnaby, BC, Canada. I was twenty-two and had dated around. I'd kissed a lot of 'frogs' and was deeply disappointed that I hadn't met that prince. In my frustration, I began to ask more profound questions, like, 'What is my purpose in life? What is something worth dying for that I can spend my life doing?'

Fuelling my angst was that, in less than a year, I had broken up with two boyfriends. Both of those men had quickly moved on to date new women and were engaged. And both were attending my church with their wives-to-be. It was so awkward for me. I felt profoundly sorry for myself even though I knew neither of these men were suitable for me, and I'd felt no emotion when I broke up with them.

My imagination went wild as I wondered, 'Where is my significant other? Will people perceive me as defective because I am not dating anyone?' For a month after learning of the engagements, I would cry on a daily basis, for hours on end, because it had made me question the meaning of my life.

Sometimes, I wept in my car with my good friend 'SungMo', a sensitive young man with an extreme stuttering problem, beside me. One night, I was driving aimlessly on a mountain road to think and get some space. I felt so desperate for answers that I was ready to drive off a cliff if I didn't get one that night. I was desperately searching for a sign.

I suddenly remembered a line that I'd heard in a message at church about serving others and working to fulfil the purpose of your generation. It was my moment of clarity. I had a purpose to make a difference in my generation and the world, and it was unfolding. I knew I was on the cusp of it, and that was enough. At the very least, it was enough to step back from the brink.

A Calling Confirmed

As a senior student at university, I struggled to figure out my career path and what success meant to me. It wasn't until a few of my perceptive friends suggested I pursue a career as a TV journalist, reporting live updates, that I truly began to consider it. Fast forward a few years, and I found myself working in TV news, fulfilling my passion for sharing important stories with the world.

During those early years of my career, I didn't care too much about making a lot of money. Even though I felt confused about my purpose and career path, I was more invested in the idea of striving for excellence than a big salary—in honing my skills as a broadcast journalist and writer and moving up the career ladder.

I once received a compliment from a manager at a public broadcasting company, who praised my enterprising spirit and writing skills. Little did I know that this same spirit would eventually lead me to travel the world for my daily work. I now recognize that taking on innovative work that has never been done before is what truly ignites my passion and motivation.

One friend advised me to consider what kind of job I would do for free. Another said the best way to discern the work you naturally gravitate to is to imagine yourself near the end of your life and think about what you would be doing.

I was a blank page at that time and wasn't leaning towards any kind of work except for writing. I had always wanted to write books, though I never had the confidence to believe I could finish one. It was a combination of low self-esteem and a lack of self-awareness.

I wish I could go back in time and tell my younger self all that I've learned, to spare her the hardship and heartache. I would tell her that the desires and dreams in our hearts are not an accident and often indicate our purpose and gifts. There is a very good reason I had no desire to become a rocket scientist—I dislike studying math and science.

For years, writing was the way I expressed my emotions. It was how I processed and made decisions. I often say it's my personal therapy. Ever since I was in the fifth grade, I was devoted to documenting my milestones and observations in my journals. Even now, I still save words of encouragement on my iPhone notes! (There are more than 8,000 notes saved over many years). Perhaps even my profound and often crippling insecurity about writing was a confirmation it was for me. Writers are notoriously insecure about their work.

While at university, I made an appointment to speak with Eugene Peterson, the renowned and prolific late author. I was struggling and wondering if I was called to be a writer. I hadn't written much at that point, but the impulse to write was there, though stymied by perfectionism and beating myself up whenever my work wasn't exactly how I wanted it to be on my first attempt.

He gave me an excellent piece of advice that has stayed with me ever since. He said, 'Writers are compelled to say something. Do you want to say something through writing?'

These words, too, turned out prophetic. They confirmed the dream I had had of writing books at ten. They made me think of how I loved writing raw about what I'd seen and experienced and using my words to relay a message and drive home a point. Of how I loved giving forgotten people and unsung heroes a voice.

After meeting Peterson, an opportunity to write a book came along in 2001 out of the clear blue sky. While working as a TV journalist, I had written numerous magazine and newspaper articles as a freelancer after taking a course at the local university. One article in the Alliance church magazine caught the eye of a retired pastor who was advising Pastor Augustus Chao on his retirement transition at the age of ninety-one. They were looking for a writer to help him write his biography.

I felt honoured to be asked. I knew this was my project, as it fit my desire to write and document something historic—in this case, about Pastor Chao's pioneering role in launching Christian and Missionary Alliance churches across Canada, Australia, and parts of the US.

He resisted being interviewed by me in the first few months of the writing process. Then he opened up like a geyser and divulged secrets he hadn't shared with anyone else, not even his wife. We became close and finished his biography in 2002. Completing my first book was an eye-opening experience, and it ignited a fire in me to write more biographies and books to inspire others.

For a year after we finished the book, I would visit Pastor Chao to do his laundry, bring him food, and talk and watch TV together. When I moved to Beijing, despite his frail condition, he made sure to come to the airport with my family to bid farewell. I was overwhelmed with emotion when he handed me a US$100 bill after giving me a warm hug.

I knew immediately this was his traditional Chinese way of saying 'I love you'.

My mother, out of her boundless love for me, selflessly took up the torch of taking care of Pastor Chao, doing his laundry and delivering him delicious home-made food. Sadly, when his funeral was held in Vancouver, I couldn't attend due to work commitments in Beijing. But my mother went in my place. She wept for me and cried my tears.

My next book on Japanese military sexual slavery was painful to write, and I felt depressed for a few months afterwards as I processed the stories of despair and death. The words of Isabel Allende resonated with me, 'Write what should not be forgotten.'

As a seeker of truth, my mission was to unveil the hidden and unknown and bring it to the light so that future generations may learn from it. During the process, I discovered a profound growth within myself. Despite penning two books, it was not until I began writing my memoir in 2020 that I knew without a shadow of a doubt that I was born to be a writer.

The Thing that Scares You Most

No risk, no story.

This is the story of my life: Plunge in, take a risk, and never turn back. Learn to push through your fears. Taking risks is key to fulfilling your purpose in life, as it is how you build confidence. A sense of accomplishment gives you courage—you gain faith in yourself knowing that you made a decision, pulled it off and could do it all again.

The beginnings of my new life in Beijing after I moved there in 2004 were fraught with risks as I spoke no Chinese, knew hardly anyone, and could barely get around in the first three months without having addresses written down on paper in Chinese. One of the first words I learned was the Chinese word for 'toilet'!

I was single, free, and ready to leap into the great unknown of living abroad. I had no job lined up and no friends or support system there. Moving to a city where hardly anyone spoke English was more challenging than expected. I was in culture shock for months and felt depressed as I tried to forge new friendships. I was wracked with doubt and wondered if I had made the right decision.

Yet, I felt in my gut that I was where I was meant to be. My risk proved to be the right decision when it came to doing work that I loved and that gave me a sense of purpose and calling. Just a year after I moved, I led international philanthropists around the city and negotiated with government officials to make humanitarian initiatives happen—all despite my limited Mandarin!

When I was shifting back to full-time TV journalism in Hong Kong after years of mainly working in philanthropy, after the first month, I was sent on an international trip to produce a film on sex trafficking. I was expected to take on the massive challenge of filming exploited women in some of China's most notorious red-light districts—something that had never been done before.

Huge risk! Once again, I had to face my crippling fear. I got the footage despite being forced to erase some of it during a dangerous altercation with thugs and mamasans. The three-part documentary series on sex trafficking won a prestigious award; later, it became a book and spawned the development of a TV series and a feature film.

Over the years, I've stuck my neck out by going to gritty and dangerous far-flung places. I could do so only by overcoming my fear. The unusual access I had and my experiences of meeting people like pimps, traffickers, mamasans, drug addicts, and exploited men, women, and children changed my perspective and made me more generous with my time and more empathetic.

I found my vocational calling—to help make the world a better place.

For much of my life, I struggled with fear. Many years ago, a wise friend challenged me when debating whether to take on an intimidating role that I didn't feel qualified for. She said, 'Always do the thing that scares you the most. Just face it and don't think about the fear.' Those words have stayed with me over the years.

As Robin Sharma said, 'The fears we don't face become our limits.' Without risk, there is no testimony. So, take that risk. Don't let fear hold you back. The rewards will be worth it.'

Take it from Ralph Waldo Emerson: 'She who is not every day conquering some fear has not learned the secret of life.'

Risk Takers

My Korean immigrant parents had hoped I would find a career in law, accounting, or medicine.

I planned to study law to fight the Japanese government on behalf of the survivors of Japanese military sexual slavery and, in part, to appease my parents instead of pursuing my love for theatre, film-making, and the creative arts.

In hindsight, I would have thrived in film production earlier in my career. Fortunately, I could get back on track with my original dream of making TV and films about the untold stories from history, which I hoped would inspire people to make a difference in the world.

It's important to find inspiration in those people—both contemporary friends and heroes from history—who have risked it all to live, work, and give radically. Those who understand the importance of taking risks are shining examples of how to live and make a difference.

But not all those we draw inspiration from must be world leaders, saints, or historical figures. One of those who has inspired me is Jin Kang. As a young man, Jin was scouted to join the national soccer team and has since travelled the world leading athletic programmes in Asia and the Middle East. Today, he is the vice president of the East Global of the Fellowship of Christian Athletes (FCA).

But he struggled with his identity like me. Jin grew up in a Korean community in a small backwater city in northeastern China, near the North Korean border. Though he lived in China, Koreans were the majority in his town. But when he went to university, he was surrounded by Han Chinese and struggled to fit in. His Mandarin was poor, so when he spoke to Chinese people, they considered him Korean—some made fun of him. Yet when he spoke to Koreans, they considered him Chinese. He felt rejected by both sides and paralysed by the question, 'Who am I?'

'I felt weak, ugly, and stupid. I didn't have confidence. I had imposter syndrome,' he recalled. He felt stuck. Jin's outlook on life began to change soon after his Korean American friend Sam Kim shared with him how he resolved his own identity crisis through his Christian faith. Sam told Jin the Old Testament story of Moses, a Jew born in Egypt, who was confused over who he was, yet later became a national hero. He also told him the story of Joseph, who was sold into slavery in a foreign country by his jealous brothers, yet overcame adversity and eventually became the second most powerful person on earth.

At this time, Jin was graduating from university in Beijing and was discouraged that he didn't have a clear career path. Shortly after, he had a chance encounter with his friend Chris Lee, who helped him find his true calling. Jin confided in Chris that he had considered going on a humanitarian mission trip to Africa but had given up on the idea due to financial constraints.

Chris, who had just graduated from law school, shared an inspiring story about how his family and friends had given him US$5,000 to support his mission trip to Mozambique, South Africa, and Zambia to work with orphans. He told Jin, 'I'd like to help support you.' Chris then surprised him by giving him a sum of money, which happened to be the exact amount Jin needed to cover his mission trip to Africa. His act of kindness and generosity deeply touched Jin.

Jin spent three months in Africa teaching sports to vulnerable children and youth, where he discovered his passion for using sports to impact people, especially the youth. Jin recalled, 'I found my calling there, where I could use my gifts, sports, and athletics to bring others hope. I realized that was my dream job. Finding my calling and passion helped heal my pain over my identity, and I found my true self through it.'

Jin's bi-cultural identity, which once caused him so much angst, is now one of his greatest superpowers. It allows him to bridge different cultures and facilitate connections between diverse groups of people.

Today, Jin uses sports as a powerful platform to bring people from all walks of life together to make a positive difference in society.

'Doing Something Beautiful for God'

The British BBC journalist Malcolm Muggeridge told the story of Mother Teresa to the world through a documentary and the book, *Something Beautiful for God*. 'Doing something beautiful for God,' is how Mother Teresa described her dedication to Kolkata's poorest of the poor and the dying. Her motto was that anything we do for God is beautiful, no matter what it is.

Muggeridge was captivated by the joy she radiated as she served the forgotten, and he called her a 'light which could never be extinguished'. As quoted in *Something Beautiful for God,* she described her mission as:

> That's the spirit of our society, that total surrender, loving trust and cheerfulness. We must be able to radiate the joy of Christ and express it in our actions. If our actions are just useful actions that give no joy to the people, our poor people would never be able to rise up to the call which we want them to hear, the call to come closer to God.

Muggeridge was a worldly sceptic who dramatically converted to Christianity because of Mother Teresa's unusual calling to serve the people no one wanted to reach. I also felt an affinity for Muggeridge, as

I identified with his commitment to telling the story of an indomitable woman doing extraordinary things. I could relate to him as a journalist, as I have had a similar fascination with some of the people I've interviewed for articles and films.

One legendary story about Mother Teresa has stayed with me. She was the keynote speaker at a fancy Washington, DC luncheon filled with the highly influential and she berated them for not doing more to love the poor. She wasn't a warm and fuzzy people pleaser, and that showed me that you can boldly stand up for what you believe in and speak truth to power.

The Power of Dreams

Wilma Rudolph was the twentieth of her father's twenty-two children from two marriages. So, you could say she was used to taking on the odds. She was infected with polio as a child and was told by a doctor that she would never walk again.

Her mother, though, had other ideas. She instilled faith in Wilma that she would indeed walk again. Wilma developed an indomitable will by overcoming her early challenges, going on to become a world-record-holding Olympic champion in track and field. She found her purpose in something she excelled at and became an inspiration to countless people over the years.

An example of overcoming all odds, Wilma once said, 'Never underestimate the power of dreams and the influence of the human spirit. We are all the same in this notion: The potential for greatness lives within each of us.'

Mother to AIDS Orphans

During my work trips for my philanthropy in China, I met Cheryl Wilkins, a jovial American woman in her late thirties.

She wanted to make her life count and felt a sense of calling to move to southern China. Soon after, she adopted two adorable Chinese daughters. Cheryl sensed that there was more for her to do, and through an expat friend, she came across some AIDS orphans. With her can-do spirit and kind heart, she opened a home for a dozen vulnerable children and provided education and opportunities for growth in every area of life.

We kept in touch via email and phone and she gave me the encouragement I needed, especially following my divorce. She urged me to leave Beijing and go back to television work and use my talents in broadcasting. She urged me to fulfil my potential. I later heeded her advice.

Sadly, she passed away about a decade after I met her. I believe her legacy continues in her two daughters and her indelible impact on the orphans she cared for. I still think of her from time to time with great fondness.

Gold from Pain

When you're firm on your overarching purpose, it changes your life.

It's a wonderful foundation to base all your decisions, actions, feelings, and goals on, and it can bring a profound sense of gratification like few things can. It also helps nourish and influence your relationships and creates meaning. Researchers on healthy ageing have found that those who see meaning in their lives are much happier overall. They also tend to be healthier, achieve more, earn more, and enjoy stronger personal relationships.

In the tapestry of my life, I see various themes leading to and weaving together my calling and values. Nothing is ever wasted: no experience, good or bad. In my reflections, I came to understand that it was my pain that led me to my purpose. I found meaning in my past suffering in a terrible first marriage. I found meaning in the brutal humiliation of racial discrimination at school.

These first-hand experiences are what compel me to fight for girls and women and to tell the world about sex trafficking in Asia through my philanthropy work, my books, films and TV series. While growing up, there were no Asian role models to look up to or advise me on my media career. I want to be there for the next generation.

Only You

Lastly, I want to say that there is no one else with your experiences, your talents, your unique personality. You were made for something greater. You're set apart for something that only you can accomplish.

Someone described 'calling' as when all our talents, passions, connections, and character converge, where all the dots line up. Ultimately, what matters most is who we become and how well we have loved those important to us.

An award-winning photographer, Lisa Kristine worked on a series dubbed the *Ancients* about people over 100 years old. She asked each of these centenarians through a translator, 'What advice would you offer the world?'

What I found awe-inspiring was that nearly all of them offered the same simple answer: 'Help one another.'

These wise ones selflessly thought of others and the greater good. When we help others, we also feel more fulfilled, and our reservoirs of hope are renewed. And hope can never be extinguished.

I would love to see more young people and professionals—especially women—who have the gift of choice to use their abilities, talents, and finances to bring more hope by influencing social change for the most disenfranchised people on earth.

I would love to be a part of the coming women's movement in Asia to bring positive changes for other women and girls. This justice awakening movement for the next generation will be bigger than anything we've seen in our lifetimes.

As I reflect upon the legacy I wish to leave for future generations, I hope we can someday tell them that we have brought healing and restoration to the broken lives of at-risk children, trafficking victims and the poor. This is the dream that's burning in my heart, and I hope that it burns in the hearts of the next generation, too.

Chapter 5

How to Find Your Voice—and Use It

As part of my work overseeing the philanthropic donations of ultra-high-net-worth family offices, I had the privilege of travelling to the farthermost reaches of China.

I met with government officials, representatives of global bodies, and heads of organizations. I was very often the only young woman in a man's world. At ceremonies and dinners, government officials often seemed amused to see me, a Korean Canadian woman. Presumably, they would have been expecting an older white American male.

It didn't help that I still looked like I was in my early 20s. Unless they were toasting me with alcoholic drinks or practising their Korean, most avoided speaking to me and gravitated to the men in the room. At this time, I didn't have a thick skin and still cared about what others thought.

I felt apologetic to be in the seat of honour and speaking on behalf of the company. I lacked confidence in what I stood for, which meant my insecurities got the better of me. My voice was like a whisper.

At several meetings, my shoulders shrank inwards, like an exclamation mark punctuating their judgement. Imposter syndrome was taking over, and I didn't know how to shake it off. Was I really supposed to be here? Was I good enough?

It wasn't just government officials. Some other non-profits also expected someone older and perhaps a man. One mainland Chinese non-profit director in his fifties with a PhD from Cambridge seemed surprised to see me when he picked me up at the airport in China and asked me how old I was. His condescending attitude irritated me.

I sensed it was because I was a young Korean woman and he had expected a much older man. I tried not to let his reaction bother me and let my work speak for itself. Later, I led the post-meeting discussion with ease and confidence and his disrespectful edge disappeared, and he became friendlier.

Another time, a Canadian non-profit caring for orphans that I had been in contact with sent me an email asking to speak with the person in charge. After pondering the proper response, I wrote matter-of-factly: 'I am the one making the decisions.' They were taken aback. At first, I was offended that they couldn't see a young woman as the most senior person, but eventually came to accept it as their personal limitation, not mine.

It was liberating because I didn't use the usual apologetic tone. Years later, I resolved never to let my gender, age, or ethnicity hinder me whenever I'm surrounded by men at work or to shrink myself to accommodate others.

When I feel discouraged, I often remind myself that had I been born in China more than 100 years ago, a woman like me would have had her feet bound; across Asia, I would have been considered property and not even given a name until I married. These reminders of the little-to-no rights Asian women had only a few generations ago—when my grandmothers were coming of age—always make me feel grateful to be living at this time and for having all the opportunities I have to speak out and the freedom to make choices. It also motivates me to stop taking for granted the ability to use my voice and speak up for those who are silenced.

In the words of Malala Yousafzai, 'We realize the importance of our voices only when we are silenced.'

At a young age, Malala was a powerful voice for educating girls in Pakistan. She was shot by the Taliban, who wanted to stop her from campaigning for the rights of girls and women.

But that didn't stop Malala. She was taken to a hospital in England, and after recovering, she set up the charity Malala Fund to continue the fight for educating girls. Just two years after she was almost killed, she received the Nobel Peace Prize in recognition of her activism.

Her journey of extraordinary courage has inspired countless people around the world. From Malala, I learned there is power in expressing ourselves. That in championing our beliefs and values, we can bring hope to others and ultimately inspire change.

It took me years to find my voice and to understand the importance of using it; still more years to use it wisely and not feel self-conscious or fear being rejected or perceived as bossy and controlling. As I learned what I really wanted in life, I also learned to refine my ability to articulate my purpose and desires.

I came to know my virtues and weak points, in part by asking friends for honest feedback. Knowing my gifts and working on my shortcomings helped me to grow in confidence. Most importantly, growing a thicker skin enabled me to be fearless and not care about what others thought. Being afraid of others stifles you from being your true self. Lastly, I made a plan to keep checking in on my progress and to take action when I needed to improve in a particular skill.

I've often seen women struggle for acceptance in leadership roles or be criticized simply for being strong. In Asia, they're called 'dragon ladies' or 'tiger women'. Men, however, are never pilloried for being strong. My husband Matt noticed this double standard while I led an anti-trafficking movement called the 852 Freedom Campaign (852 is the country code for phone numbers in Hong Kong).

Through this grassroots organization, we mobilized over 25,000 people at more than fifty-five events that raised awareness about modern slavery in Hong Kong. Every event we hosted was ridiculously successful, and we had gatherings at least twice a week. Dozens of people described the movement as 'miraculous' because we had new opportunities, partnerships, and open doors to corporations like Goldman Sachs, universities, and government bodies.

We produced and hosted media projects, anti-slavery weeks at universities, and our Sweatshop Challenge (a simulation of forced labour) while undertaking new initiatives, like training speakers and hosting student groups from around the world, and fundraising. Matt was the mastermind of the activities, and I was the operations lead driving the movement along with an amazingly talented team. We partnered with more than 120 churches, NGOs, and universities, and our core value was 'passionate compassion'.

Despite the apparent success, some people criticized me for being too assertive and strong. While I know that I am bold and sassy, I am never petty or mean. Our team wondered if we were attracting negativity from people who felt threatened by our unusual success.

Matt felt I was being treated unfairly and with disrespect because I was a woman leading a highly successful movement in Hong Kong. One pastor was angry that several members from his church group were volunteering with our programme and though I had not met him in person, I heard that he would slander me among his members. I was shocked that he would say hurtful things without taking the time to get to know me. It was never my intention to steal members from another church.

Feeling misunderstood had a hidden benefit. I was forced to address my fear of being gossiped about and learned that it doesn't matter one whit what others say.

Let people gossip. Never worry about it.

Who cares about what people think when those people have no substantive thoughts other than to talk about others? I embraced the on–off switch that my husband employs with challenging people. Finally, I grasped what he had been talking about all this time!

Once, Matt heard some people from another United Nations department gossiping about him at a conference. He stood there listening for a short while and then introduced himself. Instead of getting angry, he turned the 'off' switch that enabled him to not care about how others respond. He was able to steer that potentially awkward moment into a dialogue and an opportunity to understand where they were coming from. After some practice, I can flip that switch to the 'off' mode. It takes some willpower, but it enables me to block out negative people and thoughts.

My experience with the 852 campaign also made me ponder what it means to be a woman leader with strong opinions and a voice. I examined why I was so upset over feeling misunderstood and told myself not to allow another person to control me by making me mad. After wrestling with my fear of what others think, I came to conclude that I must not listen to the critics but move forward resolutely with my mission, trust myself, and follow my own path.

It was a turning point. Not too long after that, I fully embraced my assertiveness, and now I have no qualms in standing up for myself and fighting for what I believe in. I embraced the power of sincerity and accepted my whole authentic self. I no longer needed a mask or anyone's approval to be who I am.

Researchers say that by being genuine, by being our true selves, we inspire trust in others. Doing so boosts our self-esteem, fulfilment, and personal happiness. When we walk our talk and our actions align with our true nature, we are more likely to be more confident, pursue our passions, and speak out for others when necessary.

Today, those who disrespect me are best advised to run away as fast as they can. It's taken me many years to get to this place of freedom. As Madeleine Albright said, 'It took me quite a long time to develop a voice, and now that I have it, I am not going to be silent.'

Invisible Women

Many Asian women have told me how they have felt silenced by our hierarchical culture, which has its roots in Confucianism, a patriarchal philosophy that assigns women a low status. The teachings of the Chinese philosopher from more than 2,000 years ago are deeply entrenched in East Asia and Southeast Asia. They have embedded a pervasive oppression, granting all the power to the men and no rights of any kind to the women.

Ancient tradition dictated that women were not given names and identities until they married, and even then, they were considered the property of their husbands. Women were prohibited from deciding who they married while family inheritances and property were passed to male heirs. We've had thousands of years of this misogyny where women and girls are perceived as inferior and devalued.

In Korean, one of the words for wife literally means 'house person'—a reflection of how their roles were bound within their families and household. A woman was seen as second-class, within both society and her own family, and defined by her relationship with the men in her life—her father, husband, and even her sons.

In pre-Communist China, polygamy for men and abuse of women were commonplace.

Girls had their feet bound for life, which limited them from venturing too far outside the house. Today, polygamy and foot binding are both banned, but sexual discrimination remains rampant.

Enduring Confucian values has kept women dependent and submissive, and these ways of thinking remain entrenched in East and Southeast Asia. In China, unmarried professional women in their late twenties prioritizing their career and educational achievements over marriage are called a derogatory name 'sheng nu' or leftover women. These women experience a painful pressure, rooted in shame, to get married so they can avoid that label.

Even now, in parts of Asia, boys are preferred over girls, as only sons can carry on the family name. Parents still believe raising girls is to water another person's garden, since daughters marry into another family. Commonly, sons are offered an education over daughters in impoverished families. Women in Asia and Asian women in the West are often expected, due to their culture, to be submissive and silent, never outspoken, and loyal to their families.

As a brash tomboy in my childhood and teens, my mother often reprimanded me for being unfeminine. She had gone to a finishing school and was very elegant in how she carried herself. She walked like a runway model and always had each hair in place and a beautiful smile on her face. For years, we locked horns—she was horrified at my loud manner of speaking and the boyish way in which I walked with a swagger, and tried to correct me. I didn't want to be a woman living up to Asian cultural standards—it made me feel angry and frustrated.

I cursed the stiflingly sexist, patriarchal attitudes that were prevalent in my Korean culture and raged against them. As a result, I rejected my Korean heritage. However, as I grew older, I began to embrace my mother's blueprint and admonishment to be more polite and to lower the volume of my voice. This led me to adopt a more reserved and courteous demeanour.

While working as a youth pastor at a Korean immigrant church in Vancouver, I was paid a quarter of what the other Korean Canadian male youth pastors made every month. Yet, I was doing the bulk of the work. It was scarring to find out the wage disparity and to be treated less than a leader. The oppressive cultural stereotypes and influence of Confucius still ran deep in the Korean culture, even in Canada.

This experience left me with a chip on my shoulder for years, though eventually I learned to forgive the Korean male leaders. That journey to forgiveness was in no small part thanks to the church I have attended in recent years, where I'm surrounded by several incredibly supportive Korean men.

Their encouragement has been all the more powerful because they grew up with the same Confucian value system as me, which valued boys over girls. Yet, they moved in the opposite spirit by lifting up women.

I have a kind and considerate friend named Joon Imm, who is originally from Seoul, South Korea. He has been a constant source of encouragement for my efforts to reconcile the unhealed war wounds between the Japanese, Chinese, and Koreans. Whenever I need moral support, I know I can turn to him and his amazing wife, Grace Chae.

I received a beautiful hanbok from Grace, who felt compelled to give it to me one day. It was a timely and meaningful gift. Receiving and wearing the gorgeous hanbok serendipitously affirmed my Korean identity and gave me a sense of cultural pride for the first time.

My dear friend Chris Lee, who is Korean Australian, has also been an incredible source of healing and encouragement for me, always genuinely respecting my gifts and abilities as a leader. Chris is a successful law partner, and his charisma and compassion make him an inspiration to everyone who knows him. Many people have even given him the nickname 'Korean Jesus' due to his unwavering faith in God and loving personality.

His kindness has helped me rise above the hurt I felt from the pastors many years ago at the Korean immigrant church. Chris and his beautiful wife, Aimee, lead a weekly church community group that my husband Matt and I attend. Their loving support and prayers have been a powerful motivation for us. They are shining examples of radical generosity and faith.

Over the years, they have selflessly served at our church and donated to worthy causes like supporting at-risk children, sacrificing their needs for the greater good. Their humble and down-to-earth lifestyle and testimony have deeply impacted everyone who has heard about them. It's rare to see people willing to give until they feel uncomfortable and until it hurts, but Chris and Aimee have done so with a level of humility that is truly extraordinary.

I cannot thank them enough for how they've transformed my life. Their unwavering commitment to serving others has inspired me to do the same. I am forever grateful for the role they've played in helping me to grow in faith and live a more fulfilling life.

I have often contemplated whether living a life of sacrifice that affects my finances and time is truly worth it. At times, I feel tempted to remain within my comfort zone, but I remind myself that reconciliation is a fundamental theme in my work. Thanks to the extraordinary impact of men like Chris and Joon, it has become a theme in my personal life as well.

They have showed me that though men can wound, so can they heal.

Speak Up and Make a Change

A significant part of my two-track career in philanthropy and journalism that I gravitated to was related to addressing cultural misogyny and the abuse of women—a deeply personal issue for me because I experienced gender discrimination from my father. As I gained confidence in what I believed in, I found a healing power in speaking out for others who were marginalized. Indeed, there is nothing more satisfying than to take a stand for what's right and advocate for the oppressed.

In 2001, I was introduced to Kim Soon-duk in Washington, DC She was the first survivor of forced prostitution by Japan's military I had met. She changed my life's direction and inspired my decades-long journey to campaign and write about wartime sexual slavery and the cycle of modern-day sex trafficking that continues with impunity today.

Yet, it wasn't until 2007, when I went through a painful divorce, another turning point in my life, that I finally had the motivation to finish that book—*Silenced No More: Voices of Comfort Women*—and help amplify the voices of Kim and other victims of sexual servitude.

After my divorce, I struggled for years with a sense of shame and shattered confidence over my failed marriage. I turned the anguish into fuel to write. This experience of personal suffering gave me the willpower and empathy to be a voice for voiceless women. When I focused my writing on those less fortunate than myself, I felt this righteous anger rise up, and I was able to put my issues and problems into perspective.

It also opened my eyes to my ability to make a difference for these women who had suffered far more than I ever did and showed me I could use my life to effect social change. This was the beauty that came from the ashes of my first marriage.

I spent fourteen years writing a book about these women and girls to expose the truth of what happened to them. It was the largest case of government-sponsored human trafficking and sexual slavery in modern history, and it happened within living memory. I wanted to lay a foundation of historical truth for the next generation.

Unsurprisingly, people in various countries tried to hinder my research. The competitive activists and researchers writing their own books were the hardest to deal with. In LA, one Korean American academic researcher blocked me from spending time with one of the survivors.

It was during this period that I toughened up and it dawned on me that I should not be too trusting. Out of necessity, I developed the skin of a rhino. Through these hindrances, I developed courage and perseverance that helped me continue researching and writing my book. I dug my heels in and took a stand. I wanted to live for something meaningful, something worth dying for.

For months, during the writing of *Silenced No More*, I threw myself into a gruelling schedule from nine in the morning until eleven in the evening. From my bed, I would walk to my wooden desk around six steps away, often in my pyjamas. So engrossed was I in my writing that I would forget to eat or comb my hair. My extraordinary mother would bring down a tray of food for lunch and dinner. With my easily distracted personality, the only way I could finish this book—especially given its dark material—was to be obsessed with it.

Passion is derived from the Latin word meaning 'to suffer'. If you desire and believe in something so much that you're willing to suffer for it, that is passion. But while I was writing, I couldn't feel that passion, only anguish about whether I could actually help these women by documenting their experiences.

I reminded myself repeatedly that I was writing in a safe place while the women I was writing about were constantly violated and tortured in the worst ways imaginable. Their torment put my anguish in perspective and that helped me keep going.

Constantly, I battled self-doubt and fought the whispers in my mind that said I couldn't do it.

I had to steel myself and train my mind to focus on the positive, to imagine the book with the cover. When I finally finished, it was truly incredulous. I had fulfilled an impossible dream.

Elated though I was at one level, the birthing of this book had taken its toll on me. For a year after its release, I lacked the energy to speak on the topic. I had to take breaks from campaigning and raising awareness. It is draining and traumatic for one's mind to constantly learn how innocent girls and women were tortured and murdered.

Particularly taxing for my emotions was when we toured universities, high schools, companies, and churches to show the film *Healing River*. Countless people have been so touched by the love and bravery of this Japanese reconciliation group that they feel their generational pain and racial hatred for the Japanese have been healed on some level.

In 2015, at a school in Nanjing, China, I asked the students to close their eyes and asked them this question: 'Who wants to forgive the Japanese and release their hatred after seeing the compassionate reconciliation team in the film?' Almost all of them raised their hands to say yes. It was an exhilarating feeling.

After speaking at dozens and dozens of venues, I began to doubt whether I should repeat the same message again and again. Then, one day, I came across a message in one of the bestselling author Elisabeth Elliot's books. She talks of how she, too, felt repetitive in her talks about her late husband's martyrdom in Ecuador by Waorani tribesman in 1956.

Jim Elliot was a young man in his prime, at twenty-eight, and a father of a baby girl when he and four other missionaries were speared to death and their bodies thrown into a river by the very people they wanted to reach—members of the Auca or Huaorani tribe. In a journal, Elliot wrote a quote that he is most famous for, 'He is no fool who gives what he cannot keep to gain that which he cannot lose.'

Elisabeth Elliot felt increasingly tired of having a singular message. However, she appreciated that her audiences were always moved by her testimony of Jim's faith and willingness to risk his life. While to her, it was repeated but with each new telling, audiences were always hearing it anew. She overcame her doubts by embracing that sharing her life's message was her calling.

My reading of Elliot's words came at a serendipitous time. They were enough to reassure and encourage me to continue my quest to defend the voiceless. I see now that the challenges of campaigning helped me develop a resilience that would sustain me in my work in the long term. It is where I found the capacity to transcend painful trials, to be shaped positively by them and, ultimately, to flourish.

Discovering the Power Within

Years ago, during my first media interview about *Silenced No More: Voices of Comfort Women*, I felt like a deer caught in the headlights: stunned, awkward, and unaccustomed to speaking my mind on the record.

As a journalist, I was always on the other side, asking questions and keeping my opinions to myself. It was disorienting to no longer be in control as the interviewer. I had to find the boldness to speak my mind with compassion.

What motivated me was knowing it wasn't about me but about the victims. I closed my eyes to see in my mind the faces of the people I had met: impoverished migrant women struggling to make ends meet and living in slums; gaunt and hopeless street kids in Beijing begging for their next meal; traumatized young women forced into brothels in Southeast Asia and China; anguished North Korean trafficked women; elderly women survivors of sexual slavery in Japanese military brothels whose personalities had changed forever from a lifetime of isolation, rejection, shame, and the despair many felt for never bearing their own children because of the injuries they had suffered at the hands of their tormentors.

In short, I had to triumph over my doubts and insecurities. I was my own worst enemy. It reminded me of how, when climbing a mountain, it isn't just the vertiginous trail that challenges me, it is myself that I must conquer.

I remember going on a three-hour hike with a friend. It was on soggy terrain that had been soaked from the rain overnight and for the first thirty minutes, my feet kept slipping. I could feel the aches in my legs and my heart stopping at times, while searching for safe footing on the steep dirt path.

As I looked up at the seemingly endless steps ahead—the humidity was stifling—I gulped and deeply regretted beginning the journey. *Madness*, I thought to myself as I felt tempted to give up and turn around. But what kept me going was shutting out all thoughts of quitting and the long journey ahead and deliberately focusing on putting one foot ahead of the other. One simple step at a time. That's the only way to take on a seemingly impossible goal.

Gradually, I have become accustomed to giving media interviews on TV, radio, and for publications. In June 2023, I had one of the most memorable interviews via Zoom from my home in Hong Kong. It was about the largest case of government-sponsored human trafficking and sexual slavery in modern history. I had an engaging conversation with radio host S.J. Lee of Arirang radio to mark the 1,600th Wednesday Demonstration by the elderly survivors of Japanese military sexual slavery and their supporters in front of the former Japanese Embassy in Seoul.

Back in 2004 and 2005, I gave a speech calling on Japan to sincerely apologize to these survivors at this weekly protest, which is one of the longest-running demonstrations in the world against sexual violence in armed conflict.

Suddenly, in the middle of this interview with S.J. Lee, tears began to flow from my eyes—tears I was powerless to stop. I had no tissue box nearby and could not blow my nose. I was mortified. Flashing before me were the faces of the elderly women who had passed away before receiving closure for what they endured.

Initially, I was greatly embarrassed by my lack of control over my emotions, but after the interview ended, I received one of the most heartwarming messages from Jeesun, the producer of the show. I felt sure that I had bombed the interview due to my embarrassingly raw display of tears. But Jeesun helped me to see that being real and authentic is the key to unleashing the power of one's voice. She wrote:

Thank you so, so much. I cried my eyes out when you started crying.

I loved your passion, and the whole team and the listeners did, too.

When is the production of the TV series coming out? We would like to have you on the show again to introduce the TV series to our listeners.

Thank you so much. It was such a touching moment, and you made me realize that this world is still so beautiful.

Best,
Jeesun

I said in the interview that a time of reckoning over this issue is coming in Korea. We have waited so very long because the older generation hasn't wanted to face this tragic part of history. Unfortunately, this has played into the hands of the Japanese government and what many activists say is part of Tokyo's cynical strategy of waiting for the survivors to die off.

But I promise this: though these women will pass away, their stories will live on.

Their cause will be taken up by a new generation of Koreans, mainland Chinese, and people from all over the world, a generation committed to the fight. The young are joining the weekly demonstrations and will not back down. The activism we needed may have skipped a generation, but it is building now and not before time.

It has been nearly eighty years since the end of World War II, yet a sincere apology from the Japanese government remains nowhere in sight. Instead, over the years, it has done its best to deny this wartime system of sexual slavery ever happened. Instead, it insults the victims by calling them willing prostitutes.

The lack of closure for these women is the seeping wound of history that prevents many Chinese, Koreans, and others from being able to let go of their lingering distrust and resentment of the Japanese. Any kind of closure and apology from Tokyo has to be victim-centred and satisfy their demands.

I have recommended that the governments consider exploring a Truth and Reconciliation type of forum. A critical first step in this would be a sincere apology that satisfies the demands of the survivors and their families.

This issue is important personally and generationally. It is a matter of historical record and it's about public memory. We need to resolve this issue from the past before we can move forward into a new future of peace.

The UN Committee on the Elimination of Racial Discrimination has urged the government of Japan to do more for victims of wartime sexual slavery and to offer full redress and reparations. 'It is a wound that has been festering for far too long,' in the words, as reported by *France24,* of renowned civil rights attorney Gay McDougall, who authored a landmark UN report on Japanese wartime sexual slavery.

I first spoke with McDougall in 1999 when I couldn't find enough information in English about the plight of the wartime sex slaves. She has been a pivotal figure in investigating this crime against humanity. I teared up when I learned she was still fighting for the survivors' dignity and closure at the UN Committee on the Elimination of Racial Discrimination. She inspires me endlessly to keep advocating for change.

Sadly, time is running out. The surviving women are primarily in their late eighties and nineties now. They have been fighting for justice and an apology for decades, and now only a handful remain.

I earnestly hope these women will get justice before they pass on.

If we do not deal with the trafficking of women and girls in our past, we will be condemned to watch it recur in our present and future. There comes a time when an issue must be dealt with once and for all. This is that time.

Remember the Forgotten

Before I moved to Beijing in 2004, I was part of a study group that toured sixteen cities to research the impact of Japanese war crimes. I'm embarrassed to admit that I was expecting a rural town with dirt roads (dare I say rickshaws?) and was pleasantly surprised to find a sleek urban jungle at my first stop in Shanghai.

It was there that I met a man, one of the many forgotten victims of biological warfare, who moved me deeply and convinced me to move to Beijing to write and support those without a voice.

For sixty-three years, Chen Chong Wen had been changing the bandages on his leg daily. His home-style remedy for his oozing wound was to use a playing card to stop the flow. He would slide it onto the outer edges of his wound, then wait until the liquid pooled before scooping it up. 'There's no medicine for this,' he said. 'It hurts very much, and it itches.'

The stench of rotting flesh was overwhelming as he showed me his leg. All these years later and the open sore still looked terrible. It had a tofu-like texture. He told me he felt like a burden to his family because they had to care for him. 'It's my bad luck,' he said, looking down at the ground.

During World War II, when the Japanese were trying to take Zhejiang province, Chen had been forced to flee to the mountains to escape from the advancing Japanese Imperial Army in 1942. That's when he believes he became infected with 'rotten leg disease'.

Researchers believe the Japanese used biological weapons or germ warfare on civilians through bombs and clothes containing germs and plague-infected fleas. They spread glanders, the disease caused by bacteria called bacillus anthracis, and anthrax. Once infected, the skin begins to blister and eventually, it rots, often to the bone.

Chen's mother was also infected. And not too long after her heel rotted off, she died in terrible pain. At the time, he had no idea why he had met such misfortune, but Chen now knows that he was a victim of biological warfare.

When I met him, Chen had had several costly surgeries in the previous eight years with no government support. He was considering a lawsuit against the government of Japan, hoping to force it to fund some of his treatment.

Since June 1995, several other lawsuits have been brought against Tokyo by Chinese victims of Japanese war crimes, according to Kang Jian, a Beijing-based human rights lawyer. She estimates there have been around twenty-four cases brought by survivors of biological warfare, the Rape of Nanking, and sexual slavery. She has helped lead many of these lawsuits.

'We're asking relatives to testify and we have survivors to bear witness on the use of biological warfare dropped on villages, and chemical bombs and canisters that are still being unearthed in China,' she says.

Soon after I met Chen, I met another survivor of biological warfare in southern China. I visited seventy-seven-year-old Li Meitou in her village near Tang Xi township. The tiny woman limped along ahead of me as we walked to her home. She smiled gently and often despite the chronic pain she was in. Li, too, had rotten leg disease. She'd had it since she was twelve when she fled the Japanese army's invasion of her region.

'I've had difficulty walking, and I experience pain, a fierce burning feeling,' she said. Because she couldn't afford medical treatment, she would use over-the-counter medicine and apply salt to her open wounds.

Li's home was a small, dark one-room place with a dirt floor and dingy walls; one small table and bench lined the back. I felt sick that she had to live this way.

Why wasn't she receiving adequate financial support?

As she sat and took off her bandage to show me her rotting leg, one of my friends had to turn away because of the putrid smell of her open wound. She asked us to tell her story to the world so that all would know what the Japanese had done to her and others in her village.

The exact number of deaths caused by Japanese biological warfare can never be known. But, according to Justin McCurry's piece in *The Guardian*, China's most famous champion of biological warfare survivors, Wang Xuan, who has gathered evidence for lawsuits launched in Tokyo, estimates that in Quzhou alone, as many as 50,000 people died in 1940 from a plague spread by germ-warfare. That same plague took 300,000 lives as it spread to neighbouring areas before it finally petered out eight years later. And that is only one example.

Wang, whose home village in Yiwu was devastated by biological warfare, says the Japanese air force dropped 'balls' containing germ-carrying fleas mixed with contaminated grains, fibres, beans, and cotton. They dropped these balls from the sky and let them float down. The local rats then ate the grains while the fleas jumped onto small animals and infected people.

The fleas were specially raised to carry germs at the infamous Unit 731 laboratory that the Japanese military set up in northern China to conduct biological warfare experiments. According to *Xinhua Net*, one Unit 731 veteran has testified in a Japanese court about how rats and fleas were raised and how 600 kg of anthrax was produced monthly in the compound.

Several decades ago, farmers from Wang's home village decided to fight for their rights and dignity, and seek justice for the immense suffering and countless deaths caused by the Japanese army. They sent a petition to the Japanese Embassy in Beijing.

Somehow, a group of Japanese peace activists heard about the village and decided to find out more. The Japanese activists reported their findings at an international symposium in Harbin, China, which the *Japan Times* covered. Wang, who was living in Japan then, read the article. The rest is history.

She got in touch with people from her village again and eventually became a vocal activist, researcher, and translator for the Japanese legal team. The illiterate villagers set up a committee to investigate Japanese biological warfare. They were able to obtain the diary of a Japanese military doctor who was stationed with the occupation army in Yiwu. He was a Christian and humane, says Wang. He condemned the war crimes and documented biological warfare activities in his diary.

The Japanese peace activists, scholars, villagers, and local Chinese government spent three years preparing their case. They had an annual medical check-up to trace evidence of the plague in the area. Researchers caught 100 rats every year to determine whether plague antibodies remained in their blood.

Plague germs continued to be found in these rats until 1996.

In 2001, a Chinese doctor testified that the lingering effects of biological warfare still threatened the Chinese people. International news agencies covered his testimony. The villagers lost their first lawsuit in August 2002. However, the Tokyo District Court confirmed the use of biological warfare by the Japanese Imperial Army.

> For the first time in history, an office of authority in Japan admitted biological warfare in China. The verdict is in history. The [Japanese

> court] said biological warfare was in violation of the Geneva Treaty and international agreements and that Japan was responsible for that [. . .] But they said the issue of responsibility was resolved because China gave up her rights [to seek war reparations] in the 1972 Sino-Japan Joint Communiqué.

Over the years, in the war of words and diplomatic tensions between China and Japan, the most critical voices have not been heard. Many Chinese victims of Japanese war crimes are living in squalid conditions and cannot afford basic medical treatment.

I was shocked that survivors like Chen Chong Wen and Li Meitou had been forgotten. They spurred me on to use my writing and journalism to share their stories with the world, which I have done in a column on CBC on my blog, and now in this book.

It was mind-boggling to me that the Japanese prime ministers Junichiro Koizumi and the late Shinzo Abe both visited the Yasukuni shrine that honours infamous war criminals (no one responsible for biological warfare was ever convicted for crimes against humanity) and is seen as a source of tension between its neighbours and a symbol of past Japanese military aggression.

Shockingly, and to the ire of China and Korea, Japan's current Prime Minister Fumio Kishida sent an offering to the Yasukuni shrine in April 2023. China urged Japan in a stern message to reflect on its historical atrocities and to break away from militarism. At the same time, Korea expressed deep disappointment with Kishida and urged Japan to face its history and 'show true remorse for the past with its actions'.

Later, I learned that between 1997 and 2007, the lawsuits launched by Wang and plaintiffs like Chen and Li had gone all the way to the Supreme Court in Japan, yet all their appeals were ultimately rejected. The judge upheld the ruling that the Chinese victims did not have the right to demand compensation from the state of Japan. However, the higher courts also upheld the lower court verdict that acknowledged, for the first time, that the Japanese military had used biological weapons against Chinese civilians.

'Why have I gone to the courts more than 40 times? And why have I continued to search for men and women with rotting legs almost 10 years after the closure of the lawsuit? It's because evil must be pursued,' Wang told *China Daily* in 2016.

Meeting these survivors personally had a profound effect on me. I will never forget the sight of Chen Chong Wen weeping. 'I don't want anything else. I just want the wound to close. That's the only thing I want,' he sobbed.

I cannot erase Chen's cries from my mind. They are part of what motivates me to write and advocate for those who are downtrodden and powerless. I learned from Wang that it is possible to persevere and be fearless in the face of obstruction from a government; to be a voice of compassion and truth for those in agony and in need of justice. Her lifelong dedication to these survivors and to those who have passed on is nothing short of inspirational.

In Search of Abby

It struck me recently that my documentation of these stories is a critical step in ensuring that the experiences of trafficked and exploited women, both past and present, are never erased from history.

By recounting the untold stories of the abused and oppressed, we are not only doing justice to those who have suffered but also showing them love and respect. We must look back at history to learn from it. As someone who has met countless victims of forced prostitution across Asia, I believe that the cycle of sex trafficking is repeating.

As part of my documentary series on modern slavery, I went in search of contemporary sex trafficking victims to interview on camera in Hong Kong in 2013. I was told by the Hong Kong government and local NGOs back then that the city had no victims or survivors.

It seemed like an impossible assignment but I decided to scrutinize this assumption, to find out for myself if it is indeed true. I made it my mission to do everything in my power to shed light on the victims of sex trafficking in this city so that they can get the necessary aid and support.

For nine months, I scoured the red-light districts and notorious bar strips with the help of frontline workers to locate hidden victims. Having already produced documentaries on sex trafficking in Thailand, Cambodia, and mainland China, I felt confident as I walked most of the seedy neighbourhoods. But, in some of the smaller side streets, there was a darkness that made me edge closer to my companions. I would have held their hands if that were acceptable for a grown woman and an investigative journalist like me.

One night, we met 'Abby' on the street and approached her as if we were tiptoeing close to a frightened deer. I zoomed in on her because I sensed a tiny crack of an opening in her heart. I held my breath as I asked a non-threatening question about the time.

After a few meetings with us on the streets, Abby eventually admitted that she had been forced into prostitution. In January 2012, she was flown on a tourist visa to Shenzhen, China, from East Africa.

I asked to interview her on camera. She agreed, as long as we didn't film her face. She told me that she had been lured by the promise of a job, earning more money to pay for her twelve-year-old daughter's education. Her traffickers paid for her air tickets and expenses. When she arrived in China they told her: 'You are a slave. We hold your passport until you have paid up.'

She was forced to have sex with several men daily, with her earnings for the first three months going towards paying off her 'debt' of US$4,000.

She wasn't the only one. 'They bring girls from Africa, like a business [. . .] They were like sex slaves,' she said.

Later, she was brought to Hong Kong. Her traffickers had told her that they knew where her daughter lived. It was enough to keep her in line even though she walked freely on the streets every night—forced to find clients who buy sex. She sighed deeply when I asked if any man had hit her.

'Prostitution is a dangerous thing,' she said with a deadness in her eyes. I imagined she had been once a joyful woman, full of life. Once.

Soon after, we went to see Abby again in the hopes of helping her escape her traffickers. A missionary and I didn't know exactly what to do. We asked my husband Matt for advice, since he had helped hundreds of victims of modern slavery over the years through his roles at the United Nations and with the US government. He urged us to proceed cautiously because her traffickers would know where her family lived in Africa and could harm them.

We asked Abby to join us at a church service and afterwards took her out for a meal. Over dinner, I asked her if she wanted to escape her traffickers. But she was too scared and didn't answer.

She decided to return to her hostel room in Kowloon's Chungking Mansions—a sprawling, rundown building notorious for cheap accommodation, drugs, prostitution, and illegal immigration.

We were in uncharted waters and felt very nervous. Were we doing the right thing in asking her to consider escaping her enslavers? Would we actually be able to help her or would our actions make things worse? She was the first victim of trafficking that we had met in the city.

Perhaps because her traffickers had seen us the other day, her mobile was unexpectedly disconnected. We went to visit her after she didn't answer her phone, but she was nowhere to be found.

In the subsequent weeks and months I thought often of Abby and her daughter as I reached out to terrified looking women in the red-light districts of Hong Kong. Several times, I thought I spotted her on the streets and called her name. Each time, I was met with silence. Meeting Abby was a turning point because it deepened my commitment to giving my life to help others in need.

It was the first time one of my interviewees had disappeared ominously after I spoke to them. We were naive in our approach.

Now, I know how to help a victim like Abby.

Change Things for Others—and Yourself

Being a voice and advocating for the voiceless is vital because it is part of how we make our world a better place for the exploited and the poor. It is also how we learn about the global issues that affect our societies.

Using my voice to help others was how I reached my full potential. I benefited at least as much as, if not more than, those I spoke out for.

I'm the one who changed as I pursued and learned about a cause that I felt strongly for. Advocacy work and campaigning helped me step out of my comfort zone and grow exponentially as I took on speaking engagements. These intimidated me greatly at first but through perseverance, I have eventually become a seasoned, global keynote speaker.

I gained confidence as I raised awareness and taught countless people about historical wartime sexual slavery and modern sex trafficking and slavery. Most of them had never heard of these issues before. A handful of the younger ones went on to pursue human rights degrees and are working in non-profits today.

It's disheartening to realize that 6.2 million girls and women are currently enslaved worldwide. But it's only through awareness that we can even begin to bring about a change. I hope that we professionals, especially women, will step up and volunteer to help our sisters and daughters who are trapped and languishing in modern day sex trafficking.

My empathy grew as I listened to survivors' stories and shared their messages with the world. Bridges were built and people were enlightened. We can use the power of our voices, talents, and decision-making to transform our communities and world. We can uplift people to look higher and to do good, to show others an alternate vision of what a world of beauty and inspiration looks like and what they can do to contribute to it.

Harriet Tubman said, 'Every great dream begins with a dreamer. Always remember, you have within you the strength, the patience, and the passion to reach for the stars, to change the world.'

That's why I wrote about my personal journey to interview and document the personal stories of survivors and victims across Asia, as well as about human traffickers and frontline workers. I want to spur more people on to help. I want to inform the international community about their desperate need for aid and to take coordinated action to stop the modern slave trade. I have raised international awareness of these issues through my memoir, *A Long Road to Justice*, and through speaking engagements and media interviews.

Lastly, after meeting survivors of unimaginable tragedy, one thing has become abundantly clear: even in the darkest of times, hope never fails. They have left an indelible mark on me, and I am certain it will do the same for anyone who hears their stories.

Let's fight for something greater. Together, we can change our generation.

Chapter 6

The Changemakers

One way to reach your fullest potential is by making a difference in the world. Through helping others, whether it be through philanthropy or being a changemaker, you not only contribute to improving lives but also cultivate personal growth, leadership skills, and a profound understanding of the world's interconnectedness.

Your actions have the power to ignite positive change and inspire others to join the journey towards a better world. Doing so will bring you a greater sense of fulfilment and happiness.

Through my philanthropic work, which took me across China, I was inspired by the forgotten people—people who are blind, orphans, drug addicts, poor, street kids, and victims of modern slavery. The projects I pioneered not only helped drive social change at regional and national levels but they also transformed me as a person.

To have that kind of exposure to profound human suffering and to see frontline workers sacrificing their own lives to help others ruined me for the ordinary and expanded my heart and my understanding. I committed to working with a sense of love and compassion at the heart of all I would do.

E.M. Forster wrote 'Only connect' in the epigraph to his book *Howards End* to encourage the reader to make the connection between the head and the heart and between thoughts and feelings because that is the only way we can live a life of purpose and be a force for good.

I came to conclude that philanthropy must be a way of life, a lifestyle of love and passionate compassion. While I contributed in some small way by bringing a financial solution to social issues, I was surprised to find myself transformed by the work itself and the inspirational unsung heroes, the changemakers taking action, and solving problems through creativity, empathy and collaborative leadership.

Revolutionizing the World of the Visually Impaired in China

Bright Angel Fund (BAF) has changed the lives of people who are blind in China. In Beijing on May 2011, I met some visually impaired, wonderful musicians. They were beneficiaries of the BAF. Through my company's consulting work for ultra-high-net-worth individuals, multinational corporations, and family foundations, I directed funds to BAF's free job training project for the blind.

One of the highlights of when I had my own philanthropy advisory is building relationships with heroes who are making a difference in the lives of the impoverished and vulnerable. The late Mary Chiang was the founder and director of BAF and she never failed to inspire me with her colossal vision for those visually impaired in China. She used her vast influence to affect social change.

For me, philanthropy is a way of life, a passionate pursuit of changing lives and communities.

The young people who were supported by BAF are all highly sensitive. Due to their loss of sight, their other senses, particularly their intuition, have been heightened, and they possess an innate ability to perceive a person's character and determine whether they can be trusted. They can sense the aura of a person and instantly form an impression of them.

A few of these young people performed at the opening ceremony of the Special Olympics in 2008. Mary brokered the first Chinese presidential visit to the US—for President Jiang Zemin. To illustrate how connected she was: there was a glossy magazine that targets elites in China that had former premier Wen Jiabao on one side and she graced the other cover.

In many media interviews, she has boldly spoken of how her faith motivates her to defend people with visual impairment, who are extremely vulnerable to exploitation, slavery, and abuse. Mary passed away on January 2024, but her legacy lives on. Her contributions have been truly extraordinary.

The Children of Poipet

One experience that transformed my life came when I was on the Thailand–Cambodia border filming a documentary about sex trafficking for a TV channel years ago. Seeing so many children, some as young as three, either with paedophiles or selling themselves on the streets, left me speechless and overwhelmed.

It was heartbreaking and led me to dedicate more of my time to helping abused children.

As we filmed in Poipet, Cambodia, we saw something that made our eyes widen. These kids who were begging on the streets began to speak out for their friends. One girl named 'Maley', with dishevelled hair and dirt marks on her olive-skinned face, came near us. She looked traumatized and fearful and yet was open to answering our questions about what she had witnessed in her neighbourhood and the areas where she begged for food and money to support her family.

She told us in a soft voice, 'I am afraid of getting beaten. I knew a girl in my village. A foreigner gave her a snack and asked her to come with him to get more snacks at another place. A few days later, I saw the girl dead. The foreigner had raped her. I'm very afraid.'

To avoid trouble, Maley would stop begging before nightfall. She spoke of her fears and her hope to have enough money to support herself and her family. She was only eleven. And we couldn't ask the police to get Maley and others off the streets. At least not without direct 'evidence' of abuse. It was tragic to leave them behind.

It was nearly impossible not to cry in front of the kids during the interviews. I'll never forget meeting the children of Poipet. It was so incredibly difficult to walk away from them, back in the direction of the Thai border.

The women, such as Malina Enlund, I filmed on the ground who were helping these children and women were incredible. Malina was a remarkably courageous Canadian woman who dedicated her life for years to pioneering services for these exploited children in Thailand

and Cambodia. I followed her for several days and was in awe of her compassion and bravery to step up and do something for these children when most people with privileges and wealth simply ignored them because they didn't want to feel uncomfortable. I learned from this time that change is possible even from small acts of kindness and that generosity can have a meaningful impact on individuals, communities, and generations.

We can break generational cycles of abuse, pain, and poverty if we try.

That there were no social services, and no other frontline workers to help exploited children in this hellish place shocked me to the core. Malina bravely embodied the power of one to make a difference for those who can never pay you back.

The experience marked me, and I began to transform from a risk-averse, prissy professional to look more outwardly and to give back. I often struggled with the pendulum in my mind swinging between staying in my comfort zone, living a comfortable life, and helping others to the point that it hurts me and required sacrifices of my time, money, and skills.

This particular trip shaped my activist voice and lit the fire in my belly to use my talents and time to help the victims of modern slavery. After the documentary aired and was translated into Chinese, many donors gave to the programme to help the children of Poipet.

Carlos Santana said, 'There is no greater reward than working from your heart and making a difference in the world.'

We need a global movement of people to bring change.

The Power of Hope

My friend 'Ai Jin' was a staff member of the Door of Hope organization that rescued and rehabilitated women in forced prostitution in China. Ai Jin and I clicked immediately; we laughed often and linked arms as we walked around town. When we met, she was twenty-seven, spunky, funny, and slender with straight, jet-black hair that framed her square-shaped face.

She and two other young women from the same organization met every week to pray before they went to do outreach in the red-light district to speak with the women and girls there, some as young as thirteen, to offer them an alternative job making jewellery and a chance to leave that world behind.

From the get-go, she confessed she judged the women in the brothels and was afraid to shake their hands because of the stigma. She was part of an underground house church whose members had not been taught to love these women. Yet somehow, she still felt compelled by love to brave these seedy brothels and their lurking traffickers, mamasans, pimps, and mafia members.

I listened to her describe the challenges of her outreach and how she often struggled to continue. I commiserated and shared my own struggles with finishing a book on sexual slavery in Japanese wartime brothels that had already taken me more than ten years to compile by that time. She said:

> Every day, I prayed for more love for these women. Now, I can treat them like my own family. Social work is a new area in China. Most people don't want to help prostitutes because they feel prostitution is just a job to make money to support themselves. Others don't want to get involved because they don't want to get in trouble with the mafia and pimps who control the girls.

Ai Jin is part of a new generation of Christians in China's urban house churches who are involved in social justice and anti-human trafficking work. They preach about God's love for the afflicted, help mend broken hearts, and proclaim liberty to captives and freedom to prisoners in jails.

But what she does is a risky business. China has had a troubled relationship with religion ever since Mao Zedong's Communist Party took over in 1949 and introduced an authoritarian system with zero tolerance for any competing worldview.

During the cultural revolution from 1966 to 1976, communist authorities blacklisted and imprisoned Christians, demolished churches and destroyed Bibles. The Chinese government has since relaxed its stance somewhat to allow registered churches. Today, there are an estimated 100 million Christians in China, but even now, all pastors are required to support the party and abide by the laws and core values of socialism.

Unofficial churches not registered with the government remain illegal and while they are sometimes tolerated if they do not engage in political activities, China has been cracking down on them in recent years due to a perception that they are open to Western influence. Essentially, Chinese Christians are being persecuted once again.

Part of Ai Jin's motivation in helping these girls and women is that her fourteen-year-old cousin was lured into selling her body. She teared up as she told me about this:

> When I found out that my own cousin was working in a brothel and wasn't willing to leave, I was so upset that I wanted to quit the ministry. But God said to me that if I quit then other families would ask me, 'Why didn't you help my daughter?' This makes me believe that God called me here. If God is calling me, then I want to do this ministry for the rest of my life. It's an honour rather than a duty to work here.

I cried for her cousin, and we bonded over our commitment to end sex trafficking. I wondered if I would be more dedicated if I had a cousin suffering in the brothels. I was documenting the stories of the survivors using my skills as an interviewer and writer, *but should I be doing more?* I wrestled with these thoughts, and I knew that Ai Jin deeply empathized with the debate I was having within.

We were exposed to inhumane suffering and how could we not take action? We couldn't turn away. No man is an island. These women languishing in the prisons of modern-day sexual slavery were our cousins, our sisters, our mothers, our daughters, our families.

Ai Jin reminded me that ordinary people can do extraordinary acts of heroism. The power of hope motivated her and other frontline workers, both Chinese and foreign women, to reach trafficked women in some of the darkest places in China.

She was the first to admit that she, too, could be weak and was tempted to quit. But her faith in God and conviction to help the forgotten women and girls compelled her to do something and that challenged me. She inspired me and told me to continue writing. And I did.

There was a similar band of unconventional women in 1901 who formed the Door of Hope Mission in Shanghai, China, in a small, rented house with a neon sign that said 耶稣能救人 (Jesus saves) in the heart of the notorious red light district on Foochow (now Fuzhou) Road.

They helped rescue women and girls as young as five from sexual exploitation, indentured servitude, and abuse, and even offered food, medical care, and a home. They had up to 200 girls in their shelter and, eventually, some of them made a living by making exquisite hand-made dolls with heads carved out of pear wood that are highly sought after by collectors today.

The mission's encouragement of women's emancipation through education and independence meant they were way ahead of their time. Options for women—especially for working-class women or unmarried, widowed, or orphaned women—were extremely limited. Many of these vulnerable girls and women were sold into indentured servitude as domestic workers from a young age and, when they got older, were sold into prostitution against their will.

Over the years, around 5,000 women and girls were received in the home, yet despite its good work, it attracted controversy. Some of the women ran away, and there were complaints that their family system reinforced Confucian values because the missionaries arbitrarily selected husbands for the girls and accepted financial gifts from the husbands' families that were not included in the financial annual reports.

By 1912, three attempts were made to set the house on fire. In 1950, the Chinese government closed the mission down during a purge of what it saw as toxic foreign intervention.

A Dangerous Mission

Over the past few decades, one of the biggest tragedies I've witnessed is that of the North Korean women refugees who are trafficked as brides and forced to marry impoverished Chinese husbands in China.

I encountered these suffering women while working with an underground network of activists who helped North Korean refugees escape the country. Unfortunately, not every North Korean who manages to leave ends up in a happy place.

I met women who had crossed the Tumen River into China searching for jobs to send back money to their families in North Korea or the Democratic People's Republic of Korea (DPRK). But, upon their arrival on Chinese soil, they were sold immediately as unwilling brides to poor men unable to find a wife any other way. These women were living in quiet despair and struggling with depression and shame. They were invisible.

It was against this extraordinarily dark and hopeless backdrop that I learned of modern-day heroes like Tim Peters, a seventy-four-year-old American based in Seoul, South Korea, who has helped hundreds of North Korean refugees, including women trafficked as brides.

In the early years of their marriage, Tim and his wife Sun-mi were travelling missionaries focused on social justice and have since supported countless marginalized people, including the Korean tuna fishermen in American Samoa who were perceived as intruders and stigmatized.

Later, upon returning to Seoul, they turned their eyes to the plight of North Koreans and founded the non-profit Helping Hands Korea in 1996 to help North Koreans who risked their lives crossing the China–North Korea border.

His courageous group has assisted more than 2,000 North Koreans in escaping to freedom in another country along what Tim dubbed as the 'Underground Railroad'—a secretive route named after the system used in the American Civil War to help Black slaves in the South flee to freedom in the northern states and Canada. Tim saw a parallel in his work.

While he used to be on the frontlines when he was younger, he is now more involved in strategic planning from Seoul, partly because he believes he would attract unwanted attention from authorities as a Caucasian. The rescue operations team faces extreme danger. His organization provides medicine and food aid to the underground Christian networks inside North Korea.

Some missionaries and aid workers have been arrested and, as reported by *Financial Times*, allegedly, even killed by suspected North Korean agents. Pastor Kim Chang-hwan was killed by a poison needle in 2011 and Pastor Han Choong-ryul was fatally stabbed in 2016, both while undertaking covert missions, according to Peters.

I have also heard of missionaries who perished while crossing swollen rivers to guide North Koreans safely to a third country, while dozens of Korean American and South Korean pastors and missionaries have been imprisoned in China for trying to rescue North Korean refugees, which is considered illegal. North Koreans found in China are repatriated immediately to their home country where they are sent to languish in labour camps.

Another unsung hero, my friend 'Peter' who was involved in rescuing trafficked North Koreans, gave me his journals from this period of his life. They contained some of the most beautiful, noble thoughts and writings I've ever read. They made clear he paid no attention to his own life and personal safety; he was motivated by God's love and ready to lay down his life for these people in desperate circumstances.

Reading them made me wonder how a Korean American raised in similar circumstances as me, a second-generation immigrant Korean in a primarily Caucasian school and one who wrestled with the pain from an identity crisis, came to fulfil his fullest potential as a human being.

Peter found freedom in giving up his life and turning his back on a comfortable lifestyle to help others in great need. That's why he is a powerful role model for me.

Creative Methods for a Closed Dictatorship

When I first moved to Beijing in 2004, I felt a calling to be involved in North Korea-related work. As a child, I had heard of the starving North Koreans and had always hoped I would one day help give millions of dollars to that country. It felt like an impossible dream; I didn't really think I would ever achieve it.

Even so, I had this feeling deep in my bones that I needed to focus on the North Koreans in the coming years so I took small steps to learn Korean again.

Then, through my philanthropy work, the opportunity came to help direct funding to North Korean humanitarian aid projects, and I had the privilege of meeting those involved to vet them and do the due diligence on their organizations.

Many of them were high risk projects that needed to be handled with great sensitivity. I matured and learned how to be discreet as I grasped the magnitude of the life-changing impact funding can have on multitudes of people. Some of these projects involved getting food aid into the dictatorship, and at times, parts of the Bible were smuggled in creatively—via balloons, for instance.

One time, while writing up a report for donors, one of my American colleagues based in the US made a colossal blunder and emailed all the secretive information back to someone I'll call 'Ronald' the non-profit lead. This was particularly dangerous for the aid workers on the ground because we were all aware that his emails were being monitored.

Understandably, Ronald was extremely upset by this potential breach of security, and I had to explain to the clueless colleague why this had been an absolute error that could have shut down the entire project for good.

His nonchalant attitude in response was shocking. We never gave him any more paperwork related to North Korea ever again.

As a Korean Canadian, I inherently understood the risks and the dangers of anything related to North Korea. In 2003, I interviewed Pastor Hyeon Soo Lim of the Light Korean Presbyterian Church in Mississauga, Ontario, Canada, about his numerous trips to North Korea. He had rare access and was able to bring humanitarian aid into the Hermit Kingdom.

He recounted a 'miracle', in which one of his church members had asked him to track down her relative in Pyongyang, giving him only a piece of paper with a name written as guidance. He had thought it was an impossible ask and was very doubtful that he would ever be able to meet her relative. Regardless, he brought the paper with him on his next trip.

Miraculously, he ended up meeting this relative in person and could pass on the money his church member had asked him to give.

That was just one of many creative ways his church found to help North Koreans. It also opened a nursing home, an orphanage, and a nursery in Rajin to help the needy in this closed regime.

Fast forward to January 2015, and Lim was arrested and accused by the North Korean government of trying to use religion to overthrow the regime. He was sentenced to two years hard labour.

I read about his plight in the news and prayed for his release sometime after his arrest. After more than 100 trips to North Korea since 1997, despite warnings about the dangers from the Canadian government, Lim was languishing in a labour camp, forced to dig holes and break coal by hand.

After two and a half years in prison, he was released on 'sick bail' on humanitarian grounds a day after a six-member Canadian government delegation travelled to Pyongyang. He has since completed his sentence and returned home.

In an extraordinary act of magnanimity, he has forgiven the North Koreans and says he wouldn't hesitate to return if the country allowed him.

Persecuted for Their Faith

I helped direct funding to 'underground' or house churches in a country where churches that weren't registered with the government were considered illegal. I met young women and men in their twenties who were regularly detained and interrogated for attending Bible colleges and churches, and their bravery and willingness to stand for what they believed in changed my life.

One friend I'll call 'Victor', was taken in by the authorities and questioned, and he divulged the details of many leaders in the faith-based network. I was disappointed, as I had personally vouched for and helped connect Victor with a donor.

A year later, he asked to catch up and we met in a coffee shop, but I immediately sensed he was not acting like himself. I also suspected there was someone behind me, listening in, and sure enough, when I looked, there was a man dressed all in black with a pen and some kind of electronic device on his empty table. I jumped out of my chair and walked as fast as I could out of that building and into the crowds.

I have always relied on my strong intuition and am glad I didn't ignore the red flags that day.

I thought I knew Victor and that he was a friend, but I began to doubt my judgement after this experience. It drove home that I needed to be wiser when directing money and to get to know the people in charge of the programmes as thoroughly as possible.

Helping to send funds to these unregistered churches and their Christian activity was a great risk to me, as it meant I could have been deported. When I look back, I was so young and naive at that time that I wonder how I managed the stress of constantly looking over my shoulder to see if I was being tailed or not.

My phone was tapped, my computer hacked, and my emails monitored. I would lower my voice automatically into a whisper whenever I spoke of this faith-based work, even when I was visiting Canada or the US. Before taking on this work, I had to consider the risks and the pros and cons. I worried that the negative impact of the stress would outweigh the good.

In hindsight, it deepened my thinking, expanded my capacity to persevere, and deepened my convictions. My capacity to take on hard tasks is much greater now because I feel more grateful for my freedom and the power to choose.

I feel I was meant to take on this work and it has shaped and deepened my Christian faith. I grew up in Canada, where there are no restrictions on where I go to church—I have the freedom to do as I please regarding my religion.

To see the persecuted Christians in this land and those courageously continuing to practise their faith was inspiring and eye-opening. It challenged my apathy and made me examine what I truly believed in and was willing to dedicate my entire life to. It was a worthy exercise, as it helped eliminate the superficial and set more weighty life priorities. Knowing people who have been imprisoned for their faith is so very sobering.

I could never be the same person again. No longer could I entertain materialistic dreams or relate to anyone who compared themselves to others or spent their time hankering after a bigger home, bigger salary, or flashier car.

This work had given me a bigger dream—a vision of how to help the suffering, the deprived and persecuted, the trafficked, and orphans.

Philanthropy as a Way of Life

I still remember her raw courage as she gripped my hand and cried. 'Hong' had shared with me her story of poverty, crushing medical debt, and quiet desperation. She was only in her thirties. I kept thinking of her long after our meeting ended.

She reminded me that no matter how bad your situation was, there was always a chance to turn your life around.

I met her at a programme that was funded by a philanthropist I represented. I was managing a migrant fund in Beijing that focused on supporting job training initiatives and education programmes for the children of migrants in the slums and their holistic welfare at the time. Through this, I had the privilege of getting to know many 'internal' Chinese migrants who had moved from the countryside to the city.

While still in the countryside, Hong signed up for free vocational training through the social enterprise XZG in Beijing. Doing so required a leap of faith. She had read many news stories of women who had been sexually exploited by sham businesses or trafficking rings and spent many hours worrying over whether XZG was a legitimate organization.

But Hong had few other options open to her. She had become destitute and been hurt when her husband suddenly abandoned her. She had to find a way to support herself and her son, and pay for her terminally ill mother's mounting medical bills. So, she took the leap.

Each year, millions of women like Hong leave their rural villages to migrate to bigger cities in search of employment. It is the only way they can hope to support their poverty-stricken families. Yet, few find decent job opportunities because they lack education and contacts and have difficulties adjusting to city life. Many find themselves working for US$50 a month in menial jobs that are 3D—dirty, dangerous, and demeaning—while pimps lure others into forced prostitution.

Internal migrants, their children, the fatherless, and orphans are the most at risk.

Thankfully, Hong's leap of faith paid off. She received quality training to be a domestic worker and the social enterprise helped her get a stable job. The desperate risk she took ended up saving her from destitution and exploitation.

Even though it was only one meeting many years ago, I have never forgotten this encounter with Hong. It could be, in part, that I was still raw and reeling from the pain of my divorce at the time and that enabled me to identify deeply with Hong's plight.

Whatever the reason, the meeting drove home for me how job training could empower people. I learned that as donors and changemakers, we must be respectful and treat the needy with dignity. It was vital that Hong knew I didn't look down on her or make her feel inferior.

It also reminded me of how storytelling in philanthropy is crucial. Often, this involves telling sad stories, but it's important to share the bright side, too—highlighting positive change is one of the best ways to encourage more of the same.

So, I wrote about Hong's story for the donor of the training programme and recounted the impact it had had on her in the hope it would catalyse further generosity. Indeed, the donor continued funding millions of dollars into migrant programmes for a few more years.

The American children's author Timothy Pina knew well the role of storytelling in helping others. 'Philanthropy is not about money,' he once said. 'It's about feeling the pain of others and caring enough about their needs to help.'

Here are some lessons that helped me adopt philanthropy as a lifestyle:

- **Create lasting change:** Being a changemaker involves addressing the root causes of issues rather than just treating symptoms. The goal is to create sustainable and lasting change, not a quick fix.
- **Never stop learning:** Philanthropy will expose you to many challenges. The best way to meet them is to foster an attitude

of continuous learning about social issues, cultures, and ways to effect change.

- **Lead and innovate:** Engaging in philanthropy often means taking a leadership role in solving problems and developing innovative solutions to address societal needs.
- **Giving is more than paying:** Being a changemaker is all about giving, but it goes beyond financial resources. It's a lifestyle! Your time, skills, and knowledge are valuable assets in creating social impact.
- **Amplify voices:** Philanthropy and changemaking often involve giving a platform to those whose voices are not being heard. You must learn the importance of listening and elevating others.

Know the Risks

Working on the frontlines in a developing country can be very dangerous. I've learned to prepare for the unexpected, go with the flow, and, most of all, stay calm at all times.

The reward for exposing oneself to other cultures and having high-risk experiences is an unprecedented opportunity for growth. However, I wouldn't recommend taking a risk to anyone who has physical or emotional issues, such as depression, that might hinder them.

During his annual visit to China from the US, my boss 'Brian' and I flew to Myanmar with our NGO hosts from Yunnan. We were on a donor trip on behalf of a leading philanthropist.

I have had many bosses over the years, but Brian was by far the best boss I had ever had. He was brilliant and had a great sense of humour, and he made everyone laugh. He was kind and considerate towards his staff and working with him was always a joy. When I was going through a tough time with my divorce, Brian's support at work made all the difference.

Our host, Bangyuan Wang, arranged our stay at a Kachin military compound. I was not so excited about this prospect, but I told myself to keep an open mind in the spirit of adventure and learning something new about a country. I trusted Bangyuan's judgement, and it was essential to develop a good relationship with those making decisions on the ground that affect the community.

Bangyuan was a young, intelligent, and capable Chinese leader of a non-profit organization and was very experienced in HIV prevention work in Myanmar. He had a stocky build and his tanned, round face with metal-rimmed spectacles exuded a calm aura. He moved and talked slowly and almost always took a few minutes to pause and respond if asked a tough question.

As we drove into the wooded area, I saw cages holding scruffy-looking black bears and other wildlife that I suspected were being sold illegally to Chinese medicine producers. Several stern-faced soldiers in brown camouflage outfits with large machine guns patrolled around the low, brown buildings housing the military. It felt like a scene out of a National Geographic documentary. My eyes widened and my heart raced.

I was assigned a spartan room furnished only with a bed, a chair, and a wooden desk. As soon as I sat on the bed, I sensed something was not right—I suspected hidden cameras planted in the room.

But, at that moment, Bangyuan called for me so I didn't have the luxury of time to freak out. Instead, I left my locked luggage behind and headed out to visit the site of an HIV/AIDS programme that our donor was funding.

My boss was jet-lagged and we advised him to stay in his room that night. When I returned that evening, my wariness remained and my eyes scanned the room for any hidden cameras. Though I could not see them, I knew they were there. So, I wore my swimsuit in the shower and changed clothes with a jacket on because I could feel there were eyes watching me.

Our situation reminded me of a story about a hotel for foreigners in Pyongyang, North Korea, where the mirrors in the bathroom and bedroom are two-way and officials watch your every move. I was hypervigilant.

What were they thinking of me? Would they be surprised that I was hiding myself? I even felt a little smug, like I had outsmarted someone.

In the early hours of the next morning, it was a different story. I was awoken by a knock on the door and assumed it was the soldiers.

I had slept with my clothes on, including my blue fleece jacket and had my shoes beside the bed so I could be ready to leave at any time because I knew that something was not right. A rush of adrenalin coursed through me as I leaped from my bed and called out, 'Who is it?'

'It's me,' Brian said.

I sensed a different tone in his voice, which was usually calm and easy-going. I opened the door with a sense of dread. My boss came in and said several soldiers had come into his room and interrogated him for hours. I felt panicked and immediately began to say my prayers out loud because I thought we wouldn't make it out alive.

Without skipping a beat, I called out in the hallway to our host Bangyuan, who came rushing over. After discussing, we concluded that the head soldier probably wanted to practise his English with Brian, who had kind blue eyes, fair-skin and reddish hair, and they were curious about him. Brian was probably the first American man and the first ginger the soldiers had ever seen.

Our host decided to leave for the border hours earlier than scheduled, which led me to wonder if our trip was more perilous than he had actually conveyed. But I felt beyond grateful that we were getting out of there in one piece! It was a work trip that I'll never forget and one that has probably scarred us for life.

The lessons learned? Pack your swimsuit wherever you go! I'm only half-kidding . . .

Obviously, I was ecstatic to get out of there in one piece. I was glad that I got to see what it was really like for the humanitarian workers and to experience first-hand the risks they face on a regular basis. In philanthropy work, it's vital to know what's happening on the frontlines if you are to make wise decisions.

My admiration for changemakers like Bangyuan only increased after this experience. More importantly, though, I learned it's vital to push past your fear and to stay as calm and congenial as possible in a cross-cultural situation, especially if it's potentially dangerous. I was once surrounded by an angry mob of parents in a park in Beijing who were upset that foreign journalists were covering their matchmaking activities for their children. The only way we got out alive was by keeping our mouths shut and not provoking anyone, otherwise, we could have been trampled.

Since this Myanmar trip, I have decided not to put myself in unnecessarily risky situations anymore, especially in places where the military has absolute control and where it's prudent not to be the foreigner parachuting in.

I have also learned the importance of always seeking to understand your hosts. People are usually kind. I often tell myself to try not to jump to conclusions. What seemed like a threatening interrogation turned out to be a bored soldier trying to get a free English lesson from Brian! Finally, make gratefulness a virtue. When you do, you'll find reasons to be thankful, even in the most unlikely places.

Guiding Principles

Not too long after I moved to Hong Kong from Beijing in 2011, I was invited to speak at a prestigious private high school. It was my very first speaking gig in the city and I remember agonizing for hours over what to share with the students. I had to ask friends what the young people were like and the issues they were grappling with.

I ended up speaking about my philanthropy and journalism related to fighting human trafficking and documenting and exposing war crimes during World War II, such as Japan's use of biological warfare and military sexual slavery.

I asked them what career they wanted to pursue. Almost everyone said they wanted to be bankers. I encouraged these young people not to pursue money alone in their jobs but to embrace a life of significance and purpose.

I bet these kids had never heard anyone discouraging them from becoming money-hungry bankers! I urged them not to fall into blind filial piety, as many young Asians do, by following their parents' expectations without critically thinking about careers in law, finance and accounting, and medicine.

I asked them to stop and think about what their dream was and to pursue it. And if that dream was still to be a banker, I urged them to be one who gave back to those in need. I told them that achieving excellence and making a great salary were good things, but that even more important was to remember vulnerable groups as they climbed the career ladder.

I then explained how the concept of VIPS has guided me throughout my life journey as a changemaker and helped me reach my full potential. Here's what VIPS means:

- **Vision:** Have a clear vision, plan, and set of goals for *who* you want to be and what you want to achieve—in one, five, ten, and twenty years. Revisit your vision often; there's no harm in it changing over time. Having a plan gives your life a rudder. As Woodrow Wilson said, 'The person who has no vision will undertake no great enterprise.'
- **Integrity:** Strive to be honest in all you do and have a clear conscience at the end of each day. Be someone others can trust. Plato said, 'Integrity is your destiny—it is the light that guides your way.'
- **Passion:** You must nurture your passion and compassion if you are to achieve your dreams of making a difference in this world. Neglecting doing so risks them dimming due to fatigue and busyness.
- **Sacrifice:** Be prepared to do what's needed and put in the blood, sweat, and tears—to the point where it hurts—if it means completing a goal or fulfilling a dream.

Public speaking is now a big part of my life. In every message, I try to include the message of VIPS, which, after all these years, remains my North Star.

One of the most haunting quotes I know is this definition of hell: 'On your last day on Earth, the person you could have become will meet the person you became.'

A Force for Good

My most treasured insight from my years in philanthropy, journalism, and meeting countless changemakers is that love is all-important.

Without love and compassion, making change is meaningless and empty. We must guard our sense of compassion and take care not to burn out, since love is the most vital ingredient that we need to help those in desperate circumstances.

Only love can drive out fear and hate. Armed with genuine care, like Malina and Tim and countless other changemakers, we can do the impossible and be fearless in our mission. It is our responsibility to use the privileges we have—our skills, time, experiences, education, and more—to fulfil our potential and give back to our society and those less fortunate.

Small acts multiplied by millions of people can transform our world. I have supported my husband Matt Friedman's *Be the Hero campaign* to mobilize people of all ages to step up and volunteer to help make a difference in the global issues of our time.

It is my greatest hope that you will be inspired to get involved and help change the world. Your actions can create a positive chain reaction, fostering a culture of compassion and generosity.

What excites me about the young generation is that they have the greatest potential to bring about societal transformation—they have the energy, the time (because they are not bogged down with a mortgage or raising children), and the idealism to dream of doing the impossible and come up with innovative solutions to address the needs of the exploited and the pressing issues of our time.

Did you know that many of the social movements around the world that changed history were initiated and led by youth?

- **Civil rights movement** (1950s–60s): Young activists fuelled the fight against racial segregation and discrimination in the US. Youth, particularly college students, played a pivotal role in organizing protests, sit-ins, and freedom rides to demand equal rights for African Americans.
- **Anti-apartheid movement** (1970s–90s): Students and youth organizations protested against the racially oppressive apartheid system in South Africa, advocating for equality, justice, and the release of Nelson Mandela.

- **Arab spring** (2010–12): Young people across the Middle East and North Africa took to the streets to protest against authoritarian regimes, corruption, and lack of opportunities. Social media played a crucial role in organizing and spreading awareness about the movement.
- **Climate change movement** (2010s–present): The global youth-led movement for climate action is exemplified by figures like Greta Thunberg. Youth activists worldwide have organized strikes, marches, and campaigns to raise awareness and demand meaningful action from governments and corporations.
- **Anti-trafficking movement** (2013–present): Many students in schools and universities have been driving awareness and action against the global scourge of modern slavery. Their efforts have been instrumental in raising funds, and countless young people have gone on to major in human rights and are now working in roles that fight the trafficking and exploitation of people.

These social movements demonstrate the power of young people to drive significant societal change and challenge established norms and systems. Their passion, energy, and determination have left lasting impacts on history and continue to inspire future activists.

My advice is to identify the causes and issues that ignite your passion and learn all you can about them. Then, find the right organization where you can volunteer your time and talents to help a particular group of people or a cause that's close to your heart. I guarantee that you will grow as you commit and take action to help others and make a lasting impact. Your confidence will grow as you fulfil your purpose and pursue a dream.

I see another movement on the not-so-distant horizon: a women's movement starting in Asia. For centuries, women in this part of the world have been suppressed and silenced. Yet there are more Asian women in positions of influence and with higher levels of education than ever before. Their collective voices can transform culture and break generational cycles of misogyny, sexism, and more. They can help end the exploitation of girls and women in sex trafficking.

As more women with a spirit of giving back to the community enter positions of leadership in the corporate world, government, and civil society, there is an opportunity for great change.

Lastly, far more than what we do for work, what counts is who we become. In the end, it is our characters that count most. Respect others and use your privileges and gifts to help those in need through love.

That is how we will reach our fullest potential.

Chapter 7

The Importance of Good Friendships

Having true friends helps us grow and succeed. My good friends have been a vitally important source of love and support over the years. I often call them my 'second family'. We must choose our friends wisely, for they impact our lives profoundly. As the Chinese philosopher Mencius said, 'Friends are the siblings God never gave us.'

According to the American Psychological Association, friendship is a voluntary relationship between two or more people that is relatively long-lasting and in which those involved tend to be concerned with meeting each other's needs and interests as well as satisfying their own desires.

Lasting friendships provide us with support, mutual respect, and understanding. They also create a sense of belonging and purpose. They bring out the best in us, improve our health, and allow us to grow while providing care and companionship.

In high school, I was fortunate to have a best friend named 'Mike'. We talked for hours on the phone each night and hung out every weekend. We shared a passion for hip hop dancing and spending time with our mutual friends. Although we were each other's prom dates, our friendship was strictly platonic. We had an undeniable bond and emotional connection but never crossed the line. We didn't even hold hands—not once. Many of our friends wondered why we weren't dating, but we would always reply, 'We're just best friends.'

At times, we both secretly had more than friendship on our minds, but we were too afraid to ruin our special companionship. Our friendship was simple and beautiful, based on unconditional love and support. We celebrated each other's milestones and supported each other through thick and thin. It was one of the purest and most loyal friendships possible.

Mike and I grew apart during our university years, as he attended a different school. Our paths diverged even more after college—he became a wild partier and developed a drinking problem while I focused on my career. At one point, he asked me out on a date, but I turned him down, telling him I needed someone more mature. He didn't speak to me for a long time after that.

Years later, when we were both thirty years old, he reached out to me via email. In a hail Mary before he proposed to his girlfriend, he wanted to know if there was still a chance for us. Mike wrote that he had always loved me and that I was the one that got away for him. He hoped to hear that I loved him too before he proposed to his current girlfriend. I sensed it was his last attempt to avoid any future regrets about not confessing his true feelings to me.

I was surprised by his message. As much as I wanted to reciprocate his feelings, I couldn't muster any despite our amazing, shared history. I only cared for him as a close friend.

After reading his honest email several times, I wept. They were sentimental tears of gratefulness for the beautiful memories we had shared, and for his unwavering support during the ups and downs of our teenage years and the life-altering changes that came when my mother remarried. He was my rock then, and I'll always be thankful for our genuine friendship.

He set the bar high for all my other friends. I encouraged him to move forward with his girlfriend and start a new chapter in his life. We both had closure that day.

I knew our friendship would change after he got married, with more distance between us, since his spouse would become his top priority, and I supported that. We've exchanged occasional work-related messages on LinkedIn, and I still hold him dear. He was my first significant relationship with a man, and through this rare friendship, I developed better interpersonal skills and received unwavering moral support during stressful life transitions, which helped me persevere and shaped me into the friend I am today.

In an article published by the American Psychological Association, Professor Rebecca Schwartz-Mette—the director of the Peer Relations Lab at the University of Maine, who studies friendship among children, adolescents, and young adults—learning about oneself through friendship as a young adult spurs personal growth and lays a solid foundation for self-awareness. She says that sharing thoughts and feelings between friends through self-disclosure helps young adults build empathy for others, practise seeking and providing social support, and even solidify their identities.

Aristotle put it another way: 'For without friends no one would choose to live, though he had all other goods; even rich men and those in possession of office and of dominating power are thought to need friends most of all; for what is the use of such prosperity without the opportunity of beneficence?'

Long before any researcher began exploring the impact of the quality of our human connections, Aristotle understood that close friendships contributed to our overall welfare more than anything else and divided friends into three categories: utility, pleasure, and virtue.

'Utility friends' help one another reach desired goals through skills that benefit both. These friends can be found at the workplace. 'Pleasure friends' enjoy common hobbies and passions such as engaging in sports or cultural activities together, like going to the theatre. But it is the third type, 'virtue friends' that Aristotle thought was the best and most lasting. 'Virtue friends' want the best for one another and admire each other's good qualities, such as generosity, courage, and compassion.

Just how many friends do we need? For me, quality is more important than quantity. Oprah Winfrey, despite having endless resources and connections, has said that she has only three good friends. British anthropologist Robin Dunbar has theorized that people have the cognitive bandwidth to maintain and nurture only around five close friends, up to 150 meaningful connections, 500 acquaintances, and 1,500 people they can recognize.

Personally, I have around ten close friends, dozens that I can have great conversations with and hundreds of acquaintances. It took me years to understand what I needed in a friend, how to maintain friendships, and how to be caring towards them.

The Impact of Friends

Despite having enjoyed close bonds since childhood, it was only in my mid-twenties that I fully recognized the importance of friendships for my happiness, health, and professional success.

I transitioned into a career in TV journalism and found it more challenging to make and maintain good friends at work due to being more selective and having less free time.

I relocated to a new city and was fortunate to meet Dorothy, a dear friend who became a source of inspiration in my life. Along with our friend Janet Lam, we shared meals and laughter and bonded over the challenges we faced at work.

I struggled to cope with a competitive and toxic work environment, but Dorothy and Janet's unwavering support and practical advice helped me navigate the rough times. Their presence in my life watered my parched soul with care and kindness and gave me the endurance and joy to conquer the obstacles I faced, especially the ugly politics in my office, and I felt less lonely. I am forever grateful for their care and role in shaping me into a stronger person.

Developing strong social connections and building close friendships is essential to developing resilience and maintaining positive emotional well-being. Research shows that during times of great stress, these connections can reduce the risk of mental health issues and contribute to greater life satisfaction.

The American entrepreneur and writer Jim Rohn said famously, 'You are the average of the five people you spend the most time with.' This has been proven true in my life. Therefore, it's crucial to surround yourself with people who motivate and uplift you.

Healthy friendships can lead to greater success in all aspects of life—personal, academic, and professional. They help us develop healthy identities and nurture our self-esteem. You can achieve remarkable success by cultivating social skills and building strategic connections.

One study on entrepreneurs, 'Beyond Social Capital: The Role of Entrepreneurs' Social Competence in Their Financial Success', in the *Journal of Business Venturing* found that those with higher levels of social competence and an ability to interact effectively with others were wealthier. Remember, the friends you choose will affect your happiness; choose wisely and they will lead you towards a fulfilling and prosperous life.

Years later, my friendship with Dorothy deepened after I moved to Beijing and Hong Kong as we kept in touch by phone and email. Through this formative friendship in my twenties, I learned how to be a good friend because we felt safe to open up about virtually anything, from family issues to our struggles as single professional women who longed for work–life balance.

We often joked about not becoming too consumed by our careers, using the successful and single Condoleezza Rice as a reminder to prioritize our dating life. We would say to one another spontaneously in a deep, foreboding voice: 'Condi Rice, Condi Rice . . .' as an inside joke.

Around this time, Dorothy told me about reading a book on a successful international TV news executive at the top of her game and her despair at working over Christmas and being unable to hug the TV footage. It was a poignant reminder that relationships should come first before work. I came to conclude that I need to be more intentional about nurturing my relationships or else face the spectre of interminable loneliness.

The psychologist and author of *Platonic: How the Science of Attachment Can Help You Make—and Keep—Friends* Marisa Franco advises us to ask ourselves if we feel restricted or disconnected from our true selves and to use loneliness as a signal to seek out new friends who can bring out different aspects of our identities. Having friends at different stages of life can help us to grow and expand not only our social lives but our minds and identities too.

Franco suggests six behaviours that can help us become better friends: taking initiative, expressing vulnerability, being authentic, giving affection, offering generosity, and harmonizing with anger. These behaviours help enrich our friendships and resolve conflicts more effectively.

Speaking up honestly with love can also improve our relationships. I often share my opinions with friends on topics such as their busy schedules or other issues where they have a blind spot.

With Dorothy's unwavering support, I launched an event for Asian Heritage Month. My vision was to create a community for those who felt lonely, especially those of Asian heritage who felt invisible. We hosted a public event to celebrate our culture.

I also connected friends with others who I felt would be a great match as buddies because of their common career goals or compatible personalities. I discovered I had an innate talent for matchmaking friends and acquaintances; some forged lasting relationships and a community, and some even got married. Dorothy was the first to tell me that I had a connector gift. I have always found joy in bringing people together and making things happen. Hosting social events and dinner parties is something I truly love.

My mother, who can easily unite different types of people under different circumstances, passed on this skill to me. When I was young, I watched her happily work the room like a social butterfly and seamlessly bring people together like a seasoned diplomat. While playing this role with confidence, she could simultaneously host and cook a five-course gourmet dinner for up to seventy-five people from the church choir at our home, which she did every few months.

I genuinely enjoy meeting new people and have an open mind and natural curiosity. I take pleasure in introducing friends based on their common interests or helping them in their work. People often tell me, 'You know everybody.' I later learned that being an effective connector is a leadership trait vital for business success.

In his book, *The Tipping Point*, *The New Yorker* journalist Malcolm Gladwell describes connectors as people who can link many people in different worlds. Anyone can learn how to be a successful connector through trial and error. This has helped me create a sense of community for myself and others.

Connections are built on trust. A powerful connector can establish trust and loyalty with their network. Being generous with your time is an excellent way to build trust and loyalty. It shows that you are willing to go out of your way to help others, and that's a powerful connector trait. Active listening is crucial in building strong connections, as it shows your interest in what the other person is saying.

Lastly, look for opportunities to add value and make an impact. This can be done by sharing valuable content, offering advice, or introducing people to one another.

The philanthropist Drishti Bablani said, 'Never underestimate the empowering effect of human connection. All you need is that one person, who understands you completely, believes in you and makes you feel loved for what you are, to enable you – to unfold the miraculous YOU.'

Transformative Friendships

Some unexpected friendships can change your life forever. When I took on the assignment of writing the biography of Pastor Augustus Chao, the grandfather of Chinese churches in Vancouver, I encountered resistance from him. He was irritable and our age gap was considerable, so I didn't expect that we would eventually forge an unbreakable bond over six months based on unconditional love and trust.

We were polar opposites. But despite our different cultural backgrounds, personalities, and viewpoints, we managed to build a strong friendship. Through this, I learned the significance of having diverse friends—indeed, the more diverse, the better—to expand our understanding and grow as individuals.

At the time, Pastor Chao was a stoic man in his nineties who had been forced to retire by his church board. He felt bitter and increasingly cranky, which made him hesitant to allow anyone to peek into his inner world, let alone a young woman like me. Initially, he rarely spoke and gave only short, grunting answers to my questions. I had to coax his memories out of him, which only made things worse.

Clearly, he resented my presence during the first month of our meetings. I felt I had to extract his memories against his will, forcibly. But once the dam broke, Pastor Chao shared freely and I couldn't have stopped him even if I tried. His loneliness was no longer trapped and he felt a release as we talked for hours and hours.

He spoke of his profound regrets, highs, and lows, which he had never shared with anyone. As we talked for hours on end, his demeanour changed, and his wrinkly face freckled with brown age spots softened. He grinned widely while speaking, a remarkable transformation from his initially hardened, unsmiling face.

The power of listening without judgement can be truly transformative, as I learned from my dear friend, Pastor Chao. Our conversations were filled with a sacred trust, and I cherished our openness. Over time, he became like the grandfather I never had—my own grandfathers had passed away in Korea when I was a child before I could see them—and I often sought his wise counsel.

I was in Vancouver when I heard that Pastor Chao was in hospital, struggling, and I went immediately to be by his side. Seeing him so helpless was distressing. Despite his frailty, he still showed love and affection for me, and we knew how much we meant to each other. I told him I loved him very much, and he said he loved me too.

Sadly, he passed away shortly after my visit. To my surprise, years later, I would sometimes wake in the middle of the night crying because I missed him so much. Indeed, grief and pain are the price we pay for love. His bold, pioneering style, sense of self-sacrifice, and leadership legacy will always inspire me.

Morale Boosters

At another time when I felt weak and vulnerable, I was blessed to experience the true meaning of friendship. I am grateful to those who supported me when I felt overwhelming pain post-divorce. Ivan Yuen, a friend from college who lives in Shanghai, checked in on me regularly via Skype. His steady encouragement and talks gave me immense hope during a dark time of depression and low self-esteem.

My good friend in Toronto, Grace Han and I spoke regularly; she encouraged me and we prayed for one another. Our conversations were always uplifting and felt like an inspirational coaching session during a dark time. She is a gifted coach and wise counsellor and I'm grateful that we have been on the journey together since 2004. Ivan and Grace taught me that it's vital to have a strong network of relationships and I've been more intentional about it ever since. They have deepened my capacity for supporting friends who are facing challenges.

Meanwhile, my brilliant friend Jennifer Lee invited me to live with her for a few months in Beijing while I was looking for a new place to live. When I first saw Jennifer at a church event in 2005, I suddenly knew that we would be very good friends and eventually work together on something—it was a lightning bolt kind of premonition that I hadn't had before.

Eventually, we ended up bonding and could talk about any topic for hours. She became like a sister to me. Jennifer is wise and discerning and over the years, she has been instrumental in advising on how to successfully manage toxic colleagues.

Another dynamic and special couple, Albert and Wingee, hosted an informal weekly therapy group for friends. Their unconditional love empowered us to open up about things we never thought we would share with anyone. It was freeing to take off our masks and be real with each other, and it changed our lives. Our acceptance changed us after airing our addictions and raw struggles. I felt more relaxed and happier.

Ivan, Grace, Jennifer, Albert, and Wingee each played a unique role in my journey, showing me the power of love, encouragement, and acceptance. Through their unwavering support, I discovered a deeper level of connection and understanding that has stayed with me to this day. Their kindness and generosity have inspired me to be a better friend and a more compassionate person in all areas of my life. I learned to treasure great friends because of my wonderful experiences with them. Their unconditional support gave me the courage to face my new status as a single person again.

My former staff member, Princeton graduate, Nelson Chiu, who I met when I was working for the first philanthropic investment bank founded by two billionaires, was charismatic, energetic, and bright. I was his first boss and I mentored him with tough love and we eventually became the best of friends by working together. When I went through my divorce, his gentle and caring support helped build my confidence in men again. We bonded over our commitment to helping others.

He is now a professor at the University of Washington, head of a medical clinic, and committed to medical aid work in China. I admire his brilliance and compassion for others.

After moving to Hong Kong in 2011, I felt an intense loneliness during my first several months. Although I had made some new friends, I hadn't known them long enough for us to share a deep connection. We were still basking in the polite glow of a new relationship and the deep knowing and being known were yet to come. I networked a lot during that first year and connected with people I thought would be good friends, but it didn't work out that way.

Since my network was still growing, I spent more time on LinkedIn, Facebook, and Instagram to message friends and check their progress. There were times when I was alone in my apartment and wondered whether I had made the right decision to leave my close friends behind in Beijing, Vancouver, and the US, where I had spent nearly a year during a sabbatical, to move to a new city and start afresh.

Had I made a foolish decision? I was motivated to find a community that helped me meet as many people as possible with an open heart. At times, I felt the sting of rejection from a few women when our friendship failed to develop, leading us to part ways after meeting for a few meals.

However, I found solace in a church community, where I met Elizabeth Wong, a Chinese American woman and mother of eight children aged two to twenty-one. She had been changing diapers for twenty years. We bonded over our shared experiences of being from the West Coast of North America and our silly sense of humour. As we both transitioned into life in Hong Kong, which is more fast-paced, money-oriented, and frenetic, we supported each other.

Elizabeth was a 'kindred spirit' friend with whom I felt a natural affinity. I spent time with her children at home, hosting birthday parties and pizza nights. Her support was invaluable to me, and I genuinely believe that without her, I would have felt lonely and lost in Hong Kong. We encouraged each other and she offered a listening ear, which made me feel more at home.

One of the most extensive and longest studies on human life and happiness, spanning eighty-six years, has shown that good relationships and community involvement lead to health and happiness. The Harvard Study of Adult Development began in 1938, collecting data on 268 Harvard male graduates, including former US President John F. Kennedy and 456 Boston men.

Later, the study expanded to include the spouses of the original men and more than 1,300 descendants of the group. The participants were asked to complete questionnaires and share information about their physical health while their triumphs and failures in work and relationships were also documented. The findings showed that more than riches and fame, close relationships kept people happy throughout the ups and downs of their lives and had a significant impact on their health, regardless of their social status, financial wealth, IQ, or genetic makeup.

In an interview, Robert Waldinger, the study director and a psychiatrist at Massachusetts General Hospital, highlighted the importance of caring for our relationships and that it is just as crucial as looking after our physical health. He said, 'Taking care of your body is important, but tending to your relationships is a form of self-care too. That, I think, is the revelation.'

The Scourge of Loneliness

A loneliness epidemic is wreaking havoc on countless people's health and happiness worldwide. It is vastly different from enjoying solitude or being content with time alone. Being lonely is a kind of social pain; it's a subjective feeling of disconnection, even if you are married or surrounded by people. *Psychology Today* defines it as a state of distress or discomfort that arises when one perceives a gap between one's desires for social connection and actual experiences.

The pandemic's social distancing measures led to remote work, a halt to social gatherings of any kind, and many moved in droves to the suburbs, triggering an exponential spike in loneliness, mental health issues, and a feeling of emotional disconnection.

Long before the pandemic, our increasing reliance on technology and social media, a faster pace of life and longer work hours meant fewer face-to-face interactions. It was more difficult to maintain these human connections essential for our well-being, which fuelled a sense of collective loneliness and more stress.

Researchers have discovered a correlation between the use of social media and the increase in feelings of loneliness. This is partly due to the false sense of connection it creates and the opportunities it provides to compare oneself to others. Ironically, people often turn to social media when feeling alone but, ultimately, it makes them feel worse because it cannot replace genuine human connection with people who care.

In 2017, a study by the University of Pennsylvania featured on *Penn Today,* established a causal link between reduced social media use and fewer feelings of loneliness and depression. However, when social media is used in moderation for keeping in touch with friends and loved ones, the positives outweigh the negatives.

Poor social connections can have serious health consequences, including depression, anxiety, a higher risk of cardiovascular disease and premature death, cancer, stroke, hypertension, drug abuse, and even a risk of dementia in older adults, according to the US Surgeon General's 2023 report, *Our Epidemic of Loneliness and Isolation.* It also stated that the lack, or poor quality, of connections was a public health challenge that required immediate attention and that being lonely could lead to a higher risk of early death than smoking fifteen cigarettes a day.

The widespread impact of chronic loneliness results in enormous costs to workplaces, communities, and healthcare systems, running into billions in the US, Australia, the UK, and other nations due to medical expenditures associated with declining health, increased work turnover, and absences.

In the BBC's *Loneliness Experiment Study*, 55,000 people worldwide participated and one in three people of all ages reported feeling lonely. The study found that young people aged sixteen to twenty-four were the loneliest, with 40 per cent stating they felt lonely 'often or very often'.

In the UK and Japan, a ministry of loneliness was established to develop strategies to combat loneliness, social isolation, and rising suicide rates. Human beings have an innate desire to belong and thrive through social connections. Isolation triggers a fight or flight response, a physiological reaction to an event perceived as stressful or frightening, inducing stress, anxiety, and feeling alone. We can cultivate solid friendships and build social networks to counteract this response. By tending to and befriending one another, we can create a safe and supportive community that promotes positive emotions and a sense of belonging.

Did you know that social disconnection and rejection by a friend or romantic partner can cause physical pain? According to *Science Daily,* scientists have discovered that 'social pain' triggers the same parts of the brain as physical pain, which is why people often describe it as 'broken heart' or 'hurt feelings'.

As we age, relationships become more important to us than wealth or accomplishments. According to a study by William J. Chopik in the *Journal of the International Association for Relationship Research*, friends become more important to happiness and health than family as you grow older.

The study examined the findings of two pieces of research on relationships in 270,000 people in nearly 100 countries and 7,500 older people in the US. It found that having supportive quality friendships was a stronger predictor of well-being than having strong family relationships.

In today's world, friendships and genuine connections are more important than ever. We need robust support systems to navigate life's challenges.

Toxic Friends

During my childhood, I had a best friend named 'Sandy'. We used to do everything together and had a lot of fun. However, when we reached high school, I became more focused on my studies and started dating someone. As a result, I became an inconsiderate friend and failed to support Sandy when she needed me. I turned a blind eye to her requests to hang out because I was more self-centred and preoccupied with my life. Looking back, it became clear to me that my behaviour was unfair to Sandy, and I regret not being a better friend to her.

Years later, I tried to reconnect with Sandy, but sadly, she had already moved on and didn't want to. I felt terrible about losing such a good friend, but it taught me a valuable lesson about the importance of nurturing close relationships. Grieving a good friendship is hard and can be as painful as losing a romantic relationship or divorce.

Friendships can end for a variety of reasons, from misunderstandings to changing interests and values. Sometimes, it's hard to let go of a close friendship; sometimes, it's a case of out of sight, out of mind. But it's important to remember that sincere friends can bring immense joy and moral support into our lives and provide us with a sense of security that is different from what our family provides.

After I moved to Hong Kong, I met 'Melissa' at church, and we were good friends for ten years. I always admired her thoughtfulness, intelligence, and the way she cared for her friends. We used to celebrate each other's birthdays and have lunch or dinner together at least once a month.

I discovered a new side of my friend when I shared something confidential with her about our mutual acquaintance who had betrayed me in a work context. It was a side that seemed rigid and judgemental. She told me self-righteously that she wouldn't listen to gossip.

However, I didn't consider it gossip to share something confidentially with a good friend. This left me feeling hurt and misunderstood, especially, since I had always offered her my unwavering support and non-judgemental listening ear. Despite this, she continued to interrupt me when I tried to open up to her on other occasions, too.

During one lunch with a mutual friend, Melissa turned away from me and looked out the window while I was talking. Her hurtful gestures made me question our friendship's value. If I couldn't divulge my struggles to a safe friend then what was the point of the relationship? I did attempt to talk to her about how I felt but there was a stony wall on her side—she was unresponsive and seemed unwilling to address the issue.

Despite the strain in our friendship, I felt obligated to maintain the relationship and made excuses for her behaviour. I rationalized it away by remembering that she was caring for her mother, who had a chronic illness, and her burden was heavy. I later discerned that I was in denial about how toxic our friendship had become.

Eventually, I spent less time with Melissa. After I got married, we gradually lost touch, as my schedule became busier. Part of the critical closure process for me was forgiving her and letting go of negative emotions.

This experience taught me that I needed to surround myself with positive and supportive people and that I want my friendships to be a source of joy. I also learned that I tend to hold onto less than stellar friendships out of a false sense of loyalty, even when it's not in my best interest. While I'm open to seeing Melissa in a group setting, I've learned to prioritize my well-being and happiness in my friendships.

It is always a good idea to make amends with friends whenever possible. However, if someone is causing you mental harm and stress or is abusive, it is important to put your mental health first. Just like a gardener trims bushes, you should cut off toxic friends as soon as possible.

Dr Marisa Franco, author of *Platonic* believes that trimming friends has benefits. If we fail to invest time and effort in our friendships, especially by meeting face-to-face, our most important relationships will suffer. Having many acquaintances can leave us spread too thin, making it hard to spend quality time with close friends and putting us at risk of having weak support systems.

There are several signs of a toxic friend, including someone who gossips about you, makes mean comments, disrespects your personal boundaries, and causes stress or a feeling of insecurity. Toxic friends can make you feel nervous, put you down, and expose you to unhealthy behaviours. People who have not had healthy relationships modelled for them may either exhibit toxic characteristics unknowingly or may be unaware they are in a toxic relationship.

Disagreements and arguments are common in any relationship, but when a friend—knowingly or unknowingly causes harm and dysfunction through their words and actions, it becomes more than a disagreement. Being on the receiving end of such behaviour can gradually lead to anxiety, depression, low self-esteem, stress, exhaustion, and even trauma in cases of abuse.

Once the poison has entered your system it will weave its way into your sense of self, identity, and emotions.

I encourage setting personal boundaries and understanding your limits. Respecting others' boundaries helps maintain a mutual consideration and give-and-take dynamic. There are so many potential new friends around; do not let a bad experience hinder you from moving forward and connecting with new people.

Breaking Up Is Hard

Before I divorced my first husband, I went through a painful period of reflection. I was living in Beijing at the time. Although I had wanted to call off the wedding—because deep within, I knew it was a colossal mistake—I failed to do so for a myriad of reasons. I was afraid that cancelling the big event would bring shame, and I felt paralysed by fear.

So it went ahead, but this only delayed the shame and fear because now I had to consider the prospect of divorce. I had never failed at anything in such spectacular fashion. For me, divorce was a humiliating failure.

Expatriate life in China was a revolving door of friends and acquaintances, and this made me yearn for the days when long-time friends surrounded me. I tried to keep an open mind and met a few new friends at church in Beijing who were still single. When I divulged my marriage problems, they said some insensitive and terrible things about how Christians should not divorce at all. They drifted off when they could see that I was struggling.

From then on, I decided to keep my inner circle close and not divulge too much to those who hadn't proved loyal and discreet. Initially, I became wary of making new friends, but then I eventually came to the understanding that I needed to control my suspicion and use my judgement without snap decisions.

During my most vulnerable times, I learned to treasure reliable and trustworthy friends. It's easy to see who your true friends are when you are facing hardships. Those who stand by you in your darkest moments are true sincere friends, unlike those who are only there for you during your good times.

Friends come and go throughout your life. I usually know almost immediately when a friendship is meant to last a lifetime. Some friendships bloom for a few seasons due to chance and circumstance, while some friends last decades despite long distances and you can feel like you were never apart whenever you meet in person.

Over the years, I've also had some toxic friends whom I've ultimately had to 'break up' with. I learned the hard way that I needed to be more discerning about who I let into my circle.

But good can come from the ugly.

I started dating my first boyfriend, 'John', when I was eighteen years old. He was a highly eligible bachelor, a former professional Canadian football player with a professional degree. Due to his shy nature, he had never dated anyone before. It wasn't surprising that many women desired him.

However, I was shocked when two of my friends pursued him after we broke up, ultimately leading to our friendship's demise. I have always held the core value that I wouldn't date any of my friends' ex-boyfriends. Perhaps I was naive to expect the same standard from my friends.

After John moved back to Vancouver, he expressed his undying love, saying he wanted to get back together and eventually get married. In his attempt to be transparent, he divulged that while he was single, he had slept with a random stripper during a wild boys' trip during graduate school and that he had dated an ex-friend of mine, 'Sarah'. She had pursued John aggressively and had even flown out to visit him.

Though we were not dating at the time, I felt disgusted and couldn't envisage a married life with him anymore. I turned him down, though we remained friends and continued to hang out in the same social group.

My ex-friend Sarah and I had studied together at university. Yet even early on in our friendship, I began to distance myself from her when I noticed that she used people, especially her boyfriends. She had a reputation as a narcissistic maneater. I sensed she didn't know who she was and our conversations mainly revolved around her.

I became especially uncomfortable as she, a professed anti-social introvert, began to adopt my extroverted personality and even some of my mannerisms. It was creepy as if she were taking on my identity.

Gradually, I spent less time with her and eventually we stopped seeing each other in social settings. After learning that Sarah had dated my ex-boyfriend, I decided never to contact her again, though I have contemplated telling her off by email for being a terrible friend.

Compared to my experience with the seductress Sarah, I was surprised by my friend 'Janice'. I considered her a big sister and we always joked raucously. Her younger sister was a dear friend as well. Janice and I spent more time together when John moved back to Vancouver, and looking back, I failed to recognize her ulterior motives and the stone-cold manipulation she was engaging in. She used me as a stepping stone to spend more time with John and eventually asked him out.

She asked me if it was alright for her to date him and I said I would feel uncomfortable about it because I would not do that to a girlfriend and I would only support them if it wouldn't affect our friendship. I felt like she had strong-armed me to give my blessing.

After they had been dating for a few months, she suddenly told me that we couldn't be friends anymore. I was stunned by her betrayal—it was my first painful breakup with a good friend, and it felt like it came out of the clear blue sky.

Out of sympathy for me, our mutual friend confided that Janice was jealous, insecure, and fearful that John still harboured feelings for me and that she wanted me out of their lives for good. I couldn't comprehend that a close friend would choose a guy over our friendship.

It was precisely because of this ugly betrayal that I do not actively break up with friends unless they are extremely toxic. The silver lining of the dark Janice cloud was that I began to put more thought into the type of friends I wanted in my life. I was more motivated than ever to be a good friend and to discern better in selecting those I wanted in my inner sanctum.

Over the decades, I've had only a few friends who turned toxic. One ex-friend 'Yuna' vented about her neglectful father every day to me by phone or in person for nearly a full year, and I took it in patiently for some inexplicable reason.

Then, one day, I snapped and told her that she needed to stop and see a therapist. I had hit my limit. That wake-up call showed me the long-term impact of toxicity in friendships and how it could bring unnecessary negativity and exhaustion into my life.

When I was younger, I had a greater capacity to have a lot more acquaintance friends, and I often met different people for lunch and dinners. I often tired myself out with too many social engagements. Eventually, it became clear that I needed space to recharge alone.

As I get older, I am more aware of my limited time left on planet Earth and I tend to gravitate more to those with a similar desire to make a difference in the world, and this brings a sense of meaning and fulfilment.

Researchers have discovered that when older people prune their relationships, they are more satisfied with the friendships they choose to keep.

Here are some questions to ask yourself when you're considering whether you need to add more friends or trim:

- Am I satisfied with the quality and quantity of my friends now? Do I have enough time to invest in my existing good friends? Where am I lacking?
- Can I be my authentic self with this friend? Or do I need to pretend to be someone I'm not?
- Is there mutual respect between us? Respect is a necessary foundation for any relationship.
- Treat friends with kindness, empathy, and consideration—and expect the same in return.
- Can I be honest and open with my feelings, thoughts and concerns? Listen actively when friends speak and expect them to do the same.
- Do I feel supported and uplifted? Is there give and take? Friendships are a two-way street and both sides must be willing to give and receive support, time, and attention.

How to Create a Social Support System

Let's cherish our time on earth and value our moments spent with good friends. The most important lesson I've learned about friendship is the power of investing in positive relationships. With the support of good friends, we can reach our fullest potential as individuals. True friends know us inside out, accept us for who we are, and motivate us to grow.

Having genuine friends is an essential part of a fulfilling life. They provide a strong support system encouraging you to pursue your goals and dreams. Even when you doubt yourself, they see your potential, and their belief in you can lead you to achieve what you might not have thought possible.

Friendship is an opportunity to learn and grow, as having friends exposes you to different perspectives, experiences, and knowledge. Engaging with diverse viewpoints broadens your horizons. Sharing interests and activities leads to skill development. Whether it's a shared hobby, sport, or creative pursuit, doing it together helps you hone new abilities.

Friends can provide comfort, perspective, and a listening ear during tough times. Having friends who stand by you reinforces your resilience and ability to cope with adversity. They offer honest, constructive feedback, helping you identify your advantages and areas for improvement. Their input can guide you in making better decisions.

Having friends who care about your success can be highly beneficial. They can help keep you accountable for your actions and commitments, leading to increased focus and discipline in pursuing your goals. Celebrating your achievements with friends can also make them more meaningful. Their genuine happiness for your success can boost your self-worth and motivate you to aim even higher.

Throughout history, some of the most famous friendships catalysed positive social change. These friendships demonstrated the power of unity, collaboration, and shared ideals in driving societal transformation.

One such example is the friendship between media mogul Oprah Winfrey and the late author Maya Angelou. Their decades-long bond was based on mutual respect and shared values of empowerment, education, and social justice. Through their collaboration, both women used their platforms to amplify marginalized voices, promote literacy and education, and raise awareness about social issues including prejudice and abuse.

Another example is the friendship between Nelson Mandela and Desmond Tutu, who were key figures in the struggle against apartheid in South Africa. Their friendship demonstrated the power of forgiveness, reconciliation, and unity. Mandela and Tutu shared a commitment to healing the nation's wounds and building a more inclusive society post-apartheid. Tutu's work as the chairman of the Truth and Reconciliation Commission further highlighted the significance of their collective efforts.

The influential duo of Susan B. Anthony and Elizabeth Cady Stanton propelled the suffragette movement during the late nineteenth and early twentieth centuries. Their close friendship and partnership in advocating for women's rights played a significant role in the eventual achievement of women's suffrage in the US. Their collaboration, marked by mutual support and strategic planning, paved the way for generations of women to come.

Healthy friendships can instil positive character traits in us, such as loyalty, trust, and discretion, and they can help us grow, inspire us, and keep us accountable. To make friends, a person must strive to be a kind friend and a positive influence. It is important to choose our friends carefully, as they can either help or hinder our personal growth.

As the philosopher Albert Schweitzer once said, 'In everyone's life, at some point, our inner fire goes out. It is then reignited by an encounter with another human being. We should all be grateful for those people who rekindle the inner spirit.'

It's essential to take some time to reflect on your personal relationships and recognize the positive qualities in your friends. As for me, I've pondered over the characteristics that make a good friend. Below are the traits I came up with:

Unconditional love and care: Friends are selfless, kind, and compassionate. They bring joy and a sense of safety, giving us room to grow.

Trustworthiness: Trust is the glue that holds two people together as friends. We must be able to confide and express our innermost thoughts in this safe harbour and not betray that trust.

Honesty: Being open to speaking the truth with love is essential to growth. Our friends' validation can have a powerful effect and their ability to hold up the mirror to tell us who we are can transform us to reach our full potential.

Support: Friends who give the gift of quality time are keepers. They take the time to listen and support and are there for you through thick and thin.

Respect: Mutual respect is treating each other thoughtfully and respectfully; and it's key, as it builds confidence and feelings of trust and safety while allowing you to accept someone for who they are with all their differences. It also enables you to give space when someone needs it.

Diversity: To prevent stagnation of our minds and social circles, we need friends from different backgrounds.

Joy: Friends who make you laugh are precious indeed. Hold on to the positive ones who can see the silver lining. It's a gift to be able to laugh uncontrollably together. Run away as fast as possible from those who see the negative in every situation.

Chapter 8

Kindling the Fire: The Power of Mentorship

Since I was nineteen, I've had several extraordinary mentors.

Some were like guides and others were like coaches. Some were like craftspeople, sculpting aspects of my identity. They sanded down my rough edges, chipped away the parts that jutted out, painted over my scars and added the finishing touches to the raw material of my life.

Others were more like trusted counsellors, teachers, and advisers. They provided guidance, support, and wisdom that I couldn't find elsewhere. Oprah Winfrey described it this way, 'A mentor is someone who allows you to see the hope inside yourself.'

In the fall of 2022, something crystallized for me when I was meeting young people during my speaking tour of Canada and the US. Deep in my bones, I felt that I needed to shift my focus to the next generation and prioritize mentoring the young.

It was part of my broader decision to live a life of significance rather than try to claw my way to the proverbial top or to work for material rewards only. I wanted to spend more time giving back to others and passing on all that I had learned from my mentors and experiences.

It came to me during a heart-to-heart with 'Jen', a young woman in her twenties. As she told me of her struggles to relate to her colleagues and her doubts over whether her job was the right fit, I felt like I was staring into a mirror. And I wanted to give her a hug because I had been there.

I empathized and poured out my heart to her. I told her of all the ghastly blunders I had made when I was young and how these had helped me learn from my experiences. The tears rolled down my cheeks as I spoke from my heart.

I encouraged her to persevere because she, too, would grow from her mistakes and uncertainty—as long as she made sure to learn from them. I did my best to convey that it's about experiencing the journey and not blindly racing to the destination—a message that is hard to grasp when you are young and just setting out.

When I was her age, I too struggled with finding my career and calling. I remember freezing when I didn't know how to navigate toxic colleagues. I recall one older woman in the TV industry hurled curses at me because she felt I was encroaching on her territory. At that time, I used to be quite sheltered and was caught off guard by her sudden outburst. Her viciousness took me by surprise and left me stunned.

I had many moments like that early in my career when I didn't have a work mentor to reach out to as a safe place for advice when I was in a pickle. I struggled silently with imposter syndrome and the stress of doing something for the first time with no guidance. And I had many sleepless nights.

So, it was meaningful to be able to pass on the lessons I had learned to Jen. It was so easy and natural. She cried and felt supported. Any of us can pass on our kernels of wisdom to the younger generation. It's so simple.

The week before I spoke with Jen, I gave a lecture on sex trafficking in Asia at a college in the US where I caught the eye of a smiling young Chinese American college student. I had a feeling I would connect with her after.

Sure enough, she came up after my talk and was incredibly charming and bright. She told me her name was 'Ceci' and she had been adopted by a loving family in the Midwest. We had an undeniable rapport and simply clicked. We met later for coffee on campus.

I listened to her describe her skills, passions, and experiences. She revealed her dreams of becoming a journalist specializing in human trafficking—she wanted to follow in my footsteps in China and Asia.

I shared how I was able to break barriers and produce films that were difficult to pull off, but I also tried to explain that she had her own unique path to go on. There was no 'one size fits all', I said, so it would have been futile for her to copy anyone else's career moves.

I suggested she kept her options open, even to becoming involved in politics because I recognized her innate ability to influence and lead others and to take things one step at a time. I remembered wanting to do everything when I was her age and how that often meant that I couldn't finish even one task. I hoped she would avoid making the same mistake.

It was a watershed moment because it made me treasure how much I had learned from my mentors over several decades. Now, it was my turn to pass those lessons on. It reminded me of a famous quote, provenance unknown: 'Sometimes life brings you full circle to a place you have been before just to show you how much you have grown.'

What to Look for in a Mentor

A good mentor empowers your personal development and points out your blind spots.

At a formative time in my life, my mentor for a day, the pastor Terry Bone pointed out something to me that has had a profound effect on my life. It was about the impact my father's preference for sons had on my personality. I became hardened and felt I had to overcompensate and prove myself to others and, as a result, I was competitive with all the boys in my class, in both schoolwork and sports.

I was constantly trying to prove myself in everything I put my hand to as if saying to the spectre of my father looming over me, 'Look dad, I'm good enough, I'm better than a son.'

I couldn't embrace my femininity because I felt it represented weakness. I was a tomboy, walking like a boy and acting aggressively. Pastor Bone's insights unlocked answers that I was seeking and helped shift my mindset dramatically. My friends told me that even my face softened and became more feminine, and I became less competitive with men.

Mentors can help us break through psychological barriers. Linda Rottenberg, author of *Crazy is a Compliment*, recounts a survey in which entrepreneurs were asked about who had made the most valuable contributions to their careers. Most of them said good advice was more valuable than financial backing. She believes that the biggest barrier to success in business is psychological. Therefore, finding the right mentor who believes in you is paramount.

According to *Harvard Business Review*, executives who have had a mentor earn more money at a younger age, are better educated, and more likely to follow a career plan and feel a strong obligation to mentor others.

Research from *Responsible Science, Volume II: Background Papers and Resource Documents* has also found that scientists with mentors might be more 'self-actualized'—i.e. internally motivated rather than driven by external rewards like money—than those without, while junior academics may publish more books, receive more grants for their research, and serve as leaders in more organizations.

Some of my mentors have changed my thinking and life through their contagious passion and willingness to sacrifice. According to research featured in Emily Rogers's piece for *Forbes*, having a mentor can help expand your network, bring new opportunities, and better prepare you for professional work. They can show you what's possible through their accomplishments.

The most effective mentors are those with strong and healthy personal relationships, who are non-judgemental and accepting, passionate about making a difference in those around them, and who drive meaningful growth. Most importantly, the best mentors are compelled by love.

Here are the top ten qualities to look for in a mentor:

- **Experience and expertise:** Good mentors have a deep understanding of their field or industry and are willing to share their knowledge and experience.
- **Communication:** They communicate clearly, kindly and effectively, providing guidance, feedback, and advice in a way that is easy to understand.

- **Availability:** They are accessible and willing to make time for you. They are approachable and open to questions and discussions.
- **Empathy and understanding:** Good mentors are empathetic and can understand your challenges and concerns. They are supportive and able to relate to your experiences.
- **Positive role models:** They lead by example, demonstrating the values and behaviours they expect from you.
- **Goal-oriented and result-driven:** They help you set clear goals and guide you to achieve them. They should be focused on helping you grow and achieve results.
- **Feedback and constructive criticism:** A mentor should be willing to provide feedback and constructive criticism to help you improve. They should do so in a supportive and respectful manner.
- **Networking and connections:** An effective mentor can introduce you to valuable contacts and help you expand your professional network.
- **Patience and commitment:** Mentorship can be a long-term relationship that turns into friendship. Look for qualities like patience and a commitment to your development over time.
- **Adaptability:** Effective mentors should be adaptable and able to tailor their guidance to your specific needs and goals.

Finally, remember that not all mentors will possess all of these qualities in equal measure. These are just some of the most important traits to look for when seeking a mentor. The best relationships are built on mutual trust and respect, so it's crucial to find someone with whom you have a good rapport and shared values.

The Beautiful Simplicity of Giving Back

My journey as a mentor began when I was nineteen and still in full-time studies at university. At that time, I felt this inexplicable call as though something inside of me was urging me to teach and guide youth at my church every Friday night and Sunday morning. I had a spiritual awakening in the San Francisco Bay Area while on a summer mission programme serving impoverished families in public housing projects, and that changed the course of my life. I no longer wanted to pursue a self-absorbed life of corporate ambition. Instead, I felt a strong desire to give back to my community.

Around this time, I began caring for a brother and sister whose parents were working as missionaries in Yanji, China. At first, Helen and Jack lived with a family. Later, when Jack was a senior in high school, they lived on their own. They seemed vulnerable without their parents around, so I took them under my wing and met up with them from time to time and asked them how they were doing.

Years later, they told me how thankful they were for my thoughtfulness. That surprised me because I felt I should have done more. Their response underlined to me how small acts of kindness can leave a big impression, especially on the youth, who are like sponges and really appreciate it when older people take the time to invest in them.

Later, I became a youth director at my church. I found myself taking on the role of big sister and counselling some of the high school students who had been broken by life events—their parents' divorces, emotional neglect, bullying, and loneliness. One young man's best friend had killed himself.

Every Friday night, I picked up some kids from their homes and brought them to our events. We went on retreats and outreaches and had a lot of fun activities in between. In hindsight, it was one of the best experiences I've had. It taught me so much about patience, leadership, and mentoring, and the importance of investing in the next generation.

There's something so gratifying about seeing someone you've known since they were twelve grow up and reach their full potential. Some of these kids went on to do wonderful things and excelled in various careers. One became an acclaimed indie band singer, another a family doctor, and another an actress on a Netflix show. Others became a mortgage specialist, flight attendant, Chinese medicine doctor, and more. However, it wasn't all a bed of roses. A few of them became estranged from their parents and siblings in their adulthood.

Sometimes, years later, someone I taught as a youth director reaches out to me to express how much of a positive influence I had on them.

It's moments like these that remind me of the incredible power we have to shape someone's life for the better. I'm always very surprised to hear from them. All those years ago, I was often discouraged by all the blank faces looking back at me when I tried to share a lesson. I was frustrated by rowdy boys acting up and speaking rudely.

I first met one of my mentees, Adrian, when I taught his fifth-grade class during a church summer programme. He was a terror and kept standing up and interrupting me. The only reason I kept my patience with him was that I remembered doing the same thing when I was his age. I, too, was a horrid brat in my Sunday School class, constantly interrupting the teacher and misbehaving. I wondered if this was a kind of karma coming back to bite me.

A memory popped up from when I was fifteen. I apologized to my Sunday School director, Hye-gyung, and said I was so sorry for being a brat and causing her grief when I didn't listen to her. She wept. I was surprised that my words of contrition touched her.

Years later, Adrian joined our youth group, and I learned that his family was going through some tough times. He and his brother often looked downright sad, so I decided to spend quality time with them during the weekends.

A mutual friend told me that Adrian had said I had the biggest influence on him and his spirituality. I was floored. Adrian and his brother wrote the most beautiful original songs for my wedding. Both are now married and are fathers, and it's incredible to see them thriving in adulthood.

The Power of Love

After my divorce, I hit rock bottom. I was an emotional wreck and could barely eat. I was living and working in Beijing at the time and it was hard sometimes not to feel completely alone.

I cannot stress enough how much Pastor Gideon Chiu has been a significant figure in my life. Despite being miles apart, his unwavering support and guidance made me feel I had a father figure to rely on. Whenever I was struggling or in need of prayer, he was always there to pray and offer valuable spiritual advice which helped me navigate through some of the toughest times of my life. He radiates a spiritual other-worldliness and has a kindness and special wisdom that I have not seen or heard anywhere else.

As a child, his parents ran an orphanage in Hong Kong and he behaved like an orphan too. It took him years to process the pain of having to share his parents with other vulnerable children. This experience fuelled his desire to mentor countless other people who were going through similar struggles—with a father's caring heart.

We first met more than thirty years ago when I visited his church in Vancouver and I have managed to stay in touch with him ever since, despite his extremely busy schedule. Pastor Gideon travels extensively and has countless people clamouring for his time and attention. Hundreds of people around the world consider him a father figure. But whenever I really need to speak with him, he responds to my questions or pleas for advice.

And so, it was during that dark time in Beijing, when I was wondering if I would make it through to the other side after my divorce and if I could ever feel happy again. Without me contacting him, Gideon emailed me from Vancouver out of the blue and at the end of his message wrote, 'You WILL make it!' I nearly fell off my chair. It was as if he had read my mind from thousands of miles away.

Gideon reminded me of who I was and often told me that there was a powerful redemptive purpose for the personal pain I was going through as I processed the colossal disaster that was my divorce. He was right—I felt that the anguish of that season had a humbling effect that transformed my life's focus on helping others and fighting for human rights.

Before Gideon mentored me, I had been driven by excitement and adrenaline, travelling frequently for conferences and networking opportunities. I had no focus and no idea of what to prioritize. He helped deepen my thinking, allowing me to live a calmer life. I was able to bring order to my plans and schedule. He noticed that I took charge and controlled the agenda and conversation whenever we met, which was a habit of mine as the firstborn in my family.

In a very gentle tone, he wisely challenged me to stop manipulating people or situations because I was afraid of not being in control, and he urged me to relax. I hadn't thought of it that way before and it led me to examine my actions, and I concluded that I needed to control less. I knew that if Gideon didn't care, he would not have bothered to say anything.

More than anything he said, his supportive and fatherly care spoke volumes. An example was when we had lunch in Hong Kong and shared the dishes. He ordered his favourite beef and noodles dish and at first, I didn't touch it because I wanted him to have it.

But he said he was full and that's when I reached out to taste the tender beef brisket. He waited for me to finish the meat, then he finished the noodles. He had wanted me to have the best part of his favourite meal while he ate the leftovers! It was a simple act, but showed his fatherly heart and touched me deeply.

Another mentor, Audrey Lore, has more energy at ninety-two than most young people I know. Audrey, who has mentored me for over a decade, radiates dynamism, kindness, and a hunger to learn. She has a twinkle in her eye and a constant smile. I was drawn to her warrior spirit and the way she helped counsel others in need.

Audrey is a rock for many and hosts all sorts of people—everyone from community leaders and pastors to virtual strangers—in her home several times a week to counsel them on family or relationship issues. Before her guests leave, she pulls out a bunch of hand-knit scarfs in a variety of colours and asks them to choose one. Most people her age slowdown in their retirement years and pursue hobbies like golf or taking care of their grandchildren, but Audrey chooses every day to help people reach their full potential and pass on her knowledge and wisdom. She's a natural-born leader.

Several years ago, she was hit by a car while crossing the street. This sent her flying through the air and she landed badly on her leg. By some miracle, she survived—albeit with some injuries. Yet, even more remarkable was her upbeat attitude. She had the inner fortitude to vanquish any setback.

While recovering, she was most upset about the disruption to her weekly counselling appointments and barely complained about the pain in her legs and arms. I value Audrey's listening ear and feel I can tell her anything, even my worst personal failings, and she accepts me unconditionally. That has been an invaluable source of confidence. To have someone know you—and all your flaws—yet still accept you for who you are is a rare gift.

I have always valued the invaluable wisdom of older people and actively sought them out. With support from Joy Kogawa, a Japanese Canadian literary legend and activist pioneer in her late eighties, I gained confidence in my writing and was encouraged to keep seeking justice for the survivors of Japanese military forced prostitution.

I recall feeling quite anxious before our first meeting at her Toronto home. I was on a speaking tour and had walked to her home from my hotel, pondering whether we would have anything in common to talk about. However, as soon as the conversation started, I felt at ease and it flowed naturally. I have long deeply admired Joy and the role model that she is. She has justice and activism coursing through her veins—she helped raise awareness of the internment of Japanese Canadians during World War II through her writings and her classic novel, *Obasan.*

From 1942, the Canadian government forcibly relocated and incarcerated more than 23,000 Japanese Canadians in the name of national security under the War Measures Act. They lost their belongings, homes and property. After being relocated, many lived in harsh conditions without running water or heat. Men were separated from their families and forced to do roadwork or hard labour.

Around 4,000 were sent 'back' to Japan, a country they had never been to before. It was not until 1949—years after the war had ended—that they were allowed to move around the country freely again.

Joy was a prominent voice from the Japanese Canadian community who fought for the federal government to acknowledge and apologize for its treatment of these people during the war. In 1988, then Prime Minister Brian Mulroney issued a formal apology to all Japanese Canadians and offered CAD$21,000 as symbolic compensation to each person affected by the internment. This recognition and sincere apology helped bring a measure of closure.

During our meeting, Joy poured me tea and we sat at her table bathed in sunlight. I was overwhelmed by her generosity of spirit and love. Joy is simply beautiful, full of boundless energy and curiosity, and she's wise. She's sharp and discerning and when she speaks, she is deliberate and full of compassion. It is always deeply inspiring to connect with Joy. I love her passion for peace and conciliation.

The older you get, the harder it is to find a role model. Partly, this is because as we become more seasoned in work and life, we also become pickier. Once you find a role model, treasure them and learn all you can.

Joy's pioneering work has helped me see what is possible through the efforts of one person to create something out of nothing. She has blazed a trail for the rest of us in Canada, and I am grateful for her encouragement in my fight for justice for the survivors of Japanese military sexual slavery.

Her moral support has been like water for my parched soul. It has helped me persevere in speaking and writing about the importance of reconciliation between the Japanese, Koreans, and Chinese. Joy could see the ugly effects of generational racial hatred. Even today, Japan's lack of a sincere apology has poisoned relations for the next generations of Chinese and Koreans.

Her belief in me is what showed me: it wasn't an impossible dream.

Peer Mentoring

Over the years, my dear friend Joylynn Li and I have supported each other over the phone through our respective book-writing journeys, through heartaches, and too many life events to recount. We squeal with laughter and joke often—she brings out the kid in me.

It's because of her steady support that I persevered with my previous book, *Silenced No More*. I consider Joylynn and I to be 'peer mentors'—two people with similar experience levels who help one another grow in a more informal relationship than a traditional mentoring one.

We encouraged each other as we shared our struggles in our writing or work. Her insights were always refreshing and exactly what I needed to hear. She has also been extremely generous in donating to my work to raise awareness about modern slavery.

Above all, her ability to remain youthful in her outlook and care deeply for her friends has been a great inspiration. In a beautiful example of astounding selflessness, Joylynn mobilized dozens of people around the world to pray for and send words of encouragement to her friend Nicole during the beginning of her battle with cancer.

She did the same when Nicole was in palliative care and kept up the effort until Nicole breathed her last. Joylynn spent hours on Zoom calls and writing regular updates to Nicole's friends.

There was no way that Nicole could ever repay Joylynn for her sacrifices but that was not why she made them. Perhaps this is why their friendship has moved many people so deeply. I know it has made me more intentional in asking Joylynn how she's doing and taking care of her when I can.

When I struggled with *Silenced No More*, she had a lot of timely wisdom to impart. She told me to dig within myself as if digging for treasures to explore the lessons learned from adversity. She reminded me of the hardships I had prevailed over in Beijing during and after my first marriage and how I was blessed to have a wonderful second one.

During one phone conversation, one thing lingered long after we said goodbye. It was her exhortation to keep my eyes open to beauty as I write, to appreciate wondrous things. It was a profound insight that reminded me of the concept of 'awe and wonder'—something I used to feel more often as a child and that I am keen to preserve as I get older. Not only does it help me be more creative and productive, but ultimately, it makes me more receptive to those around me.

In an article in the *Harvard Business Review,* Eben Harrell puts it this way: 'Experiencing awe produces a multitude of positive effects. It makes us calmer, kinder, more creative [. . .] It reins in the ego and makes us feel more connected to the earth and to other creatures.'

To experience awe, you do not need to be an explorer discovering unknown places or a mountaineer scaling great heights or a daredevil tempting fate. You simply need to open your eyes. Beauty is all around us.

I became alive to this myself, even while typing away at my desk for six days a week. My desk has a bird's eye view of Hong Kong's Victoria Harbour; a view my eyes will never tire of seeing. When I look out at the hues of blue and the rays of sun that peek through wispy clouds or sparkle as they reflect off the undulating waves, I am inspired and overwhelmed by joy, beauty, and the restorative power of nature. There is something deeply humbling about the vastness of the sea and sky that hints at depths, heights, and fathoms I cannot grasp.

No words can adequately describe such unspoiled visual majesty; though the words 'deep calls unto deep' from the Book of Psalms capture its transformative effect on my soul.

The view of the harbour brings a calm I cannot manufacture. It reminds me of the 'overview effect', the cognitive shift that occurs when you see yourself from a great distance, like an astronaut viewing the Earth from space.

It is as children that awe and wonder come most naturally to us. As a child, decades before bouldering and rock climbing were a thing, I would climb and shimmy my way to the top of every hallway, doorway, and jungle gym within sight.

I felt an inherent satisfaction from simply making it to the top and remaining at the summit by my sheer energy and willpower. I was in awe of the different perspective from the heights and noticed details of buildings, trees, or objects in my home that I hadn't seen before.

According to Eben Harrell's article in the *Harvard Business Review*, to find awe, 'we must look for "eight wonders of life": nature, music, visual design, and moral beauty (when we witness people helping other people), "collective effervescence" (what fans cheering together in a stadium feel), spiritual experiences, epiphanies, and, of course, births and deaths, life's beginnings and endings.'

Or, as Joylynn would have said it, 'appreciate the wondrous things'. It is good advice and I have no doubt her fun-loving nature and peer mentoring have helped me become a more generous, thoughtful, and joyful person.

The philosopher Mencius could have been describing Joylynn when he said, 'Great is the man who has not lost his childlike heart.'

Parents as Mentors

Much of what I know about advancing my career, I learned from my immigrant mother. She was instrumental as my first mentor and has always nurtured my passions and talents and supported every one of my dreams, from writing a book to being a host of a digital TV show and everything else that I've ever done. I am fortunate to have had her as my guide, as not all parents are equipped to be good mentors.

My mother helped me believe in myself and encouraged me to dream bigger than I ever imagined. She was and continues to be my role model. Being raised by her was like attending a finishing school led by a football coach. Even today, she scolds me for slouching or standing with one foot out and reminds me to always be poised. Her ability to motivate and advise is remarkable, and she has been a mentor to many young adults and pastors. Her support for the next generation is a beautiful legacy I hope to carry on.

When she was in her mid-twenties, my parents moved to Vancouver from Korea. She didn't follow a traditional career path, and eventually she ran her own business for decades and used most of her profits to help the poor and those in dire need in her church community. She was part-mom, part-social worker, and part-pastor to all she knew. Before the term social entrepreneur was coined, she was living it.

Though she was not familiar with having a career in her adopted country, she was uncannily perceptive and adept in guiding me on mine. Her instincts and intuition were always spot on. When I was stuck on how to find a job early in my career, she encouraged me to knock on every door. 'Don't ever give up!' she used to say. She exhorted me to follow up and be proactive. To call potential bosses.

When I began my first internship at a TV station, she said I needed to be indispensable and work so hard that the boss came to depend on me. She encouraged me to be a go-getter, though she didn't know the term. She embodied that persona.

She would laminate copies of my articles and send me clippings on other Korean Canadian TV hosts. 'All your dreams will come true,' she would tell me. She believed in my dreams and no matter how silly and unattainable I thought they were, her unwavering belief in me filled me with courage to go after them.

Most of all, she has believed in me unconditionally for as long as I can remember, always telling me that I could do whatever I put my mind to. She told me never to hang on to negative words and to ignore anyone spewing them.

I remember laughing when she suggested I look in the mirror and speak positive words to myself. I used to brush off my mom's advice and felt I needed to find a real expert. How wrong I was!

Though I didn't always recognize her wisdom in my twenties, as the years went by I came to appreciate her more fully. She taught me the art of thanking people immediately, which has been invaluable in my work and my social life. I once thanked a couple who hosted a dinner for a bunch of us strangers, and they told me that no one else had sent a thank you note and they were grateful to hear from me. It helped solidify a friendship.

Mom is always well-mannered and expresses gratefulness to everyone, from friends to salespeople. Often, she would charm the store staff, and I would see everyone greet her with unusual warmth—and often offer her special discounts—wherever she went shopping.

Remarkably, I do not ever recall my mom uttering a mean word to anyone. She has hardly raised her voice at me since I was a child. She is constantly doing good deeds and acts of kindness for the elderly and those in great need.

When I was young, there was a revolving door of people coming to our home to speak with mom or to collect one of the many meals she would cook for those with a terminally ill family member.

As Abraham Lincoln said, 'All that I am or ever hope to be, I owe to my angel mother.'

Anything of significance I've done is because of her. If I have succeeded in any way, it's because my mom passed on all the qualities that I needed to be a kind person doing the right thing. Words cannot describe the depth and breadth of her impact on my life.

Mom, you are my superhero.

Generational Gifts

When I was young, little did I know that I had a rich generational blessing that would propel me towards working with youth.

In my family, there is a legacy of influencing the young in a positive manner.

My great-grandmother attracted groups of children to her wherever she went. She radiated unusual love with her beautiful smile, kind demeanour, and easy laughter.

Her son, my grandfather, was a teacher, adored by his students. He passed this gift on to his daughter, my mother, who herself has inspired many young people. Many of them called her 'mom'.

Now, I am eager to follow their lead. From January 2023, I felt compelled to volunteer at the youth Sunday school class in my church, and it felt like a full-circle moment. I thought I could pass on the support and wisdom that my mom gave me. I had the privilege of offering one-on-one mentoring time with a high school graduate about to embark on one of the most significant transitions she'd ever face.

At this stage of my life, I feel more equipped to be an adviser. I'm more street-smart and experienced than I was when I was younger. This showed in my interactions with my mentee, 'Ellen', as she prepared to head to college and said goodbye to her friends. She was moving forward into the unknown and faced the daunting prospect of having to establish a new life and make a new set of friends without her parents hovering.

The older me is more sensitive and in tune with her needs than the younger Sylvia might have been. Decades ago, I wasn't self-aware and wouldn't know how to advise on major life transitions. I would have been seeing everything through a limited, personal lens.

This time, with Ellen, it was a pleasure to listen to her and to respond to whatever she wanted to discuss. Given my own experience of reconciling with my parents and releasing the nagging feeling that they were disappointed in me, I have come to recognize the importance of generational reconciliation. I advised Ellen to get closer to her parents, to express her appreciation, and to reconcile anything that needed to be resolved.

As the American social activist Gloria Steinem said, 'To me the model of success is not linear. Success is completing the full circle of yourself.'

Sometimes it's about timing. Sometimes, we have to wait to see how the dots line up again, and that's convergence.

It's a full circle moment.

Learning from Negative Mentoring Experiences

In university, I once stopped seeing a wonderful mentor, an American woman from the southern part of the US, because we had zero chemistry and she didn't fully understand my Korean cultural background.

I feel a twinge of guilt about it to this day because I just ghosted her and failed to explain my reason for not continuing our mentoring relationship. I could see the hurt in her eyes for the next three months whenever I ran into her on campus. I was immature then and I have learned since and have never repeated this mistake.

Betrayal can be a great teacher.

A leader I know once experienced what seemed to him an inexplicable betrayal by some of his closest mentees who had become friends. Two of them slandered him and spread lies in public and tried to push him out of his own organization. His heart was broken.

However, a few of us had seen red flags in these mentees and had gently warned him. They were not trustworthy—they gossiped and were controlling and unkind. But in front of him, they put on a pious act. He felt deep regret at not heeding the warnings. My heart went out to him, but I also felt he had learned a profound lesson that would make him much wiser in relationships. He used to be open and trusting, but perhaps too trusting.

His situation triggered a memory of my own. I, too, have experienced a betrayal by a once-close mentee, a young woman I'll call 'Leanne', years ago. Without hesitating, I naively embraced her and invested a lot of time and energy into our relationship. I spent time mentoring her in her work as a youth director. I got to know some of the young people, too.

But after investing in her for a few years, my support was thrown back in my face—with no explanation. Leanne ghosted me. She also divulged to others what I shared in confidence and slandered me. I heard from one friend that she had twisted my words about her ex-boyfriend and told others that I thought he was a shady person.

I remember that awful hollow feeling when I found out later from others. While I learned that she had done the same with two of her other mentors and this was a regular pattern with her, it offered no consolation and made me question my discernment. I didn't see this side of her.

It hurt deeply to be rejected by someone I had gone out of my way to care for. Her judgement was one-sided and she cut off our friendship, without a chance for conflict resolution. I was saddened, considering the strong bond we once shared.

Separately, her other mentor and I confronted Leanne for an explanation in an attempt to reconcile and understand what happened. I said that I was sorry for any way I had hurt her. But I never did get a reasonable explanation. I felt as though I had failed. Ultimately, it was a good and timely reminder to be more intentional about conflict resolution in relationships.

She eventually apologized via email during her graduate studies in the US, but the damage was done. I have not been in touch with her since.

The novelist Sherrilyn Kenyon, author of *Invincible*, said, 'Everyone suffers at least one bad betrayal in their lifetime. It's what unites us. The trick is not to let it destroy your trust in others when that happens. Don't let them take that from you.'

After some time, I began to trust my judgement again. Like the leader I had seen betrayed by his mentees, I too had learned a painful but extremely valuable lesson.

Here's my advice for anyone wanting to avoid making the same mistake:

- Take your time before deciding who to mentor.
- When you see red flags, run, don't walk!
- Take time to heal from betrayals so they don't colour and affect your current and future relationships.
- Have a circle of advisers to discern together. Don't be a lone ranger and make decisions about people alone. As Proverbs 15:22 puts it, 'Without counsel, plans fail, but with many advisers, they succeed.'
- Keep your 'inner sanctum' circle tight and close to you.
- Value what you learn from those you mentor.
- Finally, and perhaps most importantly, if you have been betrayed, don't give up on people. Keep your heart open to trusting again.

Overcoming Hurdles

Conflict is a natural part of any mentoring relationship.

Handling conflict effectively is crucial to ensuring that the mentorship remains productive and positive. While not a specific strategy, it's important to emphasize that conflicts can be valuable learning experiences for both mentors and mentees. Reflecting on conflicts and their resolutions can lead to personal and professional growth.

Setting clear guidelines and expectations at the beginning of the mentorship relationship can prevent conflicts from arising in the first place. Define roles, responsibilities, and goals for both mentors and mentees. Establish boundaries and expectations for communication frequency and methods. When both parties have a shared understanding of what is expected, conflicts related to misunderstandings or unmet expectations are less likely to occur.

Open and honest communication and active listening are crucial in conflict resolution. Mentors should attentively listen to their mentees' concerns and feelings without interruption. This demonstrates empathy and helps in understanding the underlying issues. Active listening also involves asking clarifying questions to ensure a full understanding of the mentee's perspective. Create a safe space for open dialogue.

Becoming a mentor can be a transformative experience for both the mentee and the mentor. Mentorship challenges us to reflect on our experiences and knowledge, leading to personal growth and self-awareness. It can help develop better communication skills as we learn to convey complex ideas, provide constructive feedback, and actively listen to our mentees.

Serving as a mentor fosters leadership qualities such as empathy, patience, and the ability to inspire others.

Here are some other lessons learned from mentoring:

- **Reinforcement of knowledge:** Teaching and guiding others reinforces and deepens your own understanding of the subject matter.
- **Fulfilment and satisfaction:** Mentoring can be incredibly rewarding, offering a sense of fulfilment and satisfaction derived from helping others succeed.
- **Networking opportunities:** As a mentor, you may expand your professional network by connecting with your mentees' contacts and other mentors within your mentoring community.
- **Fresh perspectives:** Mentees may bring new perspectives and innovative ideas that can challenge your own thinking and broaden your horizons.
- **Improved problem-solving skills:** Mentoring involves helping mentees navigate challenges, which can sharpen your problem-solving skills and creativity.

Overall, being a mentor often leads to a sense of purpose and personal fulfilment as you witness your mentees' growth and accomplishments. Mentoring is a two-way street, benefiting both the mentor and the mentee, and offering a transformative journey of growth, learning, and contribution to others' success.

Inspiring a Legacy of Transformative Mentorship

Life is a mosaic with countless patterns of different experiences and moments, and few images are as vibrant and enduring as those crafted by mentors. These guiding lights have the transformative power to reshape destinies and inspire others to follow in their footsteps. The mentor could be a bridge between dreams and reality, imparting knowledge and the confidence to strive for excellence.

I encourage people of all ages to mentor and lead by example—it will help you grow and mature in your gifts and wisdom. My dear friend Agnes has been like a big sister and a powerful role model for me in investing in young people. For decades, she has selflessly invested in me and others by sharing events and insights and supporting my work for women's rights. I feel I can turn to her for advice.

She embodies trust and empathy and has taught me that the most influential mentors help encourage people who carry the torch of passion, knowledge, and even success from one generation to the next. Part of her legacy is impacting a group of leaders through one goal of simply loving others. Indeed, love is the most important quality we all need as we pass on our wisdom to others.

Mentorship builds and nourishes the fabric of communities. As mentors and mentees alike give back to their networks through mentorship, they create a supportive ecosystem that fosters growth and resilience.

I remember, in my youth, standing at the crossroads of life, facing uncertainty, doubt, and the overwhelming sense of facing a vast, uncharted world. My guides have helped me clarify my goals, develop essential life skills, and find the courage to navigate the challenges that arose. I urge you to embrace the role of a mentor, no matter how old you are.

We are measured not by what we accumulate but by the lives we positively influence.

A great mentorship is a legacy of hope and the unwavering belief in every individual to reach their fullest potential.

Chapter 9

Looking for Love

During my early twenties, I met an underwear model from South Korea, who I will refer to as 'Bob'. Bob was a perfect-looking man with a chiselled face, exceptional build, and a charming personality. He had moved from Seoul to Vancouver and attended my church. Women would swoon whenever he flashed his perfect, blindingly white teeth. He always wore trendy shirts and jeans and had immaculately coiffed hair—not a single strand out of place.

Bob began calling me to hang out at least once a week. Initially, I admit it, I was also charmed by him and felt some chemistry between us. Bob was successful in his line of work and was a top model for leading brands including the South Korean underwear company BYC. That's why I nicknamed him the BYC guy when I told my friends about him.

Bob was hoping to break into acting and saw every event as a networking opportunity. At church, I noticed that if anyone spent more than five minutes speaking with him, he would whip out his laminated modelling photos, as if he were auditioning for a gig. He couldn't shut it off. Bob had a habit of talking about his modelling experiences in Korea and nothing else. I had a distinct feeling that he was accustomed to women swarming him and constantly cooing about how incredibly handsome he was. The thought of asking another person how they were doing seemingly never crossed his mind.

Aware of his habit of talking about himself, I tried to discern whether he had an active mind or interesting opinions. But after several weeks, I concluded he simply had little else to say. I imagined cobwebs forming and crickets chirping where his brain should have been.

Meeting Bob taught me that looks can only take you so far. What truly makes you stand out is your personality, intelligence, and unique perspective. So, it's essential to focus on developing yourself and your character, not just your looks or physical appearance.

We met on several more occasions, but I was utterly bored every time. Eventually, I couldn't bring myself to see him again. His self-absorption became unattractive to me. So, I decided to ghost Bob, long before it became a culturally known phenomenon.

However, I had zero regrets and felt that my time with him wasn't wasted because it confirmed that I needed an intelligent man. This was a huge revelation, as I hadn't fully understood before then what I wanted in a spouse. While some people are satisfied with a nice-looking partner with no intellectual affinity, I needed an emotional connection more than physical attraction. I couldn't be attracted to anyone who didn't have a keen intellect.

When I was twenty-one, I started dating someone I'll call 'Dan'. We dated for three years. Dan was intelligent, spiritually committed, and we had many common friends and interests, like exercising and the outdoors. We even went on a humanitarian mission trip to Tijuana, Mexico, to work with orphans and poor villagers.

At the time, I was too inexperienced to know whether we were truly connecting emotionally. As I began entering the workforce, I matured and changed in different ways and became more jaded and exposed to a wider range of different people, and the exciting chemistry that had initially brought us together started to fade on my side.

On one occasion, I shared something that was deeply troubling me about my conflict with my parents over whether I should continue dating Dan. Although Dan was caring in his response and gave me a hug, he didn't have any wise advice or comforting words to say. I asked him a few questions about what I had shared, and all he seemed able to say was, 'Oh, I'm so sorry.' I waited for more intelligent and empathic sentences but none came.

His lack of articulation was not entirely surprising and it confirmed what I had always suspected—he was emotionally shallow and a superficial thinker. He lived his life on the surface, content with that. Sometimes—on rare occasions—he shared profoundly wise statements. However, most times, he just joked around and focused on what was in front of him, like a dog captivated by a bone.

Dan talked about marriage, but I felt trapped instead of happy. I wondered if this was all there was to the most important relationship in my life. If it was, I was excruciatingly bored and empty. Dan didn't meet my need for a deeper connection, even though he was kind and considerate, and we were compatible in many ways. I ended up closing the door on him for good. I was extremely relieved when I eventually broke up with him—a telling sign.

We all go through different experiences in life, some of which may not be as fulfilling as we would like them to be. It takes time and self-discovery to truly understand what we need in a partner, but it's worth the wait when we find the right person.

While chemistry can certainly be an exhilarating aspect of dating, it's important to recognize that relying on it solely as a basis for a relationship is unreliable—it's not a foolproof indicator of long-term compatibility. Chemistry in dating is a complex combination of physical, emotional, and psychological factors that draw individuals towards each other. It often manifests as a strong initial attraction characterized by heightened emotions, physical desire, and a sense of euphoria—as if some mystical force has brought them together. I would describe it as an almost magnetic pull that makes them feel 'on fire' or 'head over heels' for someone.

Strong chemistry can blind individuals to potential red flags or incompatibilities. People may overlook important differences in values, lifestyles, or long-term goals because the chemistry feels so right. However, it does not equate to compatibility. Two people can have incredible chemistry but still struggle with fundamental differences in communication styles, conflict resolution, or life priorities.

Over time, some people may become serial daters, constantly seeking the thrill of new chemistry without ever committing to deeper, more meaningful relationships. I've been drawn to partners who are exciting but ultimately toxic or incompatible, leading to turmoil and heartbreak.

Another guy I dated, 'Nathan', checked all the boxes on paper: he was passionate about justice for survivors of Japanese military sexual slavery, sensitive, attentive, and intellectually fascinating. We had chemistry—an intense connection of mind, body, and soul. I was feeling optimistic about him.

Yet he had a horrible temper and was prone to angry outbursts over small things. His first temper tantrum flared as he got pulled over for speeding in San Francisco. We were visiting the city to spend the weekend with friends together. The policewoman asked him to pass on his driver's license. I gently touched his shoulder to express support, then suddenly he pushed my hand away and said with great annoyance, 'Don't, I'm irritated!'

The policewoman rolled her eyes and looked at me with sympathy as if urging me to run away from this man. His temper tantrum turned me off. I wondered if this was the beginning of the end of our relationship.

I met the policewoman's gaze and nodded to thank her for her support—it was a look of understanding that women sometimes knowingly give to each other in trying situations. At the time, neither was I mature enough to have strong boundaries nor did I have anyone guiding me on the importance of having them and telling others how I wanted to be treated.

In any relationship, we need to set boundaries that define our comfort zones and limits. These boundaries allow us to protect ourselves, to say 'no' when we need space, and to maintain our well-being.

Unfortunately, I didn't know how to tell Nathan that his angry outbursts were unacceptable and that I needed to feel safe and secure in the relationship. Whenever he lost his temper, I felt confused and upset, sometimes I was even in tears, while he stormed out. My feelings of unease about Nathan continued to grow and I came to see clearly that he was emotionally stunted.

However, I was torn and couldn't decide between staying in the relationship or ending it because he had some positive qualities I admired, such as his passion for human rights.

After experiencing his angry flare-ups several more times over trivial matters and seeing more of his selfish nature, I broke up with

Nathan. I am grateful that I took the time to get to know him, as this helped me to get past the 'honeymoon' phase, when each person puts their best face forward, effectively hiding most character flaws. Doing so meant I was able to dodge a bullet—quite possibly a divorce.

By getting to know Nathan, I learned that strong chemistry doesn't always lead to lasting love and that, in fact, it can cloud our judgement and blind us to red flags and incompatibilities in values, lifestyles, and long-term goals.

After we broke up, I became more vigilant about looking out for warning signs of unhealthy relationships. The three biggest red flags to look for are physical, emotional, and mental abuse. I also gained a greater appreciation for effective communication—it is the cornerstone of a healthy relationship and includes active listening, empathy, and vulnerability in fostering understanding.

Conflict is inevitable—it's how you resolve it that matters. In the heat of the moment, breathe and remember that a healthy relationship is built on respect and compromise.

In my twenties and thirties, I was a hopeless romantic addicted to the thrill of new connections. However, relying solely on chemistry often led to short-lived dating experiences, disappointment, and heartbreak because after the initial spark faded, I was aware that there was little else left.

I was often attracted to exciting men who turned out to be toxic or incompatible, preventing me from committing to a deeper, more meaningful relationship. In retrospect, I may have overlooked potentially wonderful partners who lacked that initial 'wow' factor but possessed other essential qualities for a long-lasting relationship.

I've learned that real, lasting love takes time to develop. Chemistry is just the beginning; it's the growth of mutual trust, shared experiences, and emotional intimacy that sustains a relationship in the long run. You need both chemistry and compatibility and to find a balance between them.

Working through my failed relationships helped crystallize what qualities I truly desired in a life partner. But, even then, I had no one to give me practical advice on how to prepare myself for a successful long-term relationship.

If I could go back in time, I would urge my younger self to pay more attention to my intuition. In some relationships, there are warning signs that are important to discern. It's essential to trust your gut, prioritize your well-being, and make informed decisions that safeguard your heart and soul. Choose wisely.

Searching in All the Wrong Places

Observing the mating game in nature has always fascinated me. Many a times have I witnessed a male peacock strutting around, puffing his chest out and flaunting his feathers to impress a female. It's most amusing when the female is completely uninterested and ignores his amorous advances. Less amusing is when the male jumps onto the female without warning.

The intricate dance of attraction and courtship is central to the human experience and occurs throughout the natural world. In the wild, many species engage in behaviour displays to attract potential mates. Courtship rituals are common; they signal fitness, health, and genetic quality. These rituals are fascinating, from the elaborate dances of birds to the vibrant displays of peacocks.

But the most complex and nuanced ritual of all is surely that of the modern human.

We use body language, grooming, dressing, and social media profiles to present ourselves attractively and signal our desirability.

In the wild, animals use signals and displays to communicate their interest in mating. Female fireflies emit flashes to attract males, while male bowerbirds create elaborate nests and displays to woo females. Similarly, in modern dating, flirting, paying compliments, and adopting positive body language all serve as signals of interest, while the exchange of messages, calls, and dates is like an elaborate version of the courtship displays seen in the animal kingdom.

Humans and animals tend to have specific preferences when it comes to choosing a mate. These preferences are influenced by various factors such as genetics, health, and available resources. For instance, studies show that men are often attracted to physical features that are associated with fertility and good health, while women tend to be drawn to individuals who can provide them with social status and resources. These preferences play a significant role in shaping our choices in the dating world, alongside personal and cultural influences.

One of my friends, 'Jenny', insisted on finding a wealthy husband. I introduced her to 'Larry', a friend who was quite successful. However, Larry later told me that Jenny's materialistic tendencies turned him off and that he would not go on any more blind dates set up by me. I was grieved to hear this. There are many women like Jenny who long for a luxurious lifestyle after marriage.

In my twenties, I was quite clueless and could not read the signs when a guy was romantically interested in me. Often, I was too friendly, unintentionally, and men mistakenly believed I was after something more than friendship. I naively believed that men and women could be friends without developing romantic feelings for each other, even if they spent a lot of time together. I was often taken aback by romantic gestures from someone I thought was just a friend.

One particular incident that still makes me cringe is when I asked to stay with a friend I'll call 'Alvin', a well-known artist in New York City. He was an older, short, balding man. He had a great sense of humour, but I had no attraction to him whatsoever.

I was shocked and horrified when Alvin assumed that I wanted to spend the night in his bed. I made it very clear to him that I was interested only in a platonic friendship. Unfortunately, my rejection left him feeling embarrassed and our friendship in tatters. Another friend allowed me to seek refuge at her place for the rest of my trip despite her cramped space, where her sister and parents lived with her under the same roof.

In my early twenties, I used to hope that I would find my Prince Charming soon and would often wonder where he was and why he hadn't shown up yet. In my quest to learn more about finding the right match, I would obsessively ask hundreds of people—couples and singles alike—whether they believed in the idea of there being one single person meant for them to be married to or partnered with. Most of them replied that they just knew that they had found the right person deep in their gut. However, almost everyone agreed that the concept of 'The One' was a myth and that there was instead a pool of compatible people to choose from.

My friend 'Felicia' describes this phenomenon as the 'taxi light' effect, where whenever someone is ready to date, their 'taxi light' turns on and they become more open to meeting potential suitors. Another friend, 'Charlene', thinks we all have invisible signs hovering over us that signal whether we're available or not. What's clear is that choosing wisely is paramount, especially when it comes to finding a long-term partner or spouse.

I had no idea that I needed to know myself and enjoy my own company. Like many singles, I was lonely. I couldn't bear to be alone for long, which is a red flag. I was looking for love and affirmation in all the wrong places and went from relationship to relationship.

My friend 'Denise' advised me, wisely, that in my late 20s I needed to get to know myself first and not rush into dating. Becoming whole and healing your issues is vital to being the best version of yourself. Getting to know your passions, your breaking point, and the kind of temperament that would complement yours is critical.

I wish I could say that I made wise choices, and it was happily ever after. Unfortunately, I failed to heed Denise's advice and impulsively rushed into my first marriage. I was reckless and led by my passions in most of my relationships. I settled for Mr Good Enough instead of being discerning and making a wise decision.

I paid a heavy price in the form of a terrible divorce that left me looking gaunt for several months as I struggled with the pain of failure. It triggered childhood trauma from my parents' divorce and my encounters with racial abuse and took me several years to recover and heal. I'm fortunate that I had the loving support of my parents and brothers and sister and good friends who made a world of difference.

Throughout my recovery from that divorce, I was close friends with 'Jason'. I supported his organization, which mobilized top students from the UK and North America to teach English to children in poor regions of China. He encouraged me whenever I was feeling down. We sometimes wondered if we should take our friendship to the next level, but something always held us back. In hindsight, I am glad that we didn't date.

We could talk about anything. Once, while waiting for my flight at an airport, we chatted for eight hours straight. I didn't fully comprehend the significance of his friendship until he got engaged. He flew down to Hong Kong to spend time with me and to look for an engagement ring for his fiancé. We looked for rings at several shops and he finally found one. I was thrilled for him and at the same time, I felt a strange awkwardness for the first time.

I took him to the train that would take him to the airport. Before he boarded, we both broke down and wept and hugged one another. It was spontaneous and shocked me. It was a grief that spoke volumes of our deep friendship and love for one another.

Today, I can say with certainty that I wouldn't change a thing about my past. I have no regrets after processing my decision and impulsivity. Wisdom comes through lived experiences and processing mistakes, especially costly blunders and lapses in judgement. The wounding and pain I went through in my first marriage and subsequent divorce is what motivated me to investigate the trafficking of women and girls in Asia. I'm forever grateful that it led to finding my purpose in life. As a result of that setback, I urge others never to settle.

My advice is that you must know yourself and embrace who you are before you can find a suitable partner.

My friend 'Sally' is a beautiful example of someone who prioritized her own personal development before finding love at forty-two. Sally is a statuesque blond with a vivacious personality and a self-deprecating sense of humour. She used to be needy and had low self-esteem and then decided to go to therapy to find healing and closure for the wounds from her painful childhood. Her parents were emotionally distant and neglectful. From a young age, she often struggled with social anxiety and loneliness. She explored and processed these persistent feelings of anxiety and loneliness that often overshadowed her.

Eventually, she came to a place of self-acceptance after years of counselling, and she had a fulfilling life with a vibrant community of good friends and a thriving career at a bank. Serendipitously, after nearly two decades, she met her ex-boyfriend 'Murray' at a party. He was a divorcee with two young children, and they talked all night.

Their chemistry was palpable, and they connected intellectually and emotionally.

She told me, 'I can't explain it. I just knew that we were going to be with each other.' She embraced this second chance to date Murray again and they enjoy a fulfilling marriage today.

Unlike Sally, 'Julie' buried her fear of rejection and other issues from her parents' tumultuous marriage and domestic violence. Instead of seeing a therapist, she repressed her pain. Sadly, she regrets her unwise choice of a mate. In her mid-thirties, she met and dated a medical professional, Tom, a socially awkward man in his mid-forties. They went on a series of dates and Julie found that she was not attracted to Tom at all.

Soon after, she divulged that Tom had admitted that his sister wrote all of his text messages in the early stages of their courtship. Julie felt deceived and for a month, she deliberated over whether to continue in the relationship. She was overweight and didn't feel attractive. Every man she liked flatly rejected her.

Tom also told Julie in a condescending and manipulative way that no man would want her and that he would marry her out of compassion. I was revolted by his words and urged her to pay attention to the red flags and run away from this horrid man.

After agonizing over this, she felt she had no prospects on the horizon and worried that she would never get married if she didn't take up Tom's offer. She desperately wanted children. She ended up settling and compromised her needs and desires due to her fears. While she has two lovely children, she feels trapped in a loveless marriage. Her children fulfil her emotional needs instead of her relying on her husband for that support.

Who you choose as your spouse or significant other is one of the most important decisions that you'll ever make in life. This person will affect you in profoundly good ways or bring out the worst. My unhappy first marriage was one of the most terrible things I've experienced. It affected my work and my overall sense of well-being. I couldn't flourish because the pain was overwhelming. I can't think of any other time I've felt something similar. Nothing is worse than a bad romantic partnership because this person knows you intimately and can inflict damage in every area of your life.

Don't rush in.

Evolving Courtship: A Journey from the 1900s to the Present in Asia and the West

'Juhae' and 'Yun Sung' are in their late seventies, still together forty-eight years after they wed in a marriage arranged by their parents in Gyeongju, South Korea. Their marriage was a way to bring two families together; they hardly knew each other on their wedding day. Over the years, they have developed a comfortable companionship where they take care of each other. Though they didn't initially have any romantic feelings towards one another, they united in raising a daughter over the years and have never once mentioned the word 'divorce'.

Their daughter 'Myung-ah' is in her forties and works as a doctor in Seoul. The idea of an arranged marriage was too old-fashioned to occur to her—she expected to marry a love match. And, indeed, she met her husband, 'David', at church while she was in college, and they have been happily married for a few decades. Her two sons are in college and are dating girls they met at school and on a dating app. They, too, would find it strange to have an arranged marriage and are most comfortable meeting girls online or through friends.

Arranged marriages were de rigueur for centuries, especially in East Asia. Many couples in my parents' and grandparents' generation had their marriages arranged by their parents back in South Korea. In Canada, most of my Caucasian friends' parents and grandparents met their spouses through friends or while hanging out on the weekends at a beach, school, church, or shopping mall.

But, like arranged marriages, the idea of meeting someone at a beach, church or shopping mall might also seem old-fashioned to young people today.

It's undoubtedly easier to date online than to flirt with strangers.

Courtship, the timeless dance of attraction and romantic pursuit, has undergone profound transformations over the past century. The evolution of courtship in Asia and the West reflects shifting social, cultural, and technological landscapes, bringing both challenges and advantages to the fore.

In the early 1900s, both in Asia and the West, courtship was characterized by formality, tradition, and parental involvement. In many Asian societies, especially in East Asia in countries like China, South Korea, and Japan, arranged marriages were the norm, with parents often selecting partners for their children based on compatibility of social status or caste, family reputation and honour, and economic stability. While these marriages were seen as a practical and harmonious ways to unite families, they often left little room for romantic love.

In the West, courtship rituals included chaperoned outings, formal introductions, and an emphasis on modesty and decorum. The goal was often marriage, and dating was seen as a means to find a suitable spouse. Stability and family compatibility were often prioritized, reducing the uncertainty and risks associated with modern dating.

The mid-twentieth century brought big changes to courtship. In the West, the post-World War II era saw the rise of dating culture. Young people gained more independence and began to explore romantic relationships for companionship and personal fulfilment rather than purely for marriage. The 1950s and 1960s saw the emergence of the concept of 'teenagers' and the popularization of casual dating. In Asia, rapid urbanization, increased access to education and exposure to Western influences also began to reshape courtship norms. While arranged marriages remained common, young people began to have more say in the choice of their partners.

The shift towards more individualistic courtship introduced greater ambiguity and less structure in dating. Traditional values sometimes clash with modern desires for autonomy and personal happiness. Yet, greater personal agency allowed individuals to explore their preferences and develop more emotionally satisfying relationships.

Love in the Digital Age

The late twentieth century witnessed two transformative forces in courtship: the digital revolution and globalization. In Asia and the

West, the Internet and communication technologies transformed the dating landscape.

Online dating platforms, social media, and instant messaging connected people across vast distances, expanding the pool of potential partners. Those using dating platforms are willing to pay US$20 or US$30 a month to meet, flirt, with and get to know other users, thanks to the increasing use of smartphones.

According to an article in *Quartz* magazine, global dating app revenue has increased exponentially, from US$1.6 billion in 2015 to US$4.6 billion in 2021, and is projected to surpass US$8.4 billion by 2024.

In the twenty-first century, individuals have greater freedom to define their relationship structures and romantic identities. Concepts like gender fluidity and non-traditional partnerships have gained acceptance. The evolution of dating in East Asia, from the era of arranged marriages to the contemporary world of modern romance and the quest for authentic love, reflects the region's profound transformation.

During the pandemic, it is no surprise that there was a spike in usage of online dating apps, as most people were homebound and lonelier than ever with border closures, social restrictions, and lockdowns.

But the digital era brought challenges, including authenticity, online harassment, and the pressure to curate idealized online personas. The globalized nature of dating also introduced cultural clashes and misunderstandings. Using dating apps may reduce the serendipity of meeting potential partners in real-life settings, where unexpected connections can occur.

One advantage of the digital revolution is that it offers unprecedented access to a diverse array of potential partners—it greatly expands the pool of potential romantic and sexual partners, allowing individuals to connect with people they might never have met otherwise. The apps use matching algorithms that consider users' preferences and interests to suggest compatible romantic partners, possibly increasing the chances of finding a genuine connection.

But there is such a thing as having too many options. Scrolling through profiles, messaging, and going on multiple dates can be time-consuming, leading to a sense of burnout for some users. A vast number of potential matches can be overwhelming and may lead to a paradox of choice, making it difficult for some individuals to decide.

Allison Heiliczer, author of *Rethink the Couch: Into the Boardrooms and Bedrooms in Asia*, says that since Biblical times, people have turned to matchmakers for their relationships. She says:

> Dating apps and online platforms are a modern manifestation of this. People are attracted to the idea that dating is like ordering off a menu – 'I'll have one man with solid values around family, someone who enjoys walks on the beach, and who wants three kids.' While it's important to have enough overlap in values and goals in life, there's something that happens when people are actually together.

While apps may assist people with meeting and the idea of checking certain boxes, there is no current technology that perfectly matches people in part because no technology teaches couples how to ride the currents of life and work out issues that technology cannot predict. Therefore, one of the dangers is the delusion that online dating has perfectly solved challenges that all relationships will face.

Dating apps often emphasize physical appearance, leading to superficial judgements based on photos and brief profiles, potentially overlooking deeper compatibility factors. Some users may misrepresent themselves by using outdated photos or providing inaccurate information, leading to disappointment and frustration. Online dating can be impersonal, leading to frequent ghosting (sudden cessation of communication) or rejection, which can be emotionally challenging.

'Christina' has been in long-term relationships for the past decade and is suddenly single at forty-one. She's tried dating apps and has not had any success. Around the same time she began using apps, she spent tens of thousands of dollars on facials and minor plastic surgery to lift her sagging skin. I sensed she had an unhealthy hyperfocus on the barely noticeable wrinkles around her eyes and face, which could be indicative of body dysmorphia. Her fixation has exponentially increased as she has begun to use dating apps. Behind this anxiety is a deep-seated fear surrounding her age and that she will not meet an eligible, handsome partner unless she looks younger.

My heart goes out to Christina—she's attractive and a highly successful banker but is bound by a fear of a terrible stereotype, which is also an Asian cultural norm, that she is an old maid and ineligible, as a woman well over thirty.

According to a study in the *Body Image Journal*, women who use dating apps experience daily body dissatisfaction, eating disorders, and negative moods such as depression. A research paper in the *Journal of Telematics and Informatics* reported that greater use of dating apps was detrimental to the search for love and made people feel like 'failures' if they didn't find a good match. It also reported that those engaged in excessive swiping or looking at different profiles of potential partners felt 'partner choice overload' and feared being single forever.

A study on the association between mobile dating app use and relationship status satisfaction published in *Sage Journals* has also shown that individuals using dating apps may be more likely to experience dissatisfaction in romantic relationships. This dissatisfaction can spill over into self-esteem issues, as users may question their ability to form and maintain healthy connections.

While dating apps offer opportunities for meeting potential partners and fostering connections, they can also negatively affect self-esteem. It's essential to remember that self-worth is not determined by external validation or the success of one's interactions on dating apps. Healthy self-esteem is built on a foundation of self-acceptance, self-love, and a realistic understanding of one's intrinsic value.

There is a real risk of encountering catfishers (people who pretend to be someone else) and scams on dating apps. One particularly brutal type of scam is called 'pig butchering'. This involves the targeting of white-collar professionals, college students, and vulnerable individuals who are coerced into scamming others and engaging in illegal activities such as fake crypto investments or deceptive online romances and other schemes.

Criminal networks use elaborate techniques to lure their victims, often involving deceitful job offers, before holding them against their will in compounds across Southeast Asia and other nations. The victims are then forced to scam others from wealthier nations and often face violence, torture, and even death if they refuse.

A report by the United Nations says that hundreds of thousands are thought to be trapped in these compounds, while tens of thousands of other people across the globe are being scammed by them. Some of those scammed lose their life savings—some have killed themselves as a result. Both sets of people are victims. Meanwhile, the real criminals continue to evade justice.

The proliferation of this dangerously manipulative transnational operation has become a grave concern. It involves not only human trafficking and violence but also fraud, money laundering, and crypto currency.

The complexity and sophistication of the crime and the international networks make it an enormous challenge for law enforcement and civil society to combat.

Heiliczer says, 'Because our desire to love and be loved is at the core of most people's existence, a tremendous amount of psychology goes into these scams that can bankrupt people financially and emotionally and for some steal their lives.'

I urge you to use technology wisely but always prioritize real, meaningful connections, maintain authenticity, and not fall into the trap of superficial judgements based solely on photos.

Love Finds a Way

My friend 'Cathy', who is from Singapore and works at a bank in Hong Kong, has had very little dating experience.

In her thirties, she remained happily single. But as she turned forty, she began taking the initiative and asking her friends to set her up on dates. She also started asking men out directly, sometimes to dinner or for a hike.

As she searched for a mate, she saw that her pool of choices was dwindling, which distressed her. Yet she refused to go on a dating app. Out of desperation and fear that she may be single for the rest of her life, she started dating someone she suspected wouldn't really be a good match—a single father of a young boy, who was still living in the same home as his ex-wife. Inevitably, they broke up and she was depressed for months.

I met her around this time and urged her to be more open to using a dating app, as it would enable her to meet more eligible men. I told her of a friend, 'Denise', who met her future husband in Montreal after going on an app for the first and only time. It wasn't until Cathy turned forty-eight that she finally gave in and gave it a try, signing up for a popular platform.

After going on a handful of dates with different men, she noticed that, almost immediately, she felt a connection with an intensely shy man, also forty-eight, named 'Caleb'. On their first date, he could barely look her in the eye. His hair was dishevelled, and he wore a rather ratty T-shirt and faded pants. He expressed interest in continuing to meet, yet she was not convinced. Still, she went on one more date and found a deeper connection. After six months of dating, her mom and sister flew in to meet him, but they were critical of how he dressed and his shyness.

However, by this time, Cathy was already in love and so was Caleb—they cared deeply for one another and embraced each other's families. Her love for him was giving him a newfound confidence. He blossomed socially. After nine months of dating, they were engaged and a month later, married in a civil ceremony.

Over dinner, Cathy recounted their love story. Her breathiness and the euphoric look in her eyes said it all: she was on cloud nine and had finally met her Prince Charming—all he'd needed was some tweaking to his dress sense and hairstyle. She thanked me in person for supporting her journey to find her soulmate.

Cathy's happiness was off the charts. For years, she had believed she was too old to find her significant other and now she had been proved wrong. I was so thrilled for her. And I couldn't resist saying with a twinkle in my eye, 'I told you so! I knew you would find someone on the app.'

Not all of my friends, of course, have had the same good fortune as Cathy when it comes to dating apps.

'Clinton', a thirty-five-year-old Chinese accountant, met six women through an app but all of them moved on to other men. He's been seeing 'Monica' for thirteen months but feels conflicted over whether he wants to spend the rest of his life with her. Though doubtful, he is hanging on to the relationship until a more compatible person comes along.

A few years ago, I became an unintentional matchmaker for my friend 'Siti', a survivor of child slavery, and 'Mike', the man of her dreams.

Siti's back story was complex. She was barely a teenager when a predatory agent came knocking on her parents' door in her village in Indonesia. This broker promised her impoverished parents that if they signed Siti over to him he would find her a comfortable job in the region. They forged her age on her passport so that she was ten years older and coached her on lying to immigration officials.

While the broker lied to her parents and promised Siti would have a great paying job in a hotel, she ended up as an indentured servant—first in several homes in Singapore and then in Hong Kong. She suffered physical and emotional abuse. Her agency stole her monthly salary and illegally overcharged her to cover so-called recruitment and flight costs.

She was often slapped and called derogatory names for failing to listen to instructions on cleaning or for not working fast enough. Siti was starved and had to ask for a cup of water each day from her first employer. She begged her neighbour's domestic worker to give her bread to eat several times a week.

She wasn't the only one. Tragically, child slavery in domestic work is a systemic problem in Asia. Thousands of children from Indonesia have been trafficked into Southeast Asia and Hong Kong homes over many years.

Why do they remain largely silent? Why isn't this more known? In Hong Kong, there is no law to protect victims of this type of child slavery, and anyone found with a forged passport, which such victims often have, is charged and then sent to prison.

Siti had a big heart and wanted to make a difference for others like her. She felt robbed of her childhood and often despaired for her future. Fortunately, she was eventually able to land a job as a domestic worker for a kind employer in Hong Kong. While she had to pay a crippling fee to her agent, the same man who lied to her parents, to release her—nine months of wages—she finally had stability.

Somehow, we found each other after I began investigating Indonesian child maids. I recounted her story in newspaper articles and my book, *A Long Road to Justice*. I also produced a film on Siti and other Indonesian survivors of child domestic work exploitation.

Then, I hired her to help in the production of my music videos. That's when she met her future husband, Mike, a cameraman on set. Mike is a gentle giant with a sharp mind and a kind heart. He has a solid grounding in his Christian faith and was considered an eligible guy.

It was not until more than a year later, when I met Siti for coffee, that she told me she was dating Mike. I was pleasantly surprised. Unfortunately, I was less surprised by his parents' initial reluctance—they didn't want their educated son to date a domestic worker without a penny to her name. However, his parents finally came around and before their engagement gave their blessing with tears of happiness.

Siti summed up her fairy tale to me: 'Sis, sometimes I tell him how hard my life was. I sang on the streets to survive; I became a cleaner . . . He says my story can be a real book. Yes, it is a miracle. I never imagined I would marry him. We have only met because of your projects.'

I cried tears of joy. A beautiful marriage and perhaps the pitter-patter of little feet are totally unexpected—and totally welcome—'by-product' of my research into the child slaves of Indonesia.

Wise Choices

I have been infatuated or madly in love with someone at least a dozen times. In those moments, I really thought it was true love. But, in hindsight, I can see it was more a strong feeling of liking someone for their looks, personality, or whatever else I had projected onto them from my daydreams of an idealized Prince Charming sweeping me off my feet.

In the first year after signing my divorce papers, I went on several dates with various men, which terrified me. I was still in denial and too afraid to confront my pain.

So, I abstained from dating anyone for five years. During that time, I didn't even hold a man's hand! Instead, I used that time to write my book on Japanese military sexual slavery during a sabbatical, nurture good friendships in various cities, and spend quality time with my parents. I eventually moved to a new city, Hong Kong, from Beijing.

That is where I met Matt, the man who would become my second husband.

Unfortunately, I was still traumatized and distrustful of men due to my first husband's affair. As Matt and I began to date, my deep-seated fears came to the fore. In these early months of dating Matt, I was often triggered by some event or other that would bring my simmering anger and hurt to the surface. I might not have understood it at the time, but it was precisely because I was in a loving, intimate relationship again that these emotions were coming to the fore.

I would often get angry at Matt because of my fight-or-flight response and would completely shut down emotionally. That was the turning point, and I knew then that I had some unresolved pain and went to see a counsellor. Matt continued to love me unconditionally. I didn't know the power of forgiveness until this time. With his love and my counsellor's support, I could release unforgiveness and resentment towards my ex-husband, which was clouding my relationship with Matt.

One of the most precious things I've experienced is that Matt knows all my flaws, mistakes, and weaknesses and still thinks I am a wonderful gift to him. Eventually, my trust grew to the point where we could walk down the aisle and commit to each other in marriage.

My marriage to Matt has taught me that real, lasting love is a lot more down to earth. It involves committing to be with someone through thick and thin and accepting someone entirely—their good, bad, and ugly parts. There is no idealization anymore and the masks are off.

As Heiliczer says, 'Many of us have been hurt in relationships; yet many of us also heal in them.'

She estimates that at least 50 per cent of people worldwide have an insecure attachment style based on childhood trauma from caregivers. She says:

> In fact, one of the greatest arguments in favour of being in a relationship is the potential for growth. As a couples' therapist, I often hear that one or both people in a marriage will expect the other to heal his or her wounds. I do not believe it's anyone's responsibility to heal another's pain, and no adult can control another. Rather, how the individual shows up in the context of the relationship will determine how much healing is possible. No doubt all relationships trigger some of our deepest pain.

Responding to that pain differently is what helps inform healing.

We are all deeply flawed and bound to hurt others, especially those closest to us. Unsurprisingly, scientists who study forgiveness have vouched that it is one of the most important keys to a healthy relationship. Several studies, including one entitled 'Forgiveness and Relationship Satisfaction: Mediating Mechanisms' in the *Journal of Family Psychology*, have found that couples who practice forgiveness have longer and greater relationship satisfaction.

Forgiveness is integral to love, allowing relationships to heal and grow stronger.

When you love someone, you are willing to sacrifice and understand them and mutually support one another's goals and dreams. Matt and I supported one another through our books, films, and anti-trafficking work. What I appreciate the most is that we are creating a legacy that extends far beyond ourselves, touching the lives of those who are suffering and have been exploited, and hopefully, inspiring more people to take action to help those in desperate need.

Love is a universal language that transcends boundaries, cultures, and generations. It's a profound and complex emotion that has been celebrated, analysed, and cherished throughout human history. True love can transform lives in unimaginable ways and defining it is like capturing a shooting star—it's fleeting, powerful, and deeply personal. It involves embracing imperfections, growing together, and nurturing a connection that transcends the physical.

Winnie Mandela's love for Nelson endured despite his long imprisonment. There can be no denying the sheer power of love when it comes to triumphing over even the most difficult of circumstances.

Iconic country music stars, Johnny Cash and June Carter, were married for more than thirty years. The Hollywood film *Walk the Line*, chronicles Johnny's rise to fame, his romance with the five-time Grammy singer June, and his failed marriage to his first wife. June's steadfast support helped Johnny beat a drug addiction that nearly killed him, demonstrating that true love can be a source of redemption.

Mister Rogers, a beloved figure in children's television, is widely said to have embodied the essence of true love. He once said in his book, *The World According to Mister Rogers*, 'Love isn't a state of perfect caring. It is an active noun like "struggle". To love someone is to strive to accept that person exactly the way he or she is, right here and now.'

True success is not only determined by the height of our professional achievements or the abundance of our possessions but also by the depth of the connections we cultivate with others.

True love is a journey that can be both challenging and immensely rewarding and it can light up even the darkest of paths.

Love is not just a feeling, it's a choice, a commitment, and a source of spiritual nourishment. When you find it, cherish it with all your might, nurture it, and let it lead you to a life filled with fulfilment.

Love never fails. So, be discerning.

Here are some qualities that capture some of the essence of love:

- **Love as sacrifice:** True love often involves selflessness and sacrifice. It's the willingness to put the needs and happiness of the one you love above your own. As the author Nicholas Sparks put it, 'Love is not how you forget, but how you forgive, not how you listen, but how you understand, not what you see, but how you feel, and not how you let go, but how you hold on.'
- **Love as friendship:** True love is often rooted in a deep friendship. It's a connection that goes beyond physical attraction and superficial qualities. The author C.S. Lewis once said, 'Friendship is born at that moment when one person says to another, "What! You too? I thought I was the only one."'
- **Love as acceptance:** True love accepts flaws and imperfections. It doesn't seek to change the person you love but embraces them wholly. As the Chinese philosopher Lao Tzu said, 'Being deeply loved by someone gives you strength while loving someone deeply gives you courage.'
- **Love as growth:** True love encourages personal growth and development. It inspires you to reach your full potential. As Howard Washington Thurman said, 'Don't ask yourself what the world needs, ask yourself what makes you come alive. And then go and do that. Because what the world needs is people who have come alive.'

Chapter 10

Toxic Offices and Transitions

Early in my career, I worked in a petty and toxic office in a small city. Unfortunately, I was unprepared for the viciousness of politics and had no skills or ability to handle the ugly lion's den. It became a career-defining time, and I learned invaluable lessons. I would be a different person today if I hadn't worked there. I became tougher and bitter from the battles I went through.

The transformation in my personality was so pronounced that my family and friends would say things to me like, 'You've changed. You've hardened.'

It wasn't fun at the time but, looking back, I believe the dynamics and the people in this office gave me the iron spine and ferocious toughness that eventually enabled me to stand up for myself and what I believe in—my human rights work.

I came into this office with a disadvantage from the get-go. I didn't have any TV news skills, as I had previously worked only in a national magazine, public radio, and a community newspaper covering City Hall. I wasn't ready for the acrimonious reception from the other TV anchors, who viewed any new woman as a threat.

It was like the *Mean Girls* movie, where a naive teenage girl educated in Africa by her scientist parents experiences public school for the first time. I could relate to how she is shocked by the unspoken school rules of the popular and unpopular crowd and the cruel cliques and the bullying. I initially felt that way in this company when I arrived.

For the first six months, it was like walking through a field full of landmines. The boss who hired me told me he could see my broadcasting potential and was incredibly encouraging at first. I thought this was my big break into television hosting.

I didn't know then that I was walking into an all-Caucasian office except for two other ethnic minority anchors. I also didn't notice there was resentment and a perception that I had been given an unfair advantage as a token diversity hire. Unfortunately, my lack of broadcast skills made it even harder for me to be accepted into the fold.

I had to prove myself.

I was frustrated by their assumptions and unwillingness to see that I had transferrable skills, such as writing and interviewing, from my previous jobs and that it was just a matter of time before I could learn the ropes of TV news.

Before my first day on the job, I had seen an advertisement at the bus stop for the main show featuring the TV hosts. I was intrigued by 'May', the sweetly smiling co-anchor. As someone new to the TV world, I looked forward to meeting and learning from her. I was expecting a congenial woman and a new friend.

Instead, this woman intentionally ignored me each day. I was hurt but worried about how I could work with her—in an environment where teamwork was essential—if she virtually ignored me.

A week later, when our paths crossed, she turned to me without warning and called me a bitch. Out of nowhere, she had become so enraged that her eyes were bulging and her spittle was flying in my face.

I was paralysed with shock. It was as if someone had slapped me in the face. I didn't know what to say or do and pretended nothing had happened. No one had called me an expletive before to my face. Her persona as the sweetly smiling anchor on the posters and on air was even more troubling as I saw her true colours.

I hadn't done anything to warrant this abuse. She was simply angry that I was around. And to my disappointment, not one of my colleagues intervened. Later, while May was not around, a few colleagues approached me sympathetically to say that she was a horrid and rude person with a big ego and was nasty when she didn't get her way.

The head manager was notified, but while he was dismayed, I sensed he was not surprised by May's mean girl antics. Until then, I hadn't been aware of narcissistic people; now I was getting an MBA on that very topic through May. I wondered if being on television could ruin one's character, leading to a big ego and a lack of dignity.

Years later, I came to grasp that May would have seen any new woman colleague as a threat to her position. I also had an epiphany that there are many other women like May, that this kind of insecurity is part of every office and I should not have taken it personally.

In my previous job, my managers and colleagues had been supportive. The atmosphere was collegial, and the staff were quite intellectual and discussed films and books and current events. There was also a studious focus on the work, leaving little time to gossip and for office politics. In contrast, the staff in the TV company had a small-town mentality and were territorial and gossipy. The big stories were fires in buildings, cats stuck in trees or deadly car crashes, which left me feeling bored and hungry for something more substantial.

I wasn't surprised when May, the Queen Bee in the office, rallied some worker bees against me. A few of the video editors suddenly became rude and unhelpful. One short, balding cameraman whined incessantly whenever he sat in the office between shoots. He once had a temper tantrum and pushed me by pretending not to see me during our fieldwork when I didn't use the best of his 'great' footage. Indeed, I was too inexperienced at that time to make the most of it but that didn't excuse his childish behaviour. I took the high road and ignored him even though I had a great urge to tell him to grow up and out of his diapers.

Another Asian anchor, who had been at the company for years and was initially aloof towards me, became toxic and petty. I had the distinct feeling she wanted to distance herself from another Asian woman. She was too self-absorbed to be kind and helpful.

In one of our first conversations, I had asked her where she had gone to university because that was what we usually asked in previous newsrooms. It was the wrong question to ask, and I rubbed her the wrong way. She immediately became defensive and admitted that she didn't go to university and only had a certificate in broadcasting. I was very supportive of her choice and had no judgement at all. Besides, she was great at her job. I was surprised at how offended she was. I was disappointed to hear that she gossiped about me and others. I had hoped that she was above the petty culture.

I was bewildered that a supposedly professional setting was in reality a childish playground of pettiness—and disturbed by how vastly different people's on-air personas were to their true selves.

Most surprising of all was the stooge of the place. He had a jolly demeanour but was a nasty piece of work. Perhaps he was angry at being sidelined by the management amid perceptions that he was increasingly unpopular with viewers. He once muttered under his breath that I was a diversity hire, brought in for being Asian to mix things up on air. His racist comments were unsettling.

Later, I began to suspect he believed that I was an unnecessary headcount and a threat to his job security. He wasn't the only one to complain about diversity hiring. Another senior reporter had joined the company after moving from a bigger city. He was pompous and carried himself as a big fish. He blamed minorities for his lack of upward mobility in his previous company. I didn't have the boldness back then to challenge him, but I had also learned to pick my battles and knew when it was better to remain quiet and keep my powder dry.

There was another reporter, a Caucasian, who joined around the same time as me who had no TV experience either. Yet she was supported by the Queen Bee and others. She was sweet and had a ditzy puppy dog demeanour.

I dug my heels in and decided I didn't want to be pushed out. I wanted to leave on my terms. There were days in the first six months when I dreaded going to work and being steeped in that petty culture. Over the years, I heard similar stories of childish offices from other broadcasters and we concluded that the drive to be TV famous added an extra dimension of ugliness to the usual unpleasantness of office politics. Often, I was weary and unhappy, and it showed on my face. It was so different from when I arrived, full of optimism and ambition.

One thing that helped me through this period was that I had a supporter—a senior anchor who helped train me and was a good friend. Sometimes, all it takes is that one good friend to help you persevere in challenging circumstances. I'm grateful to have had a group of kind colleagues in the office and supportive friends outside of work.

I stuck to my guns, concentrated on improving my work, and maintained an excellent work ethic and cheerful attitude. Over time, the Queen Bee and others became more amiable towards me. By the time I was ready to move to another city for work, I had won May over and we hung out during one of my goodbye celebrations.

Even as I look back at this time, I ache for the young, naive woman I was and from the fact that I had to go through such a rude awakening. It was a gruelling way to learn about the real world and how to handle nasty colleagues.

But the unfortunate truth is that the higher you climb the corporate beanstalk, the bigger the jerks you encounter. Toxic colleagues abound when the stakes are high in any industry. They come with the territory in places of power, big money, and fame.

Still, climbing that greasy pole taught me golden lessons that I wouldn't have learned otherwise. Indeed, I believe that I was able to advance in my future work and accomplish all that I have exactly because of this office. For instance, I learned not to care about the critics and rude people—their bad behaviour reflects on them, and I believe everyone faces the consequences of their negative actions in time. We all reap what we sow, good and bad.

I also learned to put on a game face and not reveal opinions or anything substantive that could be twisted and used against me, and I strived never to gossip. Initially, I was too trusting and open and shared freely, and then I saw a few rotten apples lie and use that information in deceptive ways against me with the big boss. One time, I said that I wanted to move to another city in the future and a colleague repeated that to our head boss, but distorted what I said by adding that I wanted to quit.

Staying humble and low-key was vitally important and I learned when to fade into the background to avoid provoking unnecessary jealousy and battles. During my TV job, I faced extremely stressful deadlines, which pushed me to the limits. To cope with the stress, I initially turned to unhealthy habits such as eating pizza and chips.

However, I soon figured out the importance of taking care of myself and started exercising regularly. This has been a great source of rejuvenation for me. In fact, I became certified as a personal trainer when I was nineteen and have always enjoyed spending time in the gym.

Working in a high-pressure environment taught me the value of maintaining a calm and collected demeanour—demonstrating grace under pressure—even when faced with demanding circumstances. I learned to be mindful of my attitude and behaviour, and my ability to remain unflappable and composed under stress improved significantly. This experience helped me understand it was crucial to quiet my soul and find inner peace and tranquillity, especially during moments of tension and frustration. I continue to strive towards that goal.

Most importantly, because I was underestimated—I was the underdog—I came to grasp that the spirit of excellence is fundamental. That means striving to do your best and letting your work speak for itself. No one can nitpick and criticize, or poke a hole in your work.

Remember, being underestimated can be an advantage in disguise. It can fuel your determination and allow you to prove your potential. Instead of dwelling on the negativity of being the underdog, channel your energy into self-improvement and consistent, purpose-driven action. Over time, your actions will speak louder than other people's biases and you'll rise above the noise.

I also learned valuable insights about the power of perseverance—whether in the office or at the gym—endurance is a valuable strength. These lessons have equipped me to face the challenges that lay ahead. Initially, I believed this petty and poisonous office was one-of-a-kind. But sadly, I was soon to discover that there were even uglier workplaces out there.

Take the High Road

If I could give a piece of advice to my twenty-one-year-old self, it would be to always, even when you don't feel like it, take the high road in work situations. Don't let toxic colleagues control your emotions and lead you to stoop to their level (in every office, there's someone like that).

I once worked as a TV host where we were on a rotation and everyone was fighting for more on-camera time. Yes, it sounds like a cliché—and yes, it was catty. I was the new kid on the block and was surprised to learn that one woman colleague was gossiping about me. I hadn't even exchanged a hello with her and my wide-eyed self at the time was mystified by why she hated me so much. In our communal work closet, I once found one of my favourite blazers—a lovely bubble gum pink colour—that I wore on-air had a huge rip on the sleeve and one of the buttons was missing. It definitely didn't look like an accident!

I remember standing there clutching the jacket close to my chest and feeling like someone had punched my gut. I was horrified that she would stoop to such a grossly unethical act and want to intimidate me this way.

I was left speechless that another full-grown adult and journalist could do something like this. Colleagues pointed the finger at my number one enemy. I was tempted to confront her and to fight back by lowering myself to her level. I was hurt and resolved I wouldn't allow anyone to stop me or hinder me from doing my best work. Her actions made me only more determined to succeed. I was fired up.

Thankfully, after speaking with a mentor and colleagues and wrestling with my conscience, I let it go. I did my best to forgive her, I prayed, and I chose to focus on doing my work to the best of my ability.

I won't lie—taking the high road was hard. I usually have no qualms about standing up for myself, and it ate at me for a while to not say anything. However, I put my faith in that somehow, in some way, by not escalating the conflict, justice would prevail.

Serendipitously, a few years later, I found out through old colleagues that my old arch-enemy was unhappy at work and was applying for a new role at another company. She was interviewed by my good friend with whom I had shared the story of the ripped blazer years before! As it turned out, my arch-enemy wasn't hired for the role. By this point, I had no negative feelings towards her and felt sorry for her.

Taking the high road may not be easy, and we may never see justice prevail, but it's worth it because it helps you maintain your integrity.

Remember that, as the American novelist Nicholas Sparks said, 'In the end, you should always do the right thing, even if it's hard.'

If you find yourself in a challenging situation, it's best to step back and take a moment to calm down. Deep breathing and relaxation techniques can help you centre yourself. It's important to communicate with the other person honestly and openly about what you expect and where your boundaries lie. Working together to find a mutually acceptable solution is key. Try to be understanding and see the situation from their perspective. Tasha Eurich, in an article in *Harvard Business Review*, suggests that practising compassion can help us stay composed during difficult moments.

Unsurprisingly, I have worked in TV newsrooms and offices where some women didn't support me. There was one office where I had hoped to be mentored by some accomplished older women, but they barely said a word to me.

I was reminded of a *Harvard Business Review* article that explained the 'Queen Bee' phenomenon, where senior women executives distance themselves from junior women to get ahead and to be more accepted by their male peers.

Through these experiences and the lack of support I felt at varying times, I have tried to champion other women in my circles. It's my golden rule. There was a time when I mentored many younger women to help them reach their fullest potential.

We can all do better. As sisters, we face enough challenges in this world as it is and do not need to face more barriers from other women. We need each other. When we unite as a sisterhood, nothing can stop us.

Credit Where It's Due

My experiences with toxic colleagues taught me the importance of something else too: giving credit where credit is due.

When I was a lowly intern on a live TV show, I suggested having a wedding on our cool-looking set with brightly coloured furniture. I was in touch with a couple who really wanted to tie the knot on camera. I pitched the idea at our morning meeting, but the host and executive producer were absent.

The next day, the host returned and congratulated 'Mike', a senior producer, for the brilliant wedding idea. I didn't know that Mike had taken credit for my idea until he glared at me. His message was clear, 'Don't contradict me. The wedding was *my* idea.'

I was taken aback, my innocent beliefs shattered. I tried to comfort myself that recognition wasn't necessary as I didn't plan to continue at the show after my internship, but the truth is Mike's lack of honesty put me in a tailspin and the experience has stayed with me, even years later.

This is when I vowed to myself that I would never steal anyone's ideas. I have always strived to acknowledge people for their contributions and to support and encourage my team members. I also started making sure I treated interns with respect and fairness.

Something similar happened on another occasion, when I presented a list of my documentary ideas to the decision-makers. One of my proposals was an analysis of the complicated history and relationship between China, Korea, and Japan.

Later, I found out that a producer from another show had taken my entire outline without giving me any credit. I confronted her and told her it was my original idea from years of research and several trips to these countries for my book on Japanese military sexual slavery. Without years of research, no one could have come up with that specific idea. She staunchly denied stealing my concept.

It is disheartening when someone takes credit for our ideas. In this case, I would have been satisfied if she had acknowledged the idea privately before taking it. I was disappointed by her lack of ethics.

Although my boss secretly supported me, he didn't take any action. His apathy angered me, but ultimately, it also taught me something: that there will be leaders in the workplace who look out only for themselves—I never wanted to be like that.

I'm sure everyone has experienced or seen managers or colleagues take credit unfairly or fail to endorse the 'invisible' work someone else has put in. It's a deep human need to feel acknowledged. In some circumstances, and to some people, it matters more than financial reward.

Giving proper recognition where it's due is key to motivating people, driving performance and fostering collaboration. The very best leaders and organizations truly get this and spare no effort to get it right.

The famed American basketball coach John Wooden once said, 'A strong leader accepts blame and gives credit, while a weak leader does the opposite.'

I find these words particularly helpful, and I have a couple of tips of my own to share: First, when I achieve a goal, I make an effort to appreciate publicly or privately those who helped me along the way, including quieter team members whose contributions may have been overlooked. I also confront anyone who tries to take credit for something they didn't do.

Too Many Toxic Work Environments

A 'toxic workplace' is an environment where conflict, intimidation, bullying, and other forms of behaviour negatively impact productivity. The US Surgeon General's office highlighted the detrimental effects of toxic work environments in its 2022 report, *Framework for Workplace Mental Health and Well-Being*. The Surgeon General, Vivek H. Murthy, MD, emphasized that chronic stress caused by workplace mistreatment and abuse could result in severe health issues such as depression, heart disease, cancer, and other illnesses.

Statistics paint a sobering picture of the prevalence of toxic corporate environments. A 2022 *MIT Sloan Management Review* study found that toxic work cultures are the number one reason employees quit and ten times more important than compensation in predicting turnover.

Other factors, such as job insecurity or lack of recognition for performance, are far behind. The report found that the leading characteristics of toxic work cultures included failure to promote equity, diversity, and inclusion, workers feeling disrespected, and unethical behaviour.

The pitfalls of toxic offices came to the fore during the coronavirus pandemic, when many people began re-examining their lives, environments, and work goals. According to the *MIT Sloan Management*

Review, in what has been dubbed the Great Resignation, more than 24 million Americans quit their jobs because of toxic offices and other reasons between April and September 2021—an unprecedented statistic.

Employers in the US lose nearly US$50 billion per year due to toxic workplace-related employee turnover, according to an estimate in the 2019 *Society for Human Resource Management* report, and that was even before the Great Resignation.

According to a *Gallup* poll, a staggering 60 per cent of US workers report experiencing or witnessing bullying in the workplace. Workplace stress is also a significant issue, with 65 per cent of employees stating that work is a significant source of stress in their lives, according to the American Psychological Association. In such environments, individuals are often held back from realizing their full potential due to fear, which becomes the dominant emotion.

Mindy Shoss, an industrial-organizational psychologist and professor at the University of Central Florida, says that fear is the main theme of a toxic workplace. She explains that these dysfunctional workplaces cause employees to lose enthusiasm and motivation—fear fills the gap.

Fear is a powerful and universal emotion, one that often rears its head in the context of the workplace. Fear, particularly in the workplace, can manifest in various forms, such as fear of retribution, fear of conflict, fear of job loss, and fear of not meeting expectations. When left unaddressed, these fears can have a detrimental effect on both a personal and professional level.

In terms of personal consequences, chronic fear in the workplace can result in elevated stress levels, leading to a myriad of health problems, including anxiety, depression, and even physical ailments. It can hinder self-confidence and self-esteem, eroding one's sense of self-worth over time.

Professionally, the impact of fear is no less damaging. Fear stifles creativity and innovation, discourages risk-taking, and hinders one's ability to voice concerns or ideas. It fosters a culture of conformity rather than one of growth and progress. These factors collectively thwart one's potential for career advancement and success. The fear accompanying such toxic situations can be paralysing, but it is also a crucible that, when faced head-on, it has the ability to unlock unparalleled personal and professional growth.

In the face of chronic fear, remember that you possess the capacity to rise above your circumstances. You have the power to transform toxic environments into spaces of growth and fulfilment. By embracing change, cultivating resilience, and seeking support, we can not only navigate these formidable situations but also emerge stronger, wiser, and closer to our fullest potential.

How else can overcoming fear catalyse growth?

- **Enhanced resilience:** Confronting fear head-on builds resilience. As we navigate daunting problems, we can become better equipped to handle adversity in the future. In fact, research by the American Psychological Association indicates that people who successfully confront their fears are more likely to experience personal development.
- **Empowerment:** Overcoming fear empowers us to take control of our lives. We discover that we have a choice: to be paralysed by fear or confront it and assert our agency. Empowerment leads to a sense of ownership over one's career and life trajectory.
- **Improved communication skills:** Fear often arises from the inability to express oneself effectively. Confronting fear necessitates improved communication skills. As we learn to articulate concerns and ideas despite our trepidation, we can become more persuasive and influential.
- **Innovation and creativity:** Fear inhibits creativity and innovation. By conquering fear, we open ourselves up to new ideas and approaches. We can become more willing to take calculated risks and progress in our work.
- **Career advancement:** Fear can keep us from seeking promotions or new opportunities in toxic work environments. Overcoming fear allows us to seize new prospects.

Overcoming Fear

Fear had held me back for most of my twenties and part of my thirties until I faced my demons, especially self-sabotage. For so long, I had a habit of stopping myself from going for big roles and projects that scared me—even though that went against the exact piece of advice I received from a mentor early on in my career: go for the work that scares you the most.

Many years ago, I had multiple job interviews at a major global company. After the last face-to-face meeting with the head honcho, I had a crippling fear of failure and even fear of success, and I became acutely scared of being rejected.

What if I can't take on this role? What if I don't like my new city, Hong Kong? What if, what if . . . I was knee-deep in my imposter syndrome. I decided to take matters into my own hands and pre-emptively told the human resources manager I wouldn't take the job. I took the easy path and retreated into my comfort zone, where I wasn't fully challenged and wouldn't fail.

In hindsight, I regretted it. It was an act of self-defeating behaviour. It was also a sliding doors moment, and years later, I wondered how my life would have undoubtedly taken a different path had I moved to Hong Kong earlier than I did. I wish I could tell myself then to take a risk, to leap out of the nest and try flying despite the self-doubt.

But the hidden gem in this painful lesson was that it caused me to examine more deeply my vicious cycle of self-sabotage and the roots of it: a lack of confidence and negative self-talk. A diseased mindset. Perhaps some of you can relate to this.

I had a habit of beating myself up because my identity and self-worth were based on my performance and work success. Some of this is probably a remnant of my Korean culture and upbringing.

In another instance, I held back and nearly didn't reach my goal of finishing my second book. For a decade, I procrastinated, distracted myself, and couldn't sit still long enough to write the book. I held a false belief that I didn't have what it takes to finish the project.

I am incredibly glad that I persevered with the support and guidance of my loved ones. Completing a weighty project that took me years positively impacted other areas of my life, too. Although it has been a long, challenging journey to disentangle my identity from my work, I have made good progress. I must admit that I still haven't achieved it fully. There's almost always only one thing holding you back: it's you.

Here is some advice for banishing fear:

- Shift your mindset and immediately shut down negative thoughts that can hold you back.
- Identify a few trusted people with whom you can discuss career moves and fears, and be accountable to them.
- Work on building your confidence and overcoming any feelings of inadequacy.
- Regularly journal your thoughts and feelings to help you stay on track.
- Be bold and take risks, such as saying yes to opportunities that come your way, even if they seem daunting.

Dragon Lady

Early on in my career, I was told by a few senior managers that I was too nice, too soft, and too gentle. One elder colleague 'Susan' put it simply: 'You need to be more of a "bitch".' Several others said I wouldn't make it in journalism because I wasn't tough enough. A work nemesis, 'Justin', was often disrespectful and poked fun at my trusting, Pollyanna-ish way of carrying myself. I didn't learn until much later that Justin was an unhappy person struggling to find his place in the company and was prone to being envious of others doing well. Despite how green I was, I was thriving in my work and had the strong support of my managers.

At that time, I didn't have a coping mechanism or anyone advising me on how to protect myself from people like Justin—the vultures and sharks—though I could spot them a mile away. I didn't learn about this in school. I wasn't very worldly and had been surrounded by people who were largely supportive until then.

In short, I had intellectual knowledge but lacked street smarts and mental toughness. My response to all this unsolicited feedback was to harden my heart. I became jaded and cynical and dug in my heels to prove them wrong. I truly thought I had to be meaner to get ahead and be successful. I was so wrong.

I'm relieved that I had a serendipitous intervention in the form of a mentor who had known me since college and noticed that I was stonier and callous in my interpersonal style. She lovingly called me out, rebuked me, and said, 'That's not who you are.' I examined my actions and decided to make a drastic shift to be gentler.

In hindsight, I don't know what else could have diverted me from the path I was barrelling down to becoming a cold-hearted dragon lady.

What also helped was that I attended a seminar by a therapist who shared the effects of hardening one's heart. The *Readers' Digest* abbreviated version of it was that when we fail to process and heal from life's hurts, we tend to harden our hearts, and that not only keeps the bad out but also prevents us from receiving good things.

Mental toughness is not about being unbreakable and suppressing emotions when faced with a crisis. As the writer Roy T. Bennett said, 'The hard lessons of life are meant to make you better, not bitter.'

These factors have helped me develop mental fortitude:

- Consider adversity as a stepping stone towards improvement.
- Look at the situation from a broader or aerial perspective to gain new insights.
- Face fear instead of avoiding it.
- Develop the ability to discern others' motives and learn whom to trust.
- Acknowledge even small accomplishments as progress.

'Kim Jong Sue'

The challenges I faced in toxic work environments with abusive bosses and catty colleagues seemed insurmountable at the time. Yet, in hindsight, I realize that these taxing experiences were actually instrumental in catalysing my personal growth. Surprisingly, they helped me turn my weaknesses into strengths and toughened me up in unimaginable ways.

I had an extremely toxic boss in Hong Kong who was an expat. Susan was so unbearable that I used to call her 'Kim Jong Sue' as a way to relieve the tension and for comic relief in a miserable office.

However, there were moments when the comparison to a North Korean dictator seemed too kind to describe her narcissistic ways. During my first month, I was enthusiastic and eager to exceed my personal goals in a role I enjoyed. However, Susan had an innate talent for picking on my work to the point of shredding it and making me feel like I couldn't complete even basic tasks properly.

She often criticized my work by suggesting that since I was ethnically Korean, I didn't have a good grasp of English. This jab was below the belt and she knew it. I had told her from the beginning that I grew up in Canada from age two and was fluent in English. I had also intentionally stopped learning Korean and speaking it from a young age because I wanted to fit in with my Caucasian schoolmates. Her microaggression was demoralizing, all the more so because I knew I had made no big mistakes.

At the time, I failed to comprehend that Susan was manipulating me with her 'gaslighting' behaviour. It appeared that she enjoyed belittling us to make herself feel more significant and indispensable. However, when I shared my experience with the HR manager, she suggested that I simply ignore "batty old" Susan's eccentric behaviour and concentrate on my work instead.

The truth is, she acted that way because she was highly insecure. Like a puppet master, she often played us against each other instead of celebrating our talents and empowering us to work together as a team. The entire office was divided into rival gangs, inter-departmental conflicts, or huge rows on the same team, with vicious fighting almost daily.

Her modus operandi included gossiping, and no one was immune from petty attacks that included snickering about our clothes and appearance. She once mocked my eyebrows as looking too dark, like the singer Cher's, and called my purple dress a 'Peter Pan' outfit. I stayed silent because I knew she was unhinged and drinking bottles of hard liquor every night.

Nearly every day, she would call someone 'useless' or 'incapable' after magnifying the slightest mistakes into full-blown judgements. One of her favourite things to do was to give us an assignment only to change her mind after we had spent an entire day on it. No one trusted her and we learned how to manage up, meaning we had to unite and steer her in a particular direction to prevent wasting time.

Despite my 'Canadian-ness', I was raised in a home with Korean cultural values, which meant respecting and honouring my elders was fundamental. Therefore, I struggled with how to respond to the toxicity from my leader for several months. I began to feel weary and lost my joy and confidence. There came a watershed moment when I knew it was becoming too unhealthy for me to have to constantly manage my boss. After another round of cruel criticism, I stood my ground and spoke the truth. This time, Susan was shocked. Something within me shifted seismically and I was ready to leave.

The glimmer of hope that stood out to me in all my reading on this topic was that capable people usually walk away onto a better path—though often only if they had processed well and learned from their experiences.

This terrible experience helped refine me into a more patient and empathetic person. They say we learn the most about leadership from bad managers. Working for Susan gave me practical insight into what not to do as a leader. Just like how gold can only be refined in the fire, it tested my mettle through brutal trials, ultimately preparing me and giving me longer wings to handle more challenging roles. Looking back, I see it as an invaluable cocoon time before a butterfly transformation.

Through the silly conflicts between colleagues, I learned to see a situation from a bird's eye view rather than get mired in the quicksand on the ground in times of conflict or politics. I learned to speak at the right time instead of getting exhausted and distracted by minor squabbles with foolish people.

Integrity matters. I tried to stay true to my values and principles when faced with gossip and politics. I wasn't successful at all times. But I strove to be. And that's what matters.

Staying Humble

Humility is an underrated yet essential virtue. I grasped its value years ago when I worked for a family foundation that generously donated millions of dollars to worthy causes. Despite their philanthropic work, they intentionally chose to remain low-key and did not have a website promoting their donations. They did not seek recognition or want any buildings or reports named after them.

They even requested that their giving be kept confidential in the spirit of 'Don't let your left hand know what your right hand is doing,' (Matthew 6:3 from the Bible). Their humility was a lesson I will never forget.

I had the privilege of working with Ken Kregel, one of the foundation's senior executives, who was humble, kind, and supportive. Collaborating with him and his team was one of the most rewarding work experiences, as I learned a great deal about responsible grant direction and fund management. In contrast, my former boss, Susan, stood out for her arrogant behaviour.

In today's world, it's common practice to promote oneself and share what you do and where you work at any gathering. Self-promotion is de rigueur and considered necessary to make connections and get ahead. When I started my career, friends advised me to learn the art of self-promotion and project self-confidence. However, there were times when my behaviour came across as bragging and entitled, unable to strike the right balance. It's said that arrogance is like body odour—you're the last to know you have it.

Communication is much more subtle in Asia. I have learned to adopt the communication style of the Asians here, which often means elevating someone else's expertise and not promoting my own experience. However, this is not to be done in a disingenuous way.

I have always admired the humility of the former UN Secretary-General Ban Ki-Moon, who personifies 'service before self'. During a trip to the United Nations in 2009, a diplomat once told me that Mr Ban values humility the most in a person. At that time, I didn't fully understand the significance of this statement.

Humility can be liberating. It allows us to learn from others, acknowledge our mistakes, and see the best in others. Humility avoids conflict and does not self-promote or put others down. Instead, it lifts others up and enables us to work together. It is a peacemaker and a healer.

My husband Matt once co-wrote a screenplay with a writer, Murray Watts, who rarely spoke of the numerous industry awards he had won or his Cambridge degree. Murray was very modest. Despite his towering reputation in the field, he remained humble and treated me as an equal when he provided feedback on my initial screenplay. I was apprehensive about my writing then, but his soft-spoken guidance and mentoring encouraged me to continue pursuing my passion.

Workplace humility is often perceived as a weakness, but it can improve teamwork. This quality is like a muscle that needs to be exercised in order to grow. One way to do this is to be aware of your own shortcomings and appreciate the competence of others. It's important to differentiate between self-confidence and arrogance. You should strive to add value to others and understand that success has a shadow side. Further, it's crucial to be grateful for what you have.

As Melanie Koulouris, a writer, once said, 'Be humble in your confidence, yet courageous in your character.'

Control on Steroids

In every office, there's that one control freak.

In the office I shared with Kim Jong-Sue, it was 'Carrie', her executive assistant. Susan was often on the verge of firing Carrie. It was terrible judgement that she didn't because Carrie wreaked havoc in the office and was responsible for some of the ugliest office politics. Carrie was a hyper control freak. She made it her business to take over and micromanage whatever she could. If she wasn't in control, she unknowingly or knowingly tried to sabotage the earnest efforts of others.

What made it worse was that she was mean and would bark belittling insults at others in the same vein as our toxic boss, Susan. Everyone in the company faked small talk to give her face and avoid her ugly wrath.

Her toxicity was all-consuming, and I felt like I needed a bath every time I spoke to her, even for only a few minutes. In the early days, I dreaded her micromanaging my work. I wondered how to manage and stop her controlling ways that inexplicably strangled good sense and intelligent work—all because she was so fearful of losing her job. Surprisingly, she once revealed that she had little savings and lived paycheque to paycheque.

Although I was inexperienced and naive at the time, I had an instinctive feeling that the problem at work was more profound and rooted in a much deeper problem in Carrie and also required addressing something within myself. I used to take rudeness as a personal attack, but I perceived that this was something that I also needed to change within myself.

During a meeting, Carrie broke down in tears and expressed her frustration with our CEO, seeking reassurance from the group. She revealed that she was incredibly insecure and unhappy. It was a big revelation at the time. I dug a little deeper and discovered that she had experienced severe abuse during her childhood. This newfound knowledge made me more compassionate towards her, overtaking my initial irritation. My eyes opened to see beyond the behaviour or actions and to never judge a book by its cover because there is usually more going on beneath the surface.

Whenever someone is mean or nasty, there may be other factors at play that I am unaware of. I also was conscious that I needed to work on my response to micromanagement and remain calm when my work is unfairly torn apart. It is frustrating and mindboggling when someone tries to control everything and becomes hellbent on destruction when things don't go their way. But I have come to appreciate the words of author Robert Tew, 'Don't let negative and toxic people rent space in your head. Raise the rent and kick them out!'

Here are some valuable lessons that I have learned:

- If you encounter someone with a challenging or narcissistic personality, it is crucial to understand the basic signs and characteristics of this type of personality. Narcissists are primarily self-centred and lack empathy, so it is important to understand what motivates them.

- To avoid any unnecessary interactions, try to reduce any possible contact with them.
- It is best not to gossip with or about them.
- If they turn on you, having a plan to deal with them is important. It is essential to stand your ground and assert yourself. Approach them only when you are calm and have control over your emotions.
- Finally, it is important to let go of anything that they may have done to hurt you and forgive them. This will prevent them from infecting your life and relationships outside the office.

Years later, I knew I had fully digested these lessons when my friend 'Sara' described her nightmare client, Audrey. Sara is an eloquent, confident, and highly successful senior banking executive and was a Cambridge-educated debater. Audrey would single Sara out on each conference call with the team and reserve the choicest criticisms just for her to trash her work.

This client's constant, unreasonable demands and bullying lingered long after Sara's work day ended, ruining her evenings and weekends. She became increasingly frazzled and agitated at home with her husband.

It got to the point where Sara was always unhappy because of Audrey's belittling despite welcoming her first child and hitting every milestone of success. It hit its zenith one day when she boarded a plane after one of those calls and felt mortified after breaking down and crying on the flight.

I understood her situation all too well. I shared similar experiences of how toxic bosses and colleagues had a weird control over my emotions and brought a dark cloud over me. I urged her never to let another person's bad behaviour have control over her again. To never allow her client to steal her happiness.

I reminded her that no matter how tough the situation may seem, she still holds the power to choose her response.

For years, I, too, had struggled to shake off a mean response from a colleague or a random stranger who was either 'nuts' or having a bad day.

For instance, if someone at work said something nasty, my angry response would often leave me irritable and affect the rest of my day. When I would discuss the incident with my husband, Matt, and friends, they would tell me that it reflected on the other person, not me. 'Don't take it personally and ignore them,' they would say. But that didn't work for me and failed to stop me from being triggered the next time something similar happened.

I began seeking this unflappability years ago—I so desperately wanted it for myself. I didn't like reacting with anger and irritability to bad manners. I didn't want to respond in the same vein. But how?

After a long search, I have come to believe it stems from an inner peace rooted in knowing who you are. A peaceful acceptance of self.

Tips on Finding Peace

Achieving one's full potential is a lifelong process. Here are some lessons I learned on my journey that may be helpful to you.

- Always seek inner peace and learn to love, forgive, and accept yourself.
- Be kind to others, even those who are unkind to you, because you never know the trials and pain they may be going through.
- Forgive instantly and let go of negative emotions. Holding on to negativity can spread like a speck of black paint in water.
- One technique I use is to say a prayer and touch the top of my head, asking God to remove all negative forces from my head down to the tip of my toes, washing them away.
- Another useful tactic when someone is acting badly is to pause and ask them whether they are okay because often their actions are motivated by something else that is happening in their life that may be feeding their fear and insecurity.

Let It Go

Have faith during transition seasons.

After quitting a toxic boss, I found myself in a transition, where one door had closed, but I was still waiting for the next one to open. I felt paralysed with fear and dread about the future. I also experienced performance anxiety as I embarked on a new project for which I didn't have the experience.

I remember my first few months in Hong Kong. I spent my sabbatical on an idyllic island to finish editing one of my books. I didn't have a full-time job yet and the pressure to find one was growing every week.

After networking during the day to find my next job opportunity, I remember taking the ferry and walking to my place on top of a hill through a narrow path in the forest in the pitch dark. I often wondered if I had made a mistake leaving behind my familiar surroundings and community in Beijing. Not too long after, a job serendipitously fell in my lap with the help of a friend. This city has been a place of tremendous personal development and I met my wonderful husband Matt here.

On another occasion, when I was working on an idea for a feature film and wrote the script, I felt insecure, as I had no idea what I was doing. I didn't know how to produce a film, but I went on Zoom calls with seasoned Hollywood executives and film producers during the pandemic, and with each meeting, I learned something new.

Several years ago, I was asked to give a keynote speech at a large conference. Although I had never given one to a large crowd before, I agreed to do it. One year, I also said yes to every speaking gig that came my way. Although I regretted saying yes at least half an hour before every talk I gave, I always felt so grateful for my 'year of saying yes' after it was all over. I grew so much from pushing myself to learn and take on new assignments.

Challenging myself to grow and embrace discomfort was the best thing that happened to me. It forced me to get out of my comfort zone, and my confidence increased as I began to work towards a seemingly impossible goal in my mind.

During transitions, one of the reasons for feeling fearful is the loss of control. Anxiety arises from the unknowns and the possibility of 'what ifs'. However, it has always worked out in the end. I have never been stuck in a rut. God has never left me twisting in the wind and has always been there to guide me.

Trusting in the timing of your life is crucial. As the book of Ecclesiastes says, 'There is a time for everything and a season for every activity under heaven.'

Some seasons are extremely busy and productive, some seasons are quiet and enjoyable. Letting go and releasing control is how you make the most of these seasons, your time on earth. When I know a change is coming, I remind myself to have faith in my abilities and trust that everything will work out. It usually does, often better than expected. Still, old mindsets die hard, and I must remain vigilant and work on them.

What has helped me immensely is reflecting on the changes within myself. I ask myself questions such as: Who am I becoming? Are my goals, values, and ways of working transforming too? What is causing the fear of new things and how can I conquer it?

Going through a change in life—be it in your career, family, finances, relationships, or any other aspect—means you have entered into a transition or threshold season. During this time, it helps to make a conscious decision to strive less and to let things happen more organically. Personally, I've found that whatever was meant to come my way, would happen. This was like adopting a spiritual mindset that a bigger plan was falling into place, even if I couldn't initially see or understand it.

As a result, I hustled less, didn't forcefully push to achieve my goals, and instead chose to work with people I had a natural affinity with. I was less uptight and not as driven by my usual Type A personality. Surprisingly, taking this free and easy-going approach has given me a more profound sense of peace and even more joy. Previously, I used to worry about missing out on opportunities, now I feel greater confidence knowing I don't have to sweat the small stuff.

In my younger days, I used to roll my eyes or wonder what my elders meant when they would say, 'Timing is everything.' But, eventually, I have come to appreciate the importance of the right time. Another quote from Ecclesiastes says, 'The race is not to the swift, nor the battle to the strong, nor bread to the wise, nor riches to men of understanding. Time and chance happen to all.'

There are different ways of understanding this. One might be that however much you try to ensure a particular outcome—however fast or strong you become, however much you chase perfection—there are factors that will remain beyond your control. Understanding this can bring you peace.

If that sounds defeatist, consider the flipside. That with the right timing, you can achieve things you never thought possible and your best actions will not be wasted. You may not be the strongest, but you may yet win the battle if time and chance are on your side.

For nearly two decades, I have juggled a two-track career in philanthropy, and journalism and film-making, juggling both careers simultaneously. Being a workaholic, I always worked the equivalent of two full-time jobs. Sometimes, I was more involved in working for family offices and foundations while, at other times, film-making, writing books, and journalism took precedence.

I was constantly worrying about the future and hyperfocused on what was next. It took away the enjoyment of the moment and prevented me from going with the flow. It was like trying to ride a camel out of sync, without swaying in the rhythm of the animal's gait and then wondering why it was such a bumpy ride.

The older Sylvia has learned to chill out and stop worrying about what's next. Instead, I go with the flow and have a restful attitude, knowing that things are unfolding as they're meant to—in the fullness of time.

My Advice for Transitions

- Abandon yourself to the change and go all in.
- Laugh often and try to maintain a positive attitude.
- Don't look back, keep moving forward, and let go of the perfectionist within.

- Shut that critical voice down and tell yourself to expect great things. Have faith to fly and soar higher than you thought possible—you can and you must!

Personally, I always want to dare greatly and to become more carefree and relaxed. I want to be a big kid again and truly enjoy my work and life. To say goodbye to anxiety and stress, and hello to more transformational, life-changing shifts that help me reach the next level of my potential.

You can, too. You just need to take that first step and start the journey towards your dreams.

Chapter 11

Adversity: What Doesn't Kill You, Makes You Stronger

I had a premonition it would be no ordinary appointment. My husband Matt's urologist had asked to see him in person the week before. As soon as Matt sat down, there was no small talk, only the precise dropping of a bomb, 'You have prostate cancer.'

Matt drew in his breath, and it sounded like someone had punched him in the gut.

I gasped and felt a lump in my throat constricting my breathing.

The rest of that meeting was a blur—there was talk of the various surgery options and the recovery time. However, I cannot remember the details due to the shock of the C-word. Both of us were numb as we walked home in silence, lost in our thoughts and drowning in fear. One of our biggest immediate concerns was Matt's risk of deadly blood clots, which ran in his family. This terrified us—his mother had died from one after a simple back surgery.

For a week, we did nothing. It was one of the darkest times in our married life. Matt and I felt paralysed for the first time since we had known each other. We are usually go-getters and swift to act on anything. Yet, this time, we felt hopeless, and the future looked bleak. How we managed to function each day and put one foot in front of the other remains a mystery to me.

Matt asked me not to tell anyone and this was the hardest part for me, an extrovert who liked to process verbally. It made me depressed to not be able share my husband's cancer with anyone other than our closest friends and family. He coped by writing his will in meticulous detail, sticking it in a large binder and saving it on a hard drive. He withdrew emotionally and became depressed. I ate cakes and junk and steadily gained weight.

Also dragging us down was that we had recently joined a dysfunctional church group upon the recommendation of a friend. The members were rather cold and had formed a tight, unpleasant clique. We had shared Matt's diagnosis with one of the leaders, 'Brenda', a fellow cancer survivor, and asked her to keep it confidential, only to have her blurt it out near the end of a meeting. One of the leaders then asked everyone to pray for Matt, however, the prayers were rushed and not heartfelt at all. We both felt hurt by the lack of empathy at our most vulnerable moment. We left that group soon after, and I wasn't surprised when the leaders later left the church.

On the day of Matt's surgery, we talked about light topics, prayed, and hugged several times before the nurses wheeled him away. Because of his blood clot risk, Matt had processed his deepest anxieties and was ready to face death.

I was a basket case and a bundle of strung-out nerves. I had hardly slept a wink by the time he was wheeled back into his hospital room nearly three hours later. He was alive and the tumour had been removed.

That was all that mattered. That was also the moment my head hit the pillow in the cot near him, and I slept soundly for the first time since his diagnosis.

After we returned home, Matt had stitches and a catheter to deal with. I was always on call and helped him with meals and bathing and took on all the household tasks. After several months of being the sole carer for Matt, I began to burn out.

This was exacerbated by Matt, who still didn't want to share his illness, forcing me to carry a painful secret about his cancer. There is a kind of emotional purgatory that comes when you must silence what you want to scream about. I knew that I was really burnt out during a conversation with a stranger who asked me about the cancer journey, and I couldn't stop crying for fifteen minutes.

After that, I began freely sharing what I had been through with others and felt cathartic relief. After the weeping, a peace came over my empty soul, my wandering heart. Emotional depth is carved out in tough times. In times of uncertainty, who we really are and what we're made of emerges.

Rebirth

My friend 'Winnie', a cancer survivor encouraged me by sharing, 'After going through the shock of the diagnosis and after the surgery and chemotherapy, I began to feel grateful for having cancer. I see it as a gift.' It wasn't until many months later that I could fully make sense of the meaning of her words.

Neither Matt nor I could see the way forward. However, Winnie embodied her message—she was inspiring, strong, and deep in her thinking and compassion. I have never seen anyone else with her empathy for cancer patients. She gave me hope right when I needed it.

Ultimately, it took around a year for us to find our feet again and to come out of the shadows of the cloud that a life-threatening illness could bring on. We both journaled and released all the negative emotions during the cancer journey and accepted our 'new normal'. We found that what used to hold us back before no longer did because we had faced death and prevailed over the fear.

Our agonizing experience taught us what truly mattered. It was a new beginning, a new drive, new priorities. Our fear was gone. It reminded me of what the Everest climber Edmund Hillary once said, 'It's not the mountain we conquer, it's ourselves.'

How can we learn these principles without going through something so traumatic as cancer? What we had assumed was the worst thing that could happen to us was actually the best thing. It was like beauty rising from the ashes, a reminder that fear stands for 'false evidence appearing real'.

In our busy schedules, we are easily distracted. Things that seem important, like making a lot of money, success, and status are trivial and meaningless when you're faced with death. What matters are the people you love.

Without a doubt, my husband Matt's cancer surgery was a life-changing experience. It helped us identify what to invest our time in and clarified our goals. It was a type of rebirth. We faced a life-or-death scenario, which gave me a more profound perspective, and I began to care less about the little things. Hardship transformed us.

This life-changing trauma gave me new insights, activated my creativity, and helped me focus on the projects I wanted to accomplish. I had one of the most productive periods in my career soon after. I published a memoir, *A Long Road to Justice*, wrote a film script, and was invited to speak at corporations and universities. This newfound drive helped me thrive during the pandemic. I was very productive and had regular online speaking engagements and began developing TV and film projects.

Adversity is an inevitable part of the human experience. It comes in various forms, testing our resilience and determination. It can be defined as any hardship, obstacle, or setback that individuals encounter on their life journeys and can manifest as personal struggles, external challenges, or unexpected crises.

However, it is in the face of disaster that our true character shines.

How else did I benefit from adversity? It triggered post-traumatic growth. It helped me find the good in terrible situations and reframe stress as a challenge to be risen to. Going through misfortune teaches us about ourselves, about being uncomfortable, and how to endure. Without it, we may never discover our inner fortitude.

In the wise words of Walt Disney, 'All the adversity I've had in my life, all my troubles and obstacles, have strengthened me . . . You may not realize it when it happens, but a kick in the teeth may be the best thing in the world for you.'

Indeed, difficulties change us. If we process heartbreak well, it can transform us for the better. Affliction and suffering can influence us by pushing us to be our best selves and to strive towards our goals with greater resolve. It can also teach us invaluable lessons and help us grow and develop.

I was seven when my father's first business failed. It was right before my parents split.

That fateful day, the bank ordered our family car to be seized. It was a real shock to see the tow-truck drag away our car, but it was even more distressing to feel my parents' pain. Their worst fears had come true. They were unsure how to pay the rent and put food on the table. Since that moment of turmoil and despair, I struggled for a while and felt lost.

After seeing my mother's quiet will power not succumb to discouragement and give up, a will to fight rose within me. I stood my ground and vowed never to be helpless in my life ever again and to support my parents. I grew up that day.

That shocking experience has increased my empathy for those going through difficulties and has helped me forge a deeper connection with others. It has given me a sense of gratefulness and taught me not to focus on what's missing in my life or look at things with a critical spirit. Above all, it's made me more thankful for the many blessings in my life.

Overcoming Heartache

The airport in Beijing was abuzz with the usual hordes of people dragging their luggage, tickets in hand, in search of their boarding gate. I walked through the main terminal disconnected from the five virtual strangers who were travelling with me, team members from the US and India.

We were on a mission to host a conference in Kunming, in Yunnan province, China, with a group of people working in non-profit organizations. A manager, Carol, was getting on my nerves with her passive-aggressive streak. She felt insecure in her new role because the other expat team members in China had made it clear they were not pleased with her inexperience. I disliked her pettiness, even though I knew I, too, could be petty when irritable or tired. She was disturbing my peaceful bubble.

That day, in the spring of 2007, I had barely held myself together. I had a plastic perma-smile on my face, but inside, my head felt a dull pulsating strain, and sharp pains bombarded my heart like sheets of heavy rain. I was separating from my ex-husband at the time. Just weeks before, I was hyperventilating as it dawned on me that I was getting divorced. He didn't love me anymore. I did not love him either. But the very act of failing sent me reeling. I had an aversion to it. As a performance-oriented perfectionist, I had never spectacularly failed at anything.

I had learned of his deception and cheating only by chance, through 'Meg', a friend from church. Meg knew the other woman, 'Tonya', well because they were in the same church home group. Meg was the leader of that group and Tonya had talked about her latest relationship with mixed emotions for months. One night, she confessed to the affair and said she was feeling guilty about it. When Tonya mentioned where the mystery man was living and when he'd got married, Meg suddenly detected to her horror that Tonya was talking about my then husband and let her know what she had just twigged.

Meg told me that Tonya looked horrified when she was confronted and Meg urged her to end the adulterous relationship. But Tonya continued her affair, and for weeks Meg sat on this information, pondering when to inform me.

When she finally did, rather than being angry, I was grateful. I had long suspected my husband was cheating, but the chances of me happening upon the other woman had seemed like finding a needle in a haystack.

It felt like a miracle and I cried tears of relief to have closure finally. I confronted my husband about it and there was absolutely no way he could deny it. I told him that I was relieved that our marriage was officially over.

These were the memories haunting me as I boarded that plane in Beijing. For some reason, I was seated in business class, away from everyone else, and I was soon alone with my head leaning against the window, overwhelmed by sorrow.

Tears flowed. I had to stifle the sobs and had used every inch of the balled-up tissue in my hand.

The next three days were full of group lunches, breakout groups, and a morning speech. Evenings alone were a relief. I managed to push through the pain until the end of the three-day business trip. Every passing hour seemed unbearable.

In hindsight, refocusing on work helped me avoid drowning in my emotions. I was re-energized by a new desire to make my life count for something by practising philanthropy. To live not wastefully or uselessly but purposefully—to help others in dire need.

One perspective that I've come to embrace is to appreciate the setbacks in my life. Hitting rock bottom is a great teacher. These experiences are more valuable than all the gold in the world and some of the best MBAs. They lead to wisdom, discernment, and insight, and money can't buy that. No one can teach these things—they come from lived experience and overcoming heartbreak, difficulties, sorrow, and immense personal challenges.

For so long, I had been searching for myself, for identity, purpose, and meaning. I found it when I dedicated my life to doing meaningful work. That is, when I began to live to help others who were suffering instead of living a self-absorbed life. I've found true happiness and joy in giving my time, talents, and resources to serve and support those in need and empower vulnerable women everywhere.

Rock bottom became a greenhouse for new dreams and new visions for me. Experiencing acute anguish helped clarify my priorities like few things could. I pondered how I wanted to live. I found I wanted most to impact others. I began shifting my mindset from a shattered sense of self-worth due to a failed marriage to discovering I had so much to offer others.

I became passionate about helping women appreciate their self-worth and fighting against sex trafficking. In helping others, I could stop being self-conscious and place my own struggles into perspective. I had a renewed appreciation for life that brought joy in the same measure in the opposite direction. I wanted to have more fun and more work–life balance.

I strongly believe that facing challenges and difficulties leads to success. Adversity teaches us to learn from our mistakes, ask tough questions, take responsibility, and avoid obsessing over our gaffes. Whether they are in our professional, academic, or personal lives, obstacles and failures allow us to develop grit and courage. How we respond to unexpected outcomes and difficult situations determines our progress.

We can either let hardships hold us back or use them as stepping stones towards our goals. Our attitude towards catastrophe shapes us into better, stronger people.

Another insight I had was the importance of prioritizing self-care—physically, mentally and emotionally. While I was healing from the divorce, I was depressed and had a heavy fatigue that is difficult to describe in words. I had no motivation to do anything beyond send a few emails daily. It was a murky and challenging time. I had a similar fatigue during the pandemic while waiting for some semblance of normalcy to return and solidify under my feet.

I began to make a point of resting on Saturdays—a habit that has since become non-negotiable. This day of uninterrupted rest is what I need to replenish my creativity and energy. It enables me to be more present and caring in my relationships and at work.

In the summer, it's therapeutic to spend time at the beach on gorgeous days and watch the sun's bright rays glance off the monochromatic sand and sparkle on the aquamarine water or listen to the soothing rhythm of the choppy waves. Wispy clouds, the smell of briny water, waves crashing, and a Toni Onley-esque mountain backdrop. Who could ask for anything more?

Find your happy place and be kind to yourself.

Anne of Green Gables said it best, 'Tomorrow is a brand new day with no mistakes in it.'

Breaking Barriers

One of the most formative experiences I've ever had was being a caregiver to a brilliant PhD student, Joy. She was paralysed and confined to an electric wheelchair and needed care around the clock. Joy couldn't walk or move her arms due to an illness in her childhood.

I was nineteen, studying at university, and looking for a part-time job. I saw an advertisement for a part-time caregiver to a disabled graduate student and was intrigued. I applied and was invited to interview with

Joy. We hit it off like a house on fire. She told me that this role required that I be on hand in the mornings to help her go to the toilet and give her dinner already prepared in the evenings. I couldn't toast sliced bread without burning it at this stage, so I was relieved I wouldn't be called to use my non-existent cooking skills.

In the middle of the night, I had to turn her over to prevent bed sores that could form if she slept on one side for too long. I would have to bathe her as well. She had another part-time support staff to cook meals and do other errands.

In my gut, I felt this job would help me grow in ways that I needed to, and besides, it offered housing and the salary was considerably more than a student usually makes. I told my mother about this potential opportunity, and she told me not to take it because it would be too taxing. After wavering because of my mother's objections, I took a leap and told Joy I would be happy to work for her.

The two years I worked with Joy were a masterclass in breaking barriers and conquering difficulties. She had a metal rod in her spine, and it was potentially life-threatening if she moved her neck too fast or was ever in an accident. She also had a handful of pills to keep her other illnesses at bay and prevent her legs from swelling like balloons. Despite these challenges, Joy was upbeat and happy all the time. Nothing could bring her down.

Her mind was brilliant and she dreamed of teaching students after finishing her PhD. The only part of Joy's body that she could move was her hand and she typed her doctorate thesis with the end of a pencil, one letter key at a time. I was astonished each time I saw Joy typing at her computer daily. I was ashamed of my last-minute cramming study habits. Joy's extraordinary grit lit a fire within me and showed me that no goal was impossible and no obstacle was too great. She was heroic in the way she persevered with grace and humour.

I matured in ways I wouldn't have because of the heavy responsibility of waking up at night to attend to Joy. If I had missed just one night, it would have put her life at risk. I had never had that kind of life-or-death responsibility before, and it was sobering. As I interacted daily with a mature and wise roommate, I also developed emotional intelligence. Her wisdom began to influence me. I had to learn to manage my stress and frustrations in front of Joy, so as not to add to her burden. This new restraint helped me stay calm and objective in high-pressure situations.

Due to my well-paying job, I was able to assist other students who were in need by buying backpacks or food, as well as hosting dinners for large groups of people. Giving generously has always been a core value for me and it always will be.

I met Joy when I was in need of a role model, and she changed my life. She cleared every obstacle in her way and achieved her dream of earning a PhD and becoming a teacher. It would not have been surprising if she had given up, but despite her disabilities, she blazed a trail and set a powerful example that with determination, you can achieve the impossible.

Witnessing her triumph over her physical limitations motivated me to reassess my priorities and values and helped me identify what truly matters.

Forgiveness Fosters Freedom

Many years ago, I had the opportunity to meet and interview 'Hua' for my memoir and documentary on sex trafficking in China. Her story was unforgettable. Hua was in her thirties, with a petite build and olive skin, hailing from a minority group in Yunnan province, China. Born into an impoverished farming family with six daughters, she was forced to leave her village at a young age to find work in the city and support her parents.

She was tricked into forced prostitution by other young women who had been working with her as waitresses at a restaurant. They flaunted their money and counted the bills before her, but she had no idea how they made that much. She later learned they were paid a commission for deceptively recruiting her.

Hua agreed to join their venture and followed them to a building. That's when trafficker thugs, from the local mafia, locked her in a room with a man who stole her virginity. From then on, she was imprisoned in the room and forced to sleep with men. If she didn't comply, the goons would beat her. She experienced hatred for the first time in her life.

She had grown up on a rural farm and before her enslavement had had a simple and naive way of looking at the world. As a girl, her parents had warned her never to hold hands with a man in case she got pregnant. Because of her upbringing, she had no coping mechanisms to deal with the terrible things that happened to her and was left utterly traumatized.

Twenty other girls were with Hua in the locked brothel compound, surrounded by vicious guard dogs. All of them had been tricked and deceived into selling their bodies. One girl was fourteen-years-old and five of the young women were from Vietnam. 'I was like a sex slave. I wept at night. Every girl lived in fear,' Hua recalled. She noticed that the Vietnamese women were treated the worst and beaten more often than the women from mainland China.

All over the world, when it comes to sex trafficking, there exists a cruel and racist caste system in which White or fair-skinned women can charge more money from johns than darker-skinned women. The same racist system was used in the sexual slavery system implemented by the Japanese military during World War II, which I have raised awareness about in my speeches and articles over the years.

It was not until the police suddenly raided the compound one day that Hua and others escaped out the front door. She found odd jobs to eke out a living. But she still was not truly free. One day, her mother called to say that her father was ill and needed a new heart soon, but the operation would cost hundreds of thousands of dollars. After wrestling with the decision, Hua chose to sell her body to help pay for the life-saving surgery. She continued to do so for several years until her father died.

Soon after, a group of women from a Christian non-profit, Door of Hope, contacted her and offered her job training and trauma healing. She was pregnant then and was blown away by their kindness and unconditional love as they promised to care for her and her baby. They helped transform her life.

She said her greatest breakthrough came the day she decided to forgive her traffickers and every man who had ever raped her and used her. 'I was set free,' she said. Hua finally allowed herself to become who she'd always been—she was no longer a slave to hatred and unforgiveness. She hoped her story of transformation would help other women trapped in forced prostitution.

Hua's miraculous ability to forgive the ones who violated her is a critical aspect of dealing with suffering—forgiveness can free us from the shackles of bitterness and hatred after tragedies and horrible calamities.

Forgiveness also makes you stronger when facing challenges. It can also have potent health benefits, according to a study by the Harvard Medical School that suggests it lowers your chances of depression, anxiety, hostility, and substance abuse, and boosts feelings of self-esteem and well-being. Those who are more forgiving of others are likely to have higher levels of empathy, be more open-minded towards new perspectives, and extend more positive feelings towards people in general.

Forgiveness can help us move forward with meaning and a more positive outlook on life. If you face troubles now, it's important to do all you can to overcome them. Take heart from the fact that whatever doesn't kill you can make you more determined. I encountered this personally only a short time after meeting Hua.

My Near-Death Experience

The day I was nearly killed in China was one of the most harrowing experiences I've ever had. I was in the middle of a notorious red-light district in Yunnan province.

This was a place with no streetlamps. It was so dark outside. All you could see were the glittering pink lights of the brothel areas and a smattering of makeshift stalls selling food and electronics.

I was there to film a documentary on sex trafficking and to research a book I was writing. A missionary named 'Amy' advised me to walk through the dark alley and film it with my phone while pretending to be texting someone.

I found her request rather odd but decided to place my trust in her. After all, here was a woman with several years of experience rescuing women from the clutches of sexual exploitation in deadly red-light areas.

I saw dozens of women in the buildings with sad, empty eyes and heavy makeup behind a glass partition. It was clear they could not leave of their own free will. Unfortunately, despite following Amy's advice, I was spotted. I had hurried back to my car and didn't see anyone following me. Suddenly, a group of scowling thugs and shouting mamasans were outside our car. Despite my shaking hands, I managed to delete the video footage and photos on my phone. I threw a tiny camera into the pocket of the back seat.

'What do we do? Should we drive off?' I said, my voice quivering with terror. My driver, a Chinese American woman, decided it was better to stay put. With dread, I got out of the car. The fierce mamasans and the two young men had pasty white faces and looked menacing enough that my life flashed before my eyes. I imagined we would end up in a ditch somewhere. They accused me of videotaping their girls. The screaming and intimidation continued.

I was speechless, frozen with fear. Then, out of nowhere, a man yelled, 'The police are coming! The police!' With these words, they scattered like cockroaches under a harsh spotlight. It was only later that I learned some of my friends back home had been praying for me at that exact moment.

This was my first miracle.

It was profoundly moving to stand in the shoes of the trafficked women, to feel the danger and terror they face, and to encounter such terrifying individuals myself. For several weeks afterwards, I would often wake up at the slightest creaking sound. I became extremely sensitive to noise and had a hard time falling asleep. It dawned on me that I might have post-traumatic stress and I went into counselling for several months.

This experience gave me even more compassion for women and girls forced into sexual slavery. The ultimate purpose of my trip—to understand more of what these girls suffer in the brothels—had been accomplished.

It enabled me to effectively spotlight the suffering of women and girls so that others could empathize with them. To understand became a theme of my philanthropic initiatives and investigative work on human trafficking.

I had other menacing encounters while I was filming documentaries on sex trafficking. I've sat in creepy brothels interviewing trafficker pimps and trafficked women. One pimp started to look at me with an evil gaze that startled me and I quickly ended our interview. That led me to ask my guide, a humanitarian aid worker, to leave that brothel immediately.

In one red-light district close to Myanmar, where I was doing a site visit for a philanthropist, a giant of a man who seemed seven feet tall came over to intimidate us. I beamed at him and introduced myself as a Korean Canadian tourist. He walked away with a puzzled expression. During that entire visit of the brothels to check on an HIV prevention programme, we could feel his narrowed eyes on us from a distance.

Once, a strange man grabbed me from behind on the streets in Bangkok. On another night, a group of angry African pimps pursued me and my cameraman after we filmed some of their girls. At an infamous hotel in the city, trafficked European women sat in the open like goods for sale. Men would freely come by to pick a woman. I planned to film these women with a tiny camera. Right before I was to walk through the hotel, I was suddenly overwhelmed with fear.

The cameraman with me urged me to go and get it over with. With dread, I walked into the hotel and saw several mamasans, portly women with garish brown eye-shadow and red lips. They were the female pimps. Because I was terrified, the only thing I could think of was asking these women for the time.

Then, I kicked myself for asking such a stupid question in the middle of a dangerous hotel. The mamasans looked at me suspiciously as I turned my body to film them all with the hidden camera, all while holding my breath. I forced a smile, swiftly exited the lobby, and breathed again. We hopped into our van and I asked the driver while looking back at the hotel to see if anyone was tailing us, 'Let's get out of here, fast!'

From these threatening situations, I learned that if I put my mind to it and worked hard, I could achieve my impossible goal of documenting sex trafficking victims on film in China and elsewhere—few had pulled this off before.

You can achieve your impossible dreams too. Never give up and keep pushing forward, even in the face of calamity. Believe in yourself and your abilities.

Forged in the Fire

In my early teens, I read Esther Ahn Kim's memoir, *If I Perish, I Perish* about her surviving brutality and persecution for her Christian faith during World War II (1939–45) and under the brutal Japanese colonization of Korea (1910–45) before the nation was divided into North and South. She was a school teacher in the 1930s when the Japanese ordered every Korean to bow down to Shinto shrines and to pay homage to the emperor as a god—in Christian churches, schools, and other public gathering spaces.

Because of her spiritual and moral convictions, Esther refused to bow to a pagan Japanese Shinto shrine. She was the only one to take this stand while millions of others bowed. She knew her defiance would lead to a prison sentence and eventual death. Yet, she refused to compromise her Christian faith by denying her God.

As she was tortured in the most deplorable conditions in jail, her body grew weak. Yet, she exuded supernatural love towards her jailers and fellow prisoners, winning many over during her nearly six years of incarceration before the end of World War II.

At one point during Esther's incarceration, a violent woman who had murdered her own husband and chopped him into pieces was sent to prison and placed on death row. This prisoner repulsed everyone—all the other inmates and the guards—yet Esther embraced her, prayed for her, and even shared her meagre food portions.

Esther held this woman's feet covered with excrement, warmed them in her bosom, and spoke to her with words of kindness. Esther's love transformed this woman who repented, turned a new leaf, and became a kinder person. When the day of the woman's execution came, she faced it with peace of mind. I wept over Esther's willingness to suffer for what she believed in.

Viktor E. Frankl, a Holocaust survivor and psychiatrist, wrote in his book *Man's Search for Meaning*, 'He who has a why to live for can bear almost any how.'

Esther was a young woman with remarkable courage, the only Asian and Korean female role model I knew of as a teenager, and her powerful memoir left a deep impression on me. Greatness often emerges when individuals find meaning and purpose in their struggles.

Esther reminds me of what Kenny Chan, a book industry pioneer in Singapore, said during my interview with him on LinkedIn: 'The finest and strongest wills are forged in the fiercest of fires.'

After Esther was released from captivity, her book recounting her imprisonment and unwavering faith became a bestseller in Korea, inspiring countless readers that they too could be victorious over tragedy and affliction through perseverance and faith.

Like Esther Ahn Kim, Pastor Son Yang-Won also took a stand and actively resisted the Japanese colonial government's forced worship of the Shinto state religion in Korea. For years, Son led a Presbyterian church for people with leprosy. His church denomination had a policy allowing all church members to bow as a national ritual, but Son had a fiery conviction that he would worship only the God of his Christian faith. He was arrested and imprisoned for more than five years by the Japanese and endured countless beatings before his release at the end of World War II.

Years later, in 1948, before the Korean War broke out in 1950, a Communist mob of youth went to Pastor Son's house. Communists in Korea, like in other nations, oppose all forms of religion and persecute Christians. These youth taunted his two oldest sons and killed them.

Witnesses reported that in their final moments, his sons had worshipped Jesus and urged their killers to believe in God. After hearing the tragic news, Pastor Son broke down and wept. But he did not give in to anger. Instead, Pastor Son said at his sons' funeral that he was thankful that they had died courageously, as martyrs in a dignified manner, by not begging for their lives to be spared. I have often wondered how one could be thankful in any way after the murder of one's children.

Pastor Son wanted to demonstrate the love of Jesus Christ even one step further. He relayed a message to his good friend, a fellow pastor, 'If the killer of my sons gets arrested, please do not allow him to be executed or even get a beating for the crime. Then, I will share the gospel with that person, turn him into a Christian, and adopt him as my own son.'

A young man was indeed later arrested for the murders, and Pastor Son's daughter relayed her father's message. To everyone's shock, the pastor kept to his word, adopting the young man and leading him to faith.

Pastor Son's life of radical love and forgiveness is a witness to true reconciliation with one's worst enemies. At the age of forty-nine, he, too, was martyred for his faith by the Communists in 1950. His story was written in several books and eventually made into an inspirational film in Korea. In South Gyeongsang province, a stunning Son Yang-won Memorial Hall was built to celebrate his values and spirit of resistance, sacrifice and reconciliation.

Years later, in China, I would meet several people, including young women in their twenties, who profoundly changed my life. They were part of a Bible school and woke up at four to pray and study. They had been imprisoned for their Christian faith several times and they reminded me of the heroine I had read about all those years ago, Esther Ahn Kim.

I asked 'Gloria', twenty-seven, how she could be so peaceful in jail. She shrugged her shoulders and said it wasn't a sacrifice at all. My jaw dropped. Her face shone with an unearthly beauty. She had found the secret to true happiness: to live for something worth dying for.

A friend once told me about a Chinese woman pastor, 'Ma', who was jailed years ago for her faith. The highest-ranking prison guard was fanatically fixated on her and showed more hatred for her than any other inmate. She was despised for her Christian faith. This guard beat her, harassed her, and bullied her regularly.

With each blow, Pastor Ma responded with more love and meekness. The guard stepped up the violence until she could see that there was something different and unearthly about Ma. One day, this guard knelt and cried out to know her God. Pastor Ma led her to faith.

Forgiveness melts the most hardened hearts.

Fired

We can all overcome heartbreak. Years ago, I was fired for not agreeing to move to a third-tier city in China. Through the regional director, my CEO had asked me to lead a project and told me that my salary would significantly decrease. I refused and, because he didn't have another qualified candidate, we lost the contract. I became the scapegoat and lost my job.

I was gutted. The shocking part was this boss knew that I was struggling terribly with the aftermath of my divorce. Losing my job compounded the distress I felt from splitting with my first husband around that time. I became even more depressed and felt like a major failure. I lost so much weight that even my skinny jeans were loose on me.

I alternated between anger and self-pity. But with the benefit of hindsight's 20/20 vision, I can see it worked out ultimately for the best. I wouldn't want to work for an employer so devoid of compassion.

The hardship made me tougher and increased my capacity to endure hard things. With the fateful closing of that door, I instead took a sabbatical that allowed me finally to complete my book on Japanese military sexual slavery that I had been working on for more than ten years by that time and was tempted to quit many times.

Because I was free, I was hired by a most incredible executive in charge of a consortium of family foundations. He invested in me and showed me unforgettable kindness that I could never repay in this lifetime.

They say everything happens for a reason. That's so true for my life. Despite my many mistakes over the years, I'm amazed at how I've met the right people at the right time. Things do fall into place as long as you're failing forward—it's accepting the lessons of each failure and applying them as stepping stones to future successes.

Looking back at this period, it gave me the confidence to keep moving onwards, secure in the conviction that, in time, I would make the right connections, take on more challenging projects, and ultimately reach my fullest potential.

If you're struggling through a similar difficulty, I want you to know that on the other side, something amazing awaits. Have patience and hope.

The inventor of the telephone Alexander Graham Bell said, 'When one door closes, another opens, but we often look so long and so regretfully upon the closed door that we do not see the one which has opened for us.'

The Will to Rise Above

Like many of you, I regularly hear my share of bad news. A loved one faces an agonizing wait for an ultrasound test on a liver tumour. A friend is too depressed to work and has been for nearly a year. Another friend with two kids has lost his job. A mentor was diagnosed with breast cancer.

The psychiatrist M. Scott Peck put it brilliantly, 'Life is difficult. This is a great truth, one of the greatest truths. It is a great truth because once we truly see this truth, we transcend it. Once we truly know that life is difficult – once we truly understand and accept it – then life is no longer difficult.'

I wholeheartedly agree. How we respond to life's challenges and our mindset determines everything.

It's critical to speak the truth to ourselves and to others to remind us of the unshakable hope we could have and that we could face the future with courage and even zest for life.

I'm reminded of my depression so many years ago. When I could barely eat and felt like such a failure, I was unable to see the future objectively and all looked bleak. A dark cloud obscured the truth of my situation.

What broke me out of my diseased mindset was when my youngest brother Jae, out of frustration, got angry at me for not recognizing my blessings and for wallowing in my misery. I needed someone to point that out to me. He was a great support to me at this time and we talked often.

His words woke me up from my fog—it was an 'aha' moment and completely shifted my mindset.

The reality was that I had a great job that I loved, loyal friends, and plenty of options.

I also hit a rut when I was in between jobs. I had an intense fear that I wouldn't be able to find another role I loved. I struggled with feeling like a loser without a business card. My identity had become rooted in what I did and not in who I was (I had forgotten, we are human *beings*, not *doings*).

When I got over my gloom, I was able to move forward. As the author Deepak Chopra said, 'The best use of creativity is imagination. The worst use of creativity is anxiety.'

Whenever you feel weighed down and anxious, take a moment to pause and reflect on the things that are going well in your life. Acknowledge and appreciate those positive aspects and remind yourself that you are in a better position than you may realize.

It's vital to take charge of your emotions and be aware of when you are in a negative headspace. Remember that you can choose how you respond to your feelings without letting them control you.

It's imperative to be open to discussing your thoughts with others. Sharing your feelings with others can be a great way to receive and offer support. At any given moment, many other people just like you are facing their own challenges. Life is much better when you consciously choose a positive attitude.

I would not be who I am today without those profound struggles, my humiliations, and my time in the school of 'hard knocks'. My greatest challenge has been overcoming obstacles placed in my way by colleagues or betrayals by so-called friends.

But grappling with these challenges is exactly what made me who I am. I have learned to dig deep within and be secure in who I am and to ignore bad faith actors. I've made many mistakes, but doing so has taught me that when we embrace the lessons from failures to launch forward and refuse to stew in self-pity, our setbacks can be a source of greater tenacity, conviction, and hope.

Learn from the past without letting it define you. Doing so has made me more determined and expanded my capacity to persevere through catastrophe.

When suffering is avoided or kept away from us, it hinders the growth of our character, our learning, creativity, and conviction. The paradox of suffering is that it can serve as a road to greatness. It's in the crucible of hard times that individuals forge their character.

Adversity is a universal experience, one that reminds us we are not alone in facing life's troubles. It fosters empathy and connections with others. Today, I define success as being able to do work that utilizes your talents and motivations. When that work is something you would do for free, it brings deep fulfilment and leads to one's relationships flourishing. What counts most are my family and friends—loving those in my community.

Lastly, though it may be hard to believe, handling success can be more of a challenge than enduring misery. As Thomas Carlyle, the Scottish essayist and historian, once declared: 'Adversity is hard on a man; but for one man who can stand prosperity, there are a hundred that will stand adversity.'

More of us can hang tough through a humiliating demotion than through a promotion in which we are honoured and exalted. Few can remain humble and grounded in the lap of luxury and power and still maintain their spiritual, emotional, and moral equilibrium.

As you pause to reflect on your life, don't just dwell on the hardships you've faced or the times you've come up short. Rather, cherish the moments of triumph when you overcame those obstacles and succeeded. Your life has been a beautiful blend of highs and lows, and both have played an essential role. The highs have given you courage while the lows have nurtured your growth. Therefore, be grateful for every experience that you've been through and for the times of testing. They are what make you amazing. The very thing meant to break us is what makes us stronger and wiser.

Keep pushing yourself forward and never give up because the path you are on is worth the effort.

So, go out there and chase your dreams with passion and purpose, and never forget that you can make a difference in the world.

Epilogue

A Letter to My Younger Self

Dear Younger Self,

As I write this letter, I am filled with a profound sense of awe at the incredible journey you are about to embark on. I have often wondered what I would tell you if I had the chance.

Reflecting on the seasons of my life—your life—has given me a vantage point to see the bigger picture of all that I have gone through and all the forces that have shaped me into the person you are to become.

Tremendous pain, great confusion, breakthroughs, and triumphs. And tears, lots of them. All these have forged the strong and confident woman who writes to you now. Curating these memories has been a great way to explore self-growth. I am no longer mired in the weeds that can obscure the true meaning of all our experiences.

Life is full of ups and downs. If I could press refresh and restart my life all over again, I simply wouldn't. I have come to embrace all the highs and lows, the peaks and troughs, the valleys and the mountaintops of my life—these are what make us who we are. The only way to become self-assured and confident in our identity is to face obstacles, rejection, and adversity.

If I had veered slightly to the left or right and made different choices, my life would be completely different today. Every milestone, trial, and painful experience has helped shape me into who I am. I'm not perfect, but that's okay.

If I could travel back in time and have a heartfelt conversation with you, my younger self, I would share invaluable insights about the journey you are about to embark on. My personal experiences have shaped these insights, and I hope they will serve as a guiding light on your path to understanding the complexities of life.

You possess a potential you are unaware of yet, but you were born with a purpose and a destiny. This potential is limitless—it comprises your untapped abilities, unexplored talents, and unused success. It is the sum total of who you are that remains unexplored.

Just like a seed has the potential to grow into a tree or even a forest, you have the power to become something greater, to touch the lives of others and to make a difference in this world.

If I could give you some pearls of wisdom for the exciting journey ahead, here's what they would be:

- Believe in yourself. Love yourself. Enjoy hanging out with yourself.
- Be a lifelong student. Keep learning and evolving.
- Stay humble. It is one of the most important qualities for connecting with others and for success.
- Be grateful. Don't dwell on what's missing in your life or be critical. Be thankful for the gifts in your life.
- Strive for excellence. There are no shortcuts, you have to put in the work. Excellence is trying to do your best, and it is what separates extraordinary people from the ordinary.
- Cultivate a passion for public service and helping others. The author of *Pilgrim's Progress,* John Bunyan, said it best, 'You have not lived today until you have done something for someone who can never repay you.' Sometimes, just a little bit of your time can transform someone else's life.
- Have the courage to persevere and laugh at suffering because doing so will give you greater levels of toughness and resilience.
- Aspire to a warrior mindset. Believe in yourself and keep fighting and pushing forward despite your obstacles. Remember, warriors run to the sound of battle not away from danger—they face challenges head-on and never retreat.

- Choose the path less travelled. Going out of your comfort zone is the only way to grow. Keep challenging yourself. Take the job that scares you most.
- Choose loyal friends. They bring fun, love, and meaning to the journey.
- Dream bigger. Free yourself from the limits of your mind!
- Leave no regrets. Live towards an end that will leave no remorse.
- Cultivate discernment. This crucial skill enables you to make sound decisions, navigate heartbreak, and achieve success. It involves assessing situations, considering all the angles, and making choices that align with personal and professional goals.
- Learn from older generations. Their wisdom and insights can offer invaluable lessons in every area of life.
- Forgive people. Forgiveness is a potent tool that enables you to let go of grudges and bitterness. Hanging on to them will only burden your heart and hinder the growth of love. Free yourself from these negative emotions. As people age, they may become more irritable and more crotchety, but it's essential not to let bitterness take hold of you and affect your relationships.
- Find a loving significant other. Supportive partners help each other accomplish their dreams.

We are a sum of all of the choices we make.

Our thoughts.

Our words.

Our actions.

We have a finite amount of time on earth. Use it wisely. Strategically.

Spend your life on what is meaningful and what is worth dying for.

As the physician Dr David Hawkins said, 'We change the world not by what we say or do, but as a consequence of what we have become.'

Let us continue to work towards creating a better world for the voiceless and underprivileged. We have the potential to witness the largest women's movement in history, starting from Asia and spreading worldwide. Let us stand up for those who cannot stand up for themselves and persevere in our passion to inspire and mobilize individuals in positions of power to help those in dire need.

Embrace fearlessness as a lifelong pursuit.

Never give up on your dreams because anything is possible with hard work and determination.

As I conclude this heartfelt letter, my dear Younger Self, I want you to know that the journey of life is intricate and profound. It's filled with joys, challenges, heartaches, and triumphs. Embrace each experience, learn from it and cherish the connections you make.

I want you to know I have the utmost faith in you, Younger Self. You will navigate this journey with grace, courage, joy, and wisdom. And as you walk this path, remember that you are never alone; you are surrounded by love from within and from those who cherish you.

Whatever the circumstance, always find reasons to be grateful and happy. Remember to have the time of your life.

Laugh often and have lots of fun.

With love and wisdom,

Your Older Self

Acknowledgements

I would like to express my deepest gratitude and love to the following people, in no particular order:

I am eternally grateful to Nora Nazerene Abu Bakar, the publisher of Penguin Random House SEA, for believing in me and the message of my book. Thank you from the bottom of my heart.

Andy Raine, you are a genius! Thank you for the outstanding edits.

I would also like to express gratitude to Thatchaayanie Renganathan and Sneha Bhagwat of PRH SEA for editing support.

I would like to express my deepest gratitude to Papa Gideon Chiu for his powerful love and spiritual guidance that have transformed my life. Since I was nineteen, he has been my role model and I am forever grateful for his special presence in my life. It's no surprise that hundreds of people call him their spiritual father. Thank you, Papa Gideon.

To our dear lifelong friend, Olivia Kow, I am grateful for your love, prayers, and unwavering support. Lots of love to you.

Audrey Lore, you are a wonderful best friend, always inspiring and loving me unconditionally. You have changed me in ways I cannot express.

Chris and Aimee Lee, it's because of your loving support and prayers that this book and many significant projects have been birthed since we began to walk together. Thank you for being a part of this life-changing journey. I love you both.

Agnes, Joylynn, and Miranda, thank you for walking with me, your devotion to God inspires profoundly and has transformed me. All my love to you all.

Charlene Chu, my kindred spirit, I'm forever thankful for your friendship and the depth of your understanding.

Dorothy Wong, it always feels like we saw each other yesterday whenever we talk on the phone. Thanks for being on the journey together for so many years. Sending so much love to you and your family.

Thank you Ken Kregel for all your timely, divine support that has led to my previous memoir, *A Long Road to Justice*, and this book.

Connie Lam, I am so thankful for your love, wisdom, and powerful prayers. I look forward to walking together in the years to come.

Dennis Miller, I cannot express enough how thankful I am to you for your steadfast prayers and uplifting words. You are a special friend to us.

Albert and Wingee, thanks for your unconditional love and for walking together as a family.

Mabel Tai, thank you for your prayers and loving kindness. It's an honour to know you and to journey together—you will change our generation.

Grace Han, thank you for all your wisdom and prayers over the years.

Allison Heiliczer, I am forever grateful for your lovely encouragement and kindred spirit friendship.

Gene White, you were pivotal in my China journey—thank you for your kindness.

Thanks for your prayers and friendship, Joon Imm and Grace Chae.

Fanny Vermes, thank you for your love and prayers over the decades. You're always in my heart. Also, I'm grateful to Kwok-Ying and the late Nancy Patterson, for inspiring us deeply.

A billion thanks to my trailblazing husband, Matt Friedman, for lovingly giving me the space and freedom to write this book. What a beautiful harvest season we are in—the best is yet to come!

I'm eternally grateful to my extraordinary and loving Mom and Dad, and my brilliant, talented, hilarious, charismatic, and dynamic sister and brothers, Jayne, Jae, and Jaemin. I'm so proud of you all. I wrote this book with my nieces, Zoe and Ava, in mind.

Thank you to my praying friends for supporting me over the years: My house church family, Nellie Hue, Parin Kanani, Jenny Lu, Winnie Chau, Han Shih Toh, Ivan Yuen, Peter Wang, Vivien Tam, Mary Koo and Kenny Chang, the friends on the 852 Freedom Campaign WhatsApp group, and many others.